A SHAKESPE

THE AGES

OF

MAN

Selected and Arranged
by
GEORGE RYLANDS

HARPER COLOPHON BOOKS

HARPER & ROW, PUBLISHERS
NEW YORK AND EVANSTON

THE AGES
OF
MAN

TO
ARTHUR MARSHALL

CONTENTS

INTRODUCTION

ADDENDUM

INDEX

INTRODUCTION

"The late Mr. Sheridan, on being shown a volume of
the Beauties of Shakespeare, very properly asked—
'But where are the other eleven?' "

—*Hazlitt*

SHAKESPEARE's first anthologist was Dr. William Dodd,
chaplain to the King. He was executed in 1777, twenty-five
years after his publication of *The Beauties of Shakespeare*, for
forging a bond for £4,200 in the name of his former pupil, the
fifth Lord Chesterfield. In the same year William Henry
Ireland was born, forger of Shakespearian manuscripts and
fabricator of two pseudo-Shakespearian plays. There have
been anthologists since Dodd as there have been forgers but
the study of Shakespeare has been more usually associated
with lunacy than with crime.

Samuel Johnson, most solemn of moralists, to whom none
ever appealed in vain, acted as Dodd's apologist. "I will do
what I can," he said, walking up and down his chamber in
extreme agitation. Dodd's speech at the Old Bailey, Dodd's
sermon delivered in Newgate Chapel, Dodd's Letter to His
Majesty petitioning for exile, were penned by Johnson.
And on the night before the execution Johnson wrote a
letter to the condemned man asking to be remembered in his
prayers. The pages of Boswell which tell us these things are
profoundly moving. They serve to show why it is that
Samuel Johnson is in some ways the greatest of all Shakespeare's critics. The biographer of Savage, Pope and Gray,
like the creator of Falstaff, Caliban and Jaques, has as his
device: *homo sum; humani nil a me alienum puto*. For both

these men forgiveness is the fairest of virtues and ingratitude the meanest of sins.

How different they are and yet in their Englishness and insularity how essentially the same! They supplement one another. Shakespeare created language, Johnson established it: Johnson was a man of prodigious and desultory learning, Shakespeare knew little Latin and less Greek: Shakespeare is the intuitive poet, Johnson the man of measured prose and reasoned philosophy: the one is modest and unassuming with a certain feminine sensibility, the other is masculine and assertive, although we must not make the mistake of ignoring the bawdry of Shakespeare or Johnson's tenderness for his unattractive Tetty. The one embodies the spirit of the age as the other is an inspiration for all time. Of Johnson we know everything, his tastes and table manners, his politics and prejudices, his conversation, his friendships, his religion. Of Shakespeare we know only that we know next to nothing. The meagre facts fill a sheet of notepaper, myth and conjecture overstock a library. We know the dates of his christening and his death; we know that his father was an alderman of Stratford; that his son, a twin, died at eleven years; that he was "a poor player"; that he prospered as a shareholder in the Lord Chamberlain's Company and acquired a coat of arms and became a man of property. Every schoolboy has heard of his second-best bed. And we may perhaps guess at what Shakespeare was *not*, as we turn over the pages of the folio. Not a courtier or a Catholic or an intellectual or a scholar or a satirist or an imperialist or, indeed, Sir Francis Bacon. He must, says Tucker Brooke, have been one of the last men in London with whom an up-to-date Elizabethan would have thought of discussing politics, or religion, or geography, or current affairs. Or, let us add, art for art's sake. Shake-

INTRODUCTION

speare indeed is two things; the man in a London street, the man in a Warwickshire lane.

But it is to Johnson, paradoxically enough, that we must turn for a true appreciation of Shakespeare. For both of them (and Charles Dickens is the corresponding figure in the third great creative age), literature and life are one. The Wit and Wisdom of Samuel Johnson has its place at the bed's head side by side with The Beauties of Shakespeare. They wrote "to be understanded of the people." As Johnson puts it: "All claim to poetical honours must be generally decided by the common sense of the common reader." A Coleridge explores the imaginative process, a Bradley pursues the niceties of characterisation, a Granville Barker reveals theatrical convention and histrionic technique; but for Johnson Shakespeare is the mouthpiece of *humanum genus*, the man in the street. It was the attitude of his age. The eighteenth century were not concerned with poetic utterance or dramatic artifice, but with truth to nature and the business of living. "Shakespeare," says Alexander Pope, "is not so much an imitator as an instrument of nature. His characters are so much nature, that it is a sort of injury to call them by so distant a name as copies of her." Johnson follows his lead and decides that Shakespeare's plays are not tragedies or comedies but "compositions of a distinct kind exhibiting the real state of sublunary nature which partakes of good and evil, joy and sorrow, mingled with endless variety of proportion and innumerable modes of combination." It is only just to add that the Doctor was not unaware of the nature of dramatic method and the pleasures of stage illusion. He was indeed more alive to them than his Victorian successors. He directs the reader's attention to the progress of the fable and the tenor of the dialogue, stresses the successive evolutions of the design and commends the show and bustle of the scenes. But his ultimate conclusion on the value and meaning of Shakespeare derives from Pope's critical dogmas—*First follow Nature* and *The proper study of Mankind is Man*. That conclusion must be quoted at length because it justifies the practice in which the late eighteenth and early nineteenth century delighted and which modern criticism feels obliged in high-minded and high-handed fashion to condemn; namely the practice of extracting beauties, tags, aphorisms, and purple passages from the mighty dead:

"Shakespeare is above all other writers, at least above all modern writers, the poet of nature; the poet that holds up to his readers a faithful mirror of manners and of life. His characters . . . are the genuine progeny of common humanity, such as the world will always supply, and observation will always find. His persons act and speak by the influence of those general passions and principles by which all minds are agitated, and the whole system of life is continued in motion. In the writings of other poets a character is too often an individual; in those of Shakespeare it is commonly a species. . . . This therefore is the praise of Shakespeare that his drama is the mirror of life; that he who has mazed his imagination, in following the phantoms which other writers raise up before him, may here be cured of his delirious ecstasies, by reading human sentiments in human language; by scenes from which a hermit may estimate the transactions of the world, and a confessor predict the progress of the passions."

Curiously enough, when the greatest of the romantics, William Wordsworth, asks himself in the preface to his own Lyrical Ballads, What is a Poet? the answer seems to echo the preface to Shakespeare of the neo-classic critic, Samuel

INTRODUCTION

Johnson. "He is a man speaking to men. . . . Poetry is the most philosophic of all writing . . . its object is truth, not individual and local, but general and operative; not standing upon external testimony, but carried alive into the heart by passion. . . . Poetry is the image of man and nature." And if we look on to the Victorian evangelist of culture, Matthew Arnold, we fix in the essay on Wordsworth upon the famous sentence: "Poetry is a criticism of life: the greatness of a poet lies in his powerful and beautiful application of ideas to life—to the question: How to live." Fleet Street, Helvellyn, Oriel—three poets in three different ages born—are in remarkable agreement.

This anthology then is Shakespeare's mirror of manners and life; it is Shakespeare's image of man and nature; it is Shakespeare's criticism of life. Here we may find expressed those general passions and principles by which all minds are agitated; here is truth carried alive into the heart by passion; here is the powerful and beautiful application of ideas to the question, How to live.

Maybe a Johnsonian will interrupt with the reminder that the Doctor warned off all anthologists of Shakespeare when he said that his real power is not shewn in the splendour of particular passages and that anyone who tries to recommend him by select quotations, will succeed like the pedant in Hierocles, who, when he offered his house to sale, carried a brick in his pocket as a specimen. The answer is that this anthology is intended for those who have some acquaintance with the best of Shakespeare's drama, whether on the stage or at school or from occasional reading, who perhaps carry the Sonnets in their pocket when they travel, but who lack the energy or time or inclination to re-read the plays systematically and who do not expect ever to look into, say, *Pericles*, or *Timon of Athens* or *Alls Well that Ends Well*. Besides, Johnson, it must be remembered, had no liking for Shakespeare's style as such—an anthology gives one ample opportunity for detailed study—and he provocatively asserted that no single passage was equal to some dozen lines in Congreve's *Mourning Bride*. Moreover he himself allowed that from the works of Shakespeare may be collected a system of civil and economical prudence.

The disadvantage of many previous selections has arisen from a want of plan. Extracts as a rule followed the order of the Folio from *The Tempest* to *Othello:* Poems and Sonnets were lumped together; the fault lay in the arrangement rather than in the choice. A case might well be made for a chronological selection according to the present dating of scholars, to illustrate Shakespeare's intellectual and artistic development, but such a volume would interest the student more than the common reader. The present anthologist therefore, returning to the eighteenth-century estimate of Shakespeare, chose rather to group loosely together those passages which give utterance to the same or similar passions, which express associated ideas or develop variations on a single theme, which sum up different attitudes to the common problems of daily life and record the experiences of diverse temperaments exposed to like temptation or provocation or reversal, or which on the other hand reveal affinities of style. From time to time one quotation serves as a gloss upon another. As a general scheme in which to arrange these groups, Jaques's disillusioned survey of the pageant of human life and the actors who strut and fret their hour upon the stage came readily to mind. The anthology falls into three main divisions: *Youth, Manhood, Age*. The first is sunshiny enough, including the world of Faërie and rustic life, whether of the pastoral tradition or the English scene, and passing from the birth of Marina in a storm at sea through childhood and adolescence and the Shakespearian boy-girl (as recognisable as the Chaucerian or Jane Austen heroine) to the myriad-minded passion and theme of Love. This provides the major section of the first book and casts, in its treatment of jealousy, separation and unrequited passion, the first darker shadows of what is to come. These pages outstrip all poets whose ink is tempered with love's sighs, from Catullus to Keats, and make them halt behind. Among the lovers are numbered soldier and shepherd, crown and clown, wife and mistress, the boyish and the senile, the false and the faithful, the all-conquering and the unloved. The setting may be orchard or tavern, graveyard or bedchamber, Egypt or Eastcheap or an Enchanted Island. Wooing and wedding, the heyday in the blood, the expense of spirit in a waste of shame, the marriage of two minds, selflessness and rejection, compliment and fashion, vows, tears and gifts, the sublimation of breathing human passion in the Phœnix and the Turtle's mutual flame—all are celebrated here.

Manhood spells War and Statesmanship. Ambition, the soldier's virtue, patriotism, honour, the sores of civil strife; government, authority, service, social ills. And in the last book, *Age*, maturer passions and fiercer experience, Death the Skeleton and Time the Shadow, ingratitude, remorse and guilt, "what man has made of man," are resolved at last, as in Shakespeare's own final period, in trespasses forgiven, in reconciliations and the tranquillity of white hairs.

In an anthology of Shakespeare what do we receive and what do we lose? We lose the form; that is the plot, the whole; the theatrical effect also, the dramatic moment and the particular situation; what Johnson calls the progress of the fable and the tenor of the dialogue. And we must forget or neglect the characterisation. We receive in recompense and in isolation two elements: the thing said and the way in which it is said; not the form but the content and the style, to use a rough and ready distinction. The content comprehends the general sentiments, affections, passions, moods, reflections and ideas of that sentient thinking animal, Man, whether heroic or base, whether commonplace or beyond the reaches of our own workaday life and limited experience. Thus we school our hearts, enlarge our understandings and achieve imaginative expansion. Secondly the words themselves. They are not ours but Shakespeare's. Yet each time we return to them, each time they rise up in our memory like ghosts and push us from our stools of self-complacency, we feel that double sense of recognition and surprise, a simultaneous release and intensification, and sometimes we clutch at the familiar tag as a drowning man clutches a straw. The crooked thought is made plain, the dumb emotion speaks.

We sacrifice then the *action* which is the mainspring of drama; we sacrifice *character* which comes second in importance; we ignore the whole and isolate the part. Shakespeare the dramatist gives place to Shakespeare the artist and Shakespeare the man, and we attend, I repeat, to the thing said and the way in which it is said; to the thought or passion, and to the language, the idiom, the rhythm, the single word. Nevertheless the passion is felt as it is felt and uttered as it is uttered *because* Shakespeare was a dramatist and an actor (however indifferent), *because* he wrote for the speaking voice and the miming posturing player. He holds up the mirror to nature, not as the painter does to fix a moment of suspended animation. Chaucer in his Prologue paints the speaking likeness; we admire the light and shade, the significant detail, the characteristic pose. But Shakespeare is dynamic not static. His stage had no picture frame; he did not set his figures before a drop-scene. Malvolio struts in yellow stockings, Romeo drops from the balcony, Gertrude quaffs the poisoned cup, Iago watches the Moor stalk forward amid the spectators charged with his poison, the mob tear Cinna for his bad verses, self-willed Richard throws his warder down, Imogen leaps into her husband's arms. As Blake puts it

> He who bends to himself a joy
> Does the wingéd life destroy;
> He who catches a joy as it flies
> Lives in eternity's sunrise.

Shakespeare never bends to himself a situation, a character, a passion. He catches it as it flies. And this is the secret of his language. Gray said of Shakespeare: "Every word with him is a picture." "Pictures" to-day have a further connotation and we can expand the comment. Every sentence is a moving picture, a talking picture. In Shakespeare's speech (both verse and prose) there are latent gesture and intonation, pauses, accelerations and crescendos. Not of course in his apprentice work. From *Titus Andronicus* to *The Tempest* the development in range, variation and flexibility is continuous and while his ideas became more and more subtle, his observation more and more acute, his passions more delicate or more complex, his syntax, his metaphors, his coinages, his combinations of the colloquial and the far-fetched kept pace. "His mind and hand went together (Heminge and Condell tell us) and what he thought he uttered with that easiness that we have scarce received from him a blot in his papers." Say rather his heart and voice went together. His language rings in our ears.

The secret then of the style is the secret of his drama, namely, that we are always on the move. It is the ebb and flow, the forward thrust, the change of rhythm, the rapidity of transition. We admire the ripple of the muscles of the race-horse beneath the satiny skin. And although the diction is often baffling, although the rhetorical hyperbole sometimes chills us and the verbal play and punning are always wearisome, although the Elizabethan vocabulary is not ours and "the taffeta phrases, silken terms precise" are as dated as twisted chimneys and jewelled stomachers, yet for the most part we agree with Dr. Johnson that Shakespeare's creatures "act and speak as the reader thinks that he should himself have spoken or acted on the same occasion: even where the agency is supernatural, the dialogue is level with life."

Those who believe themselves to be well acquainted with Shakespeare may like to amuse themselves with "placing" the quotations in the pages that follow and may find some lines which they have missed or may see them in a new light. Above all, the juxtapositions, as for instance Jack Cade's commonwealth and Gonzalo's Utopia, are frequently curious. But the anthology is intended first and foremost for the common reader, who may care to carry in his luggage if not in his head something more than *To be or not to be* and *To-morrow and to-morrow and to-morrow* and *The quality of mercy is not strained*.

GEORGE RYLANDS

All the world's a stage,
And all the men and women merely players:
They have their exits and their entrances;
And one man in his time plays many parts,
His acts being seven ages. As, first the infant
Mewling and puking in the nurse's arms.
And then the whining schoolboy, with his satchel
And shining morning face, creeping like snail
Unwillingly to school. And then the lover,
Sighing like furnace, with a woeful ballad
Made to his mistress' eyebrow. Then the soldier
Full of strange oaths, and bearded like the pard,
Jealous in honour, sudden and quick in quarrel,
Seeking the bubble reputation
Even in the cannon's mouth. And then the justice,
In fair round belly with good capon lined,
With eyes severe and beard of formal cut,
Full of wise saws and modern instances;
And so he plays his part. The sixth age shifts
Into the lean and slipper'd pantaloon,
With spectacles on nose and pouch on side;
His youthful hose, well saved, a world too wide
For his shrunk shank; and his big manly voice,
Turning again toward childish treble, pipes
And whistles in his sound. Last scene of all,
That ends this strange eventful history,
Is second childishness and mere oblivion,
Sans teeth, sans eyes, sans taste, sans every thing.

Book I ★ Youth

CHILDHOOD

MAGIC AND FAERY

NATURE

SPORT

LOVE

1   A terrible childbed hast thou had, my dear;
No light, no fire: th'unfriendly elements
Forgot thee utterly; nor have I time
To give thee hallow'd to thy grave, but straight
Must cast thee, scarcely coffin'd, in the ooze;
Where, for a monument upon thy bones,
And aye-remaining lamps, the belching whale
And humming water must o'erwhelm thy corpse,
Lying with simple shells.

2   Behold, my lords,
Although the print be little, the whole matter
And copy of the father,—eye, nose, lip;
The trick of's frown; his forehead; nay, the valley,
The pretty dimples of his chin and cheek; his smiles;
The very mould and frame of hand, nail, finger.

3   Thou art thy mother's glass, and she in thee
Calls back the lovely April of her prime.

4   Now, mild may be thy life!
For a more blusterous birth had never babe:
Quiet and gentle thy conditions! for
Thou art the rudeliest welcome to this world
That ever was prince's child. Happy what follows!
Thou hast as chiding a nativity
As fire, air, water, earth, and heaven can make,
To herald thee from the womb.

5   The milk thou suck'dst from her did turn to marble;
Even at thy teat thou hadst thy tyranny.

6 Lo, as a careful housewife runs to catch
  One of her feather'd creatures broke away,
  Sets down her babe, and makes all swift dispatch
  In pursuit of the thing she would have stay;
  Whilst her neglected child holds her in chase,
  Cries to catch her whose busy care is bent
  To follow that which flies before her face,
  Not prizing her poor infant's discontent:
  So runn'st thou after that which flies from thee,
  Whilst I thy babe chase thee afar behind;
  But if thou catch thy hope, turn back to me,
  And play the mother's part, kiss me, be kind:
   So will I pray that thou mayst have thy *Will*,
   If thou turn back, and my loud crying still.

7 But thou art fair; and at thy birth, dear boy,
  Nature and Fortune join'd to make thee great:
  Of Nature's gifts thou mayst with lilies boast
  And with the half-blown rose.

8 Shall I compare thee to a summer's day?
  Thou art more lovely and more temperate:
  Rough winds do shake the darling buds of May,
  And summer's lease hath all too short a date:
  Sometime too hot the eye of heaven shines,
  And often is his gold complexion dimm'd;
  And every fair from fair sometime declines,
  By chance, or nature's changing course, untrimm'd;
  But thy eternal summer shall not fade,
  Nor lose possession of that fair thou ow'st;
  Nor shall Death brag thou wander'st in his shade,
  When in eternal lines to time thou grow'st:
   So long as men can breathe, or eyes can see,
   So long lives this, and this gives life to thee.

9

HERMIONE
Come, I'll question you
Of my lord's tricks and yours when you were boys:
You were pretty lordings then?

POLIXENES
We were, fair queen,
Two lads that thought there was no more behind
But such a day to-morrow as to-day,
And to be boy eternal.

HERMIONE
Was not my lord the verier wag o' the two?

POLIXENES
We were as twinn'd lambs that did frisk i'the sun,
And bleat the one at the other: what we changed
Was innocence for innocence; we knew not
The doctrine of ill-doing, no, nor dream'd
That any did. Had we pursued that life,
And our weak spirits ne'er been higher rear'd
With stronger blood, we should have answer'd heaven
Boldly, 'Not guilty;' the imposition clear'd
Hereditary ours.

10

LEONTES
Mamillius,
Art thou my boy?

MAMILLIUS
Ay, my good lord.

LEONTES
I'fecks!
Why, that's my bawcock. What, hast smutcht thy
nose?—
They say it is a copy out of mine. Come, captain,
We must be neat;—not neat, but cleanly, captain:
Come, sir page,
Look on me with your welkin eye: sweet villain!
Most dear'st! my collop!

11
LEONTES

Looking on the lines
Of my boy's face, methoughts I did recoil
Twenty-three years; and saw myself unbreecht,
In my green velvet coat; my dagger muzzled,
Lest it should bite its master, and so prove,
As ornaments oft do, too dangerous:
How like, methought, I then was to this kernel,
This squash, this gentleman.—Mine honest friend,
Will you take eggs for money?

MAMILLIUS

No, my lord, I'll fight.

LEONTES

You will? why, happy man be's dole!—My brother,
Are you so fond of your young prince as we
Do seem to be of ours?

POLIXENES

If at home, sir,
He's all my exercise, my mirth, my matter:
Now my sworn friend, and then mine enemy;
My parasite, my soldier, statesman, all:
He makes a July's day short as December;
And with his varying childness cures in me
Thoughts that would thick my blood.

12
Boy! Lucius!—Fast asleep? It is no matter;
Enjoy the honey-heavy dew of slumber:
Thou hast no figures nor no fantasies,
Which busy care draws in the brains of men;
Therefore thou sleep'st so sound.

13
VALERIA
How does your little son?

VIRGILIA
I thank your ladyship; well, good madam.

A SOLDIER'S SON

VOLUMNIA

He had rather see the swords, and hear a drum,
than look upon his schoolmaster.

VALERIA

O'my word, the father's son: I'll swear, 'tis a very
pretty boy. O'my troth, I lookt upon him o' Wednesday half an hour together: has such a confirm'd
countenance. I saw him run after a gilded butterfly;
and when he caught it, he let it go again; and after it
again; and over and over he comes, and up again;
catcht it again: or whether his fall enraged him, or
how 'twas, he did so set his teeth, and tear it: O, I
warrant, how he mammockt it!

VOLUMNIA

One on's father's moods.

VALERIA

Indeed, la, 'tis a noble child.

VIRGILIA

A crack, madam.

14   A' shall not tread on me;
I'll run away till I am bigger, but then I'll fight.

15   **MISTRESS PAGE**

How now, Sir Hugh! no school to-day?

SIR HUGH EVANS

No; Master Slender is let the boys leave to play.

MISTRESS QUICKLY

Blessing of his heart!

MISTRESS PAGE

Sir Hugh, my husband says my son profits nothing
in the world at his book. I pray you, ask him some
questions in his accidence.

SIR HUGH EVANS

Come hither, William; hold up your head; come.

MISTRESS PAGE

Come on, sirrah; hold up your head; answer your
master, be not afraid.

SIR HUGH EVANS

William, how many numbers is in nouns?

WILLIAM PAGE

Two.

MISTRESS QUICKLY

Truly, I thought there had been one number more,
because they say, Od's-nouns.

SIR HUGH EVANS

Peace your tattlings.—What is *fair*, William?

WILLIAM PAGE

Pulcher.

MISTRESS QUICKLY

Polecats! there are fairer things than polecats, sure.

SIR HUGH EVANS

You are a very simplicity 'oman: I pray you, peace.

16

HERMIONE

Take the boy to you: he so troubles me,
'Tis past enduring.

FIRST LADY

        Come, my gracious lord,
Shall I be your playfellow?

MAMILLIUS

        No, I'll none of you.

FIRST LADY

Why, my sweet lord?

MAMILLIUS

You'll kiss me hard, and speak to me as if
I were a baby still

17

> HERMIONE
> Come sir, now
> I am for you again: pray you, sit by us,
> And tell's a tale.
>
> MAMILLIUS
> Merry or sad shall't be?
>
> HERMIONE
> As merry as you will.
>
> MAMILLIUS
> A sad tale's best for winter: I have one
> Of sprites and goblins.
>
> HERMIONE
> Let's have that, good sir.
> Come on, sit down:—come on, and do your best
> To fright me with your sprites; you're powerful at it.
>
> MAMILLIUS
> There was a man,—
>
> HERMIONE
> Nay, come, sit down; then on.
>
> MAMILLIUS
> Dwelt by a churchyard:—I will tell it softly;
> Yond crickets shall not hear it.

18

> O thou goddess,
> Thou divine Nature, how thyself thou blazon'st
> In these two princely boys! They are as gentle
> As zephyrs, blowing below the violet,
> Not wagging his sweet head; and yet as rough,
> Their royal blood enchafed, as the rudest wind,
> That by the top doth take the mountain pine,
> And make him stoop to the vale. 'Tis wonder
> That an invisible instinct should frame them
> To royalty unlearn'd; honour untaught;
> Civility not seen from other; valour,
> That wildly grows in them, but yields a crop
> As if it had been sow'd.

19

But, gracious sir,
Here are your sons again; and I must lose
Two of the sweet'st companions in the world.
The benediction of these covering heavens
Fall on their heads like dew! for they are worthy
To inlay heaven with stars.

20

ARTHUR

Good morrow, Hubert.

HUBERT DE BURGH

Good morrow, little prince.

ARTHUR

As little prince, having so great a title
To be more prince, as may be.—You are sad.

HUBERT DE BURGH

Indeed, I have been merrier.

ARTHUR

Mercy on me!
Methinks no body should be sad but I:
Yet, I remember, when I was in France,
Young gentlemen would be as sad as night,
Only for wantonness. By my christendom,
So I were out of prison, and kept sheep,
I should be as merry as the day is long;
And so I would be here, but that I doubt
My uncle practises more harm to me:
He is afraid of me, and I of him:
Is it my fault that I was Geffrey's son?
No, indeed, is't not; and I would to heaven
I were your son, so you would love me, Hubert

HUBERT DE BURGH

If I talk to him, with his innocent prate
He will awake my mercy, which lies dead:
Therefore I will be sudden and dispatch.

A BOY'S NURSING

ARTHUR

Are you sick, Hubert? you look pale to-day:
In sooth, I would you were a little sick,
That I might sit all night and watch with you:
I warrant I love you more than you do me.

HUBERT DE BURGH

His words do take possession of my bosom.—
Read here, young Arthur.

How now, foolish rheum!
Turning dispiteous torture out of door!
I must be brief, lest resolution drop
Out at mine eyes in tender womanish tears.—
Can you not read it, is it not fair writ?

ARTHUR

Too fairly, Hubert, for so foul effect:
Must you with hot irons burn out both mine eyes?

HUBERT DE BURGH

Young boy, I must.

ARTHUR

And will you?

HUBERT DE BURGH

And I will.

ARTHUR

Have you the heart? When your head did but
    ache,
I knit my handkercher about your brows,—
The best I had, a princess wrought it me,—
And I did never ask it you again;
And with my hand at midnight held your head;
And like the watchful minutes to the hour,
Still and anon cheer'd up the heavy time,
Saying, 'What lack you?' and, 'Where lies your
    grief?'
Or, 'What good love may I perform for you?'
Many a poor man's son would have lien still,
And ne'er have spoke a loving word to you;
But you at your sick service had a prince.

Nay, you may think my love was crafty love,
And call it cunning:—do, an if you will:
If heaven be pleased that you must use me ill,
Why, then you must.—Will you put out mine eyes?
These eyes that never did nor never shall
So much as frown on you?

HUBERT DE BURGH
         I have sworn to do it;
And with hot irons must I burn them out.

ARTHUR
Ah, none but in this iron age would do it!
The iron of itself, though heat red-hot,
Approaching near these eyes, would drink my tears
And quench his fiery indignation
Even in the water of mine innocence;
Nay, after that, consume away in rust,
But for containing fire to harm mine eye.
Are you more stubborn-hard than hammer'd iron?
An if an angel should have come to me,
And told me Hubert should put out mine eyes,
I would not have believed him,—no tongue but
    Hubert's.

HUBERT DE BURGH
Come forth!
    Enter EXECUTIONERS.
Do as I bid you do.

ARTHUR
O, save me, Hubert, save me! my eyes are out
Even with the fierce looks of these bloody men.

HUBERT DE BURGH
Give me the iron, I say, and bind him here.

ARTHUR
Alas, what need you be so boisterous-rough?
I will not struggle, I will stand stone-still.
For heaven sake, Hubert, let me not be bound!
Nay, hear me, Hubert!—drive these men away,
And I will sit as quiet as a lamb;

I will not stir, nor wince, nor speak a word,
Nor look upon the iron angerly:
Thrust but these men away, and I'll forgive you,
Whatever torment you do put me to.

HUBERT DE BURGH
Go, stand within; let me alone with him.

EXECUTIONER
I am best pleased to be from such a deed.

ARTHUR
Alas, I then have chid away my friend!
He hath a stern look, but a gentle heart:—
Let him come back, that his compassion may
Give life to yours.

HUBERT DE BURGH
Come, boy, prepare yourself.

ARTHUR
Is there no remedy?

HUBERT DE BURGH
None, but to lose your eyes.

*

ARTHUR
O heaven!—that there were but a mote in yours,
A grain, a dust, a gnat, a wandering hair,
Any annoyance in that precious sense!
Then, feeling what small things are boisterous there,
Your vile intent must needs seem horrible.

HUBERT DE BURGH
Is this your promise? go to, hold your tongue.

ARTHUR
Hubert, the utterance of a brace of tongues
Must needs want pleading for a pair of eyes:
Let me not hold my tongue,—let me not, Hubert;
Or, Hubert, if you will, cut out my tongue,
So I may keep my eyes: O, spare mine eyes,
Though to no use but still to look on you!

21   Lo, thus, quoth Dighton, lay the gentle babes,—
Thus, thus, quoth Forrest, girdling one another
Within their innocent alabaster arms:
Their lips were four red roses on a stalk,
Which in their summer beauty kist each other . .
The most replenished sweet work of nature,
That from the prime creation e'er she framed.

22   Stay yet, look back with me unto the Tower.
Pity, you ancient stones, those tender babes,
Whom envy hath immured within your walls!
Rough cradle for such little pretty ones!
Rude ragged nurse, old sullen playfellow
For tender princes, use my babies well!

23   Grief fills the room up of my absent child,
Lies in his bed, walks up and down with me,
Puts on his pretty looks, repeats his words,
Remembers me of all his gracious parts,
Stuffs out his vacant garments with his form;
Then have I reason to be fond of grief.
Fare you well: had you such a loss as I,
I could give better comfort than you do.—
I will not keep this form upon my head,
When there is such disorder in my wit.
O Lord! my boy, my Arthur, my fair son!
My life, my joy, my food, my all the world!
My widow-comfort, and my sorrows' cure!

24   KING LEAR
               My wits begin to turn.—
Come on, my boy: how dost, my boy? art cold?
I am cold myself.—Where is this straw, my fellow?
The art of our necessities is strange,

That can make vile things precious. Come, your
    hovel.—
Poor fool and knave, I have one part in my heart
That's sorry yet for thee.

FOOL

He that has and a little tiny wit,—
    With hey, ho, the wind and the rain,—
Must make content with his fortunes fit,
    Though the rain it raineth every day.

KING LEAR

True, my good boy.—Come, bring us to this hovel.

25

FIRST MURDERER

Where is your husband?

LADY MACDUFF

I hope, in no place so unsanctified
Where such as thou mayst find him.

FIRST MURDERER

              He's a traitor!

SON

Thou liest, thou shag-hair'd villain!

FIRST MURDERER

         What, you egg!
Young fry of treachery!

SON

        He has kill'd me, mother:
Run away, I pray you!

26

Look here upon thy brother Geffrey's face;—
These eyes, these brows, were moulded out of his:
This little abstract doth contain that large
Which dies in Geffrey; and the hand of time
Shall draw this brief into as huge a volume.

27

VOLUMNIA

This is a poor epitome of yours,
Which by the interpretation of full time
May show like all yourself.

CAIUS MARCIUS CORIOLANUS

                    The god of soldiers,
With the consent of supreme Jove, inform
Thy thoughts with nobleness; that thou mayst prove
To shame unvulnerable, and stick i'the wars
Like a great sea-mark, standing every flaw,
And saving those that eye thee!

VOLUMNIA

                    Your knee, sirrah.

CAIUS MARCIUS CORIOLANUS

That's my brave boy!

VOLUMNIA

Even he, your wife, this lady, and myself,
Are suitors to you.

28

NURSE

Faith, I can tell her age unto an hour

LADY CAPULET

She's not fourteen.

NURSE

I'll lay fourteen of my teeth,—and yet, to my teen
be it spoken, I have but four,—she's not fourteen.
How long is it now to Lammas-tide?

LADY CAPULET

A fortnight and odd days.

NURSE.

Even or odd, of all days in the year,
Come Lammas-eve at night shall she be fourteen.
Susan and she—God rest all Christian souls!—
Were of an age: well, Susan is with God;

JULIET'S 'AY'

She was too good for me:—but, as I said,
On Lammas-eve at night shall she be fourteen;
That shall she, marry; I remember it well.
'Tis since the earthquake now eleven years;
And she was wean'd,—I never shall forget it,—
Of all the days of the year, upon that day:
For I had then laid wormwood to my dug,
Sitting in the sun under the dove-house wall;
My lord and you were then at Mantua:—
Nay, I do bear a brain:—but, as I said,
When it did taste the wormwood on the nipple
Of my dug, and felt it bitter, pretty fool,
To see it tetchy, and fall out with the dug!
Shake, quoth the dove-house: 'twas no need, I trow,
To bid me trudge:
And since that time it is eleven years;
For then she could stand high-lone; nay, by th' rood,
She could have run and waddled all about;
For even the day before, she broke her brow:
And then my husband—God be with his soul!
A' was a merry man—took up the child:
'Yea,' quoth he, 'dost thou fall upon thy face?
Thou wilt fall backward when thou hast more wit;
Wilt thou not, Jule?' and, by my holidame,
The pretty wretch left crying, and said 'Ay.'
To see, now, how a jest shall come about!
I warrant, an I should live a thousand years,
I never should forget it: 'Wilt thou not, Jule?' quoth
   he;
And, pretty fool, it stinted, and said 'Ay.'
LADY CAPULET
Enough of this; I pray thee, hold thy peace.
NURSE
Yes, madam:—yet I cannot choose but laugh,
To think it should leave crying, and say 'Ay':
And yet, I warrant, it had upon it brow
A bump as big as a young cockerel's stone;

A perilous knock; and it cried bitterly:
'Yea,' quoth my husband, 'fall'st upon thy face?
Thou wilt fall backward when thou comest to age;
Wilt thou not, Jule?' it stinted, and said 'Ay.'

29   The tongues of mocking wenches are as keen
      As is the razor's edge invisible,
Cutting a smaller hair than may be seen,
      Above the sense of sense; so sensible
Seemeth their conference; their conceits have wings
Fleeter than arrows, bullets, wind, thought, swifter
      things.

30   Not yet old enough for a man, nor young enough for
a boy; as a squash is before 'tis a peascod, or a codling
when 'tis almost an apple: 'tis with him e'en standing
water, between boy and man. He is very well-
favour'd, and he speaks very shrewishly; one would
think his mother's milk were scarce out of him.

31   For they shall yet belie thy happy years,
That say thou art a man: Diana's lip
Is not more smooth and rubious; thy small pipe
Is as the maiden's organ, shrill and sound;
And all is semblative a woman's part.

32   I'll hold thee any wager,
When we are both accoutred like young men,
I'll prove the prettier fellow of the two,
And wear my dagger with the braver grace:

And speak between the change of man and boy
With a reed voice; and turn two mincing steps
Into a manly stride; and speak of frays,
Like a fine-bragging youth; and tell quaint lies,
How honourable ladies sought my love,
Which I denying, they fell sick and died,—
I could not do withal;—then I'll repent,
And wish, for all that, that I had not kill'd them:
And twenty of these puny lies I'll tell;
That men shall swear I have discontinued school
Above a twelvemonth:—I have within my mind
A thousand raw tricks of these bragging Jacks,
Which I will practise.

33 Think not I love him, though I ask for him;
'Tis but a peevish boy:—yet he talks well;—
But what care I for words? yet words do well,
When he that speaks them pleases those that hear.
It is a pretty youth:—not very pretty:—
But, sure, he's proud; and yet his pride becomes him:
He'll make a proper man: the best thing in him
Is his complexion; and faster than his tongue
Did make offence, his eye did heal it up.
He is not very tall; yet for his years he's tall:
His leg is but so-so; and yet 'tis well:
There was a pretty redness in his lip,
A little riper and more lusty red
Than that mixt in his cheek; 'twas just the difference
Betwixt the constant red and mingled damask.

34 You must forget to be a woman; change
Command into obedience; fear and niceness—
The handmaids of all women, or, more truly,
Woman it pretty self—into a waggish courage;

Ready in gibes, quick-answer'd, saucy, and
As quarrelous as the weasel; nay, you must
Forget that rarest treasure of your cheek,
Exposing it—but, O, the harder heart!
Alack, no remedy!—to the greedy touch
Of common-kissing Titan; and forget
Your laboursome and dainty trims, wherein
You made great Juno angry.

35   Crabbed age and youth cannot live together:
Youth is full of pleasance, age is full of care;
Youth like summer morn, age like winter weather;
Youth like summer brave, age like winter bare.
Youth is full of sport, age's breath is short;
    Youth is nimble, age is lame;
Youth is hot and bold, age is weak and cold;
    Youth is wild, and age is tame.
Age, I do abhor thee; youth, I do adore thee;
    O, my love, my love is young!
Age, I do defy thee: O, sweet shepherd, hie thee,
    For methinks thou stay'st too long.

36   Dost thou think, because thou art virtuous,
there shall be no more cakes and ale?

37   At my poor house look to behold this night
Earth-treading stars that make dark heaven light:
Such comfort as do lusty young men feel
When well-apparell'd April on the heel
Of limping Winter treads, even such delight
Among fresh female buds shall you this night
Inherit at my house.

38
      My salad days,
When I was green in judgement:—cold in blood,
To say as I said then!

39 When forty winters shall besiege thy brow,
And dig deep trenches in thy beauty's field,
Thy youth's proud livery, so gazed on now,
Will be a tatter'd weed, of small worth held:
Then being askt where all thy beauty lies,
Where all the treasure of thy lusty days;
To say, within thine own deep-sunken eyes,
Were an all-eating shame and thriftless praise.
How much more praise deserved thy beauty's use,
If thou couldst answer, 'This fair child of mine
Shall sum my count, and make my old excuse,'
Proving his beauty by succession thine!
 This were to be new made when thou art old,
 And see thy blood warm when thou feel'st it cold.

40   There, my blessing with thee!
And these few precepts in thy memory
See thou character. Give thy thoughts no tongue,
Nor any unproportion'd thought his act.
Be thou familiar, but by no means vulgar.
The friends thou hast, and their adoption tried,
Grapple them to thy soul with hoops of steel;
But do not dull thy palm with entertainment
Of each new-hatcht, unfledged comrade. Beware
Of entrance to a quarrel; but being in,
Bear't, that th'opposed may beware of thee.
Give every man thine ear, but few thy voice:
Take each man's censure, but reserve thy judgement.
Costly thy habit as thy purse can buy,

But not exprest in fancy; rich, not gaudy:
For the apparel oft proclaims the man . . .
Neither a borrower nor a lender be:
For loan oft loses both itself and friend;
And borrowing dulls the edge of husbandry.
This above all,—to thine own self be true;
And it must follow, as the night the day,
Thou canst not then be false to any man.

41   Be thou blest, Bertram, and succeed thy father
In manners as in shape! Thy blood and virtue
Contend for empire in thee, and thy goodness
Share with thy birthright. Love all, trust a few,
Do wrong to none; be able for thine enemy
Rather in power than use, and keep thy friend
Under thy own life's key; be checkt for silence,
But never taxt for speech. What heaven more will,
That thee may furnish, and my prayers pluck down,
Fall on thy head!

42   I know a bank where the wild thyme blows,
Where oxlips and the nodding violet grows;
Quite over-canopied with lush woodbine,
With sweet musk-roses, and with eglantine:
There sleeps Titania sometime of the night,
Lull'd in these flowers with dances and delight;
And there the snake throws her enamell'd skin,
Weed wide enough to wrap a fairy in.

43   Be not afeard; the isle is full of noises,
Sounds, and sweet airs, that give delight, and hurt
    not.
Sometimes a thousand twangling instruments
Will hum about mine ears; and sometime voices,

That, if I then had waked after long sleep,
Will make me sleep again: and then, in dreaming,
The clouds methought would open, and show riches
Ready to drop upon me; that, when I waked,
I cried to dream again.

44   Where the bee sucks, there suck I;
        In a cowslip's bell I lie;
        There I couch when owls do cry.
        On the bat's back I do fly
        After summer merrily.
    Merrily, merrily shall I live now
    Under the blossom that hangs on the bough.

45   O, then, I see Queen Mab hath been with you.
        She is the fairies' midwife; and she comes
        In shape no bigger than an agate-stone
        On the fore-finger of an alderman,
        Drawn with a team of little atomies
        Athwart men's noses as they lie asleep:
        Her wagon-spokes made of long spinners' legs;
        The cover, of the wings of grasshoppers;
        The traces, of the smallest spider's web;
        The collars, of the moonshine's watery beams;
        Her whip, of cricket's bone; the lash, of film;
        Her wagoner, a small gray-coated gnat,
        Not half so big as a round little worm
        Prickt from the lazy finger of a maid;
        Her chariot is an empty hazel-nut,
        Made by the joiner squirrel or old grub,
        Time out o' mind the fairies' coachmakers.
        And in this state she gallops night by night
        Through lovers' brains, and then they dream of love;

THE AGES OF MAN

O'er courtiers' knees, that dream on court'sies
  straight;
O'er lawyers' fingers, who straight dream on fees;
O'er ladies' lips, who straight on kisses dream,—
Which oft the angry Mab with blisters plagues,
Because their breaths with sweetmeats tainted
  are:
Sometime she gallops o'er a courtier's nose,
And then dreams he of smelling out a suit;
And sometime comes she with a tithe-pig's tail
Tickling a parson's nose as 'a lies asleep,
Then dreams he of another benefice:
Sometime she driveth o'er a soldier's neck,
And then dreams he of cutting foreign throats,
Of breaches, ambuscadoes, Spanish blades,
Of healths five-fadom deep; and then anon
Drums in his ear, at which he starts, and wakes;
And, being thus frighted, swears a prayer or two,
And sleeps again. This is that very Mab
That plats the manes of horses in the night;
And bakes the elf-locks in foul sluttish hairs,
Which once untangled, much misfortune bodes:
This is the hag, when maids lie on their backs,
That presses them, and learns them first to bear,
Making them women of good carriage.

46   Over hill, over dale,
          Thorough bush, thorough brier,
        Over park, over pale,
          Thorough flood, thorough fire,
        I do wander every where,
        Swifter than the moon's sphere;
        And I serve the fairy queen,
        To dew her orbs upon the green.

The cowslips tall her pensioners be:
In their gold coats spots you see;
Those be rubies, fairy favours,
In those freckles live their savours:
I must go seek some dewdrops here,
And hang a pearl in every cowslip's ear.

47 I am a spirit of no common rate,—
The summer still doth tend upon my state;
And I do love thee: therefore, go with me;
I'll give thee fairies to attend on thee;
And they shall fetch thee jewels from the deep,
And sing, while thou on pressed flowers dost sleep:
And I will purge thy mortal grossness so,
That thou shalt like an airy spirit go.—
Peas-blossom! Cobweb! Moth! and Mustard-seed!
Be kind and courteous to this gentleman,—
Hop in his walks, and gambol in his eyes;
Feed him with apricocks and dewberries,
With purple grapes, green figs, and mulberries;
The honey-bags steal from the humble-bees,
And for night-tapers crop their waxen thighs,
And light them at the fiery glow-worm's eyes,
To have my love to bed and to arise;
And pluck the wings from painted butterflies
To fan the moonbeams from his sleeping eyes:
Nod to him, elves, and do him courtesies.

48 These are the forgeries of jealousy:
And never, since the middle summer's spring,
Met we on hill, in dale, forest, or mead,
By paved fountain or by rushy brook,
Or in the beached margent of the sea,

To dance our ringlets to the whistling wind,
But with thy brawls thou hast disturb'd our sport.
Therefore the winds, piping to us in vain,
As in revenge, have suck'd up from the sea
Contagious fogs; which falling in the land,
Hath every pelting river made so proud,
That they have overborne their continents:
The ox hath therefore stretch'd his yoke in vain,
The ploughman lost his sweat; and the green corn
Hath rotted ere his youth attain'd a beard:
The fold stands empty in the drowned field,
And crows are fatted with the murrion flock;
The nine-men's-morris is fill'd up with mud;
And the quaint mazes in the wanton green,
For lack of tread, are undistinguishable:
The human mortals want their winter cheer;
No night is now with hymn or carol blest:—
Therefore the moon, the governess of floods,
Pale in her anger, washes all the air,
That rheumatic diseases do abound:
And thorough this distemperature we see
The seasons alter: hoary-headed frosts
Fall in the fresh lap of the crimson rose;
And on old Hiems' thin and icy crown
An odorous chaplet of sweet summer buds
Is, as in mockery, set: the spring, the summer,
The childing autumn, angry winter, change
Their wonted liveries; and the mazed world,
By their increase, now knows not which is which.

49   For never-resting time leads summer on
To hideous winter and confounds him there;
Sap checkt with frost, and lusty leaves quite gone,
Beauty o'ersnow'd, and bareness every where.

50
The fairy-land buys not the child of me.
His mother was a vot'ress of my order:
And, in the spiced Indian air, by night
Full often hath she gossipt by my side;
And sat with me on Neptune's yellow sands,
Marking th' embarked traders on the flood;
When we have laught to see the sails conceive
And grow big-bellied with the wanton wind;
Which she, with pretty and with swimming gait
Following,—her womb then rich with my young
   squire,—
Would imitate, and sail upon the land,
To fetch me trifles, and return again,
As from a voyage, rich with merchandise.
But she, being mortal, of that boy did die;
And for her sake do I rear up her boy;
And for her sake I will not part with him.

51
                    OTHELLO
That handkerchief
Did an Egyptian to my mother give;
She was a charmer, and could almost read
The thoughts of people: she told her, while she kept
   it,
'Twould make her amiable, and subdue my father
Entirely to her love; but if she lost it,
Or made a gift of it, my father's eye
Should hold her loathed, and his spirits should hunt
After new fancies: she, dying, gave it me;
And bid me, when my fate would have me wive,
To give it her. I did so: and take heed on't;
Make it a darling like your precious eye;
To lose't or give't away were such perdition
As nothing else could match.
                    DESDEMONA
                         Is't possible?

OTHELLO

'Tis true: there's magic in the web of it:
A sibyl, that had number'd in the world
The sun to course two hundred compasses,
In her prophetic fury sew'd the work;
The worms were hallow'd that did breed the silk;
And it was dyed in mummy which the skilful
Conserved of maidens' hearts.

52   All the infections that the sun sucks up
From bogs, fens, flats, on Prosper fall, and make him
By inch-meal a disease! His spirits hear me,
And yet I needs must curse. But they'll nor pinch,
Fright me with urchin-shows, pitch me i' the mire,
Nor lead me, like a firebrand, in the dark
Out of my way, unless he bid 'em: but
For every trifle are they set upon me;
Sometime like apes, that mow and chatter at me,
And after bite me; then like hedgehogs, which
Lie tumbling in my barefoot way, and mount
Their pricks at my footfall; sometime am I
All wound with adders, who with cloven tongues
Do hiss me into madness.

53   I'll show thee the best springs; I'll pluck thee berries;
I'll fish for thee, and get thee wood enough.
A plague upon the tyrant that I serve!
I'll bear him no more sticks, but follow thee,
Thou wondrous man.
I prithee, let me bring thee where crabs grow;
And I with my long nails will dig thee pig-nuts;
Show thee a jay's nest, and instruct thee how
To snare the nimble marmoset; I'll bring thee
To clustering filberts, and sometimes I'll get thee
Young scamels from the rock. Wilt thou go with me?

54   Come, now a roundel and a fairy song;
Then, for the third part of a minute, hence;—
Some, to kill cankers in the musk-rose buds;
Some, war with rere-mice for their leathern wings,
To make my small elves coats; and some, keep back
The clamorous owl, that nightly hoots and wonders
At our quaint spirits. Sing me now asleep;
Then to your offices, and let me rest.

Song.

You spotted snakes with double tongue,
   Thorny hedgehogs, be not seen;
Newts and blind-worms, do no wrong,
   Come not near our fairy queen.

Weaving spiders, come not here;
   Hence, you long-legg'd spinners, hence!
Beetles black, approach not near;
   Worm nor snail, do no offence.

   Philomel, with melody
   Sing in our sweet lullaby;
Lulla, lulla, lullaby; lulla, lulla, lullaby;
     Never harm,
     Nor spell nor charm,
   Come our lovely lady nigh;
   So, good night, with lullaby.

55   PUCK
My fairy lord, this must be done with haste,
For Night's swift dragons cut the clouds full fast,
And yonder shines Aurora's harbinger;
At whose approach, ghosts, wandering here and
   there,

Troop home to churchyards: damned spirits all,
That in crossways and floods have burial,
Already to their wormy beds are gone;
For fear lest day should look their shames upon,
They wilfully themselves exile from light,
And must for aye consort with black-brow'd night.

OBERON

But we are spirits of another sort:
I with the Morning's love have oft made sport;
And, like a forester, the groves may tread,
Even till the eastern gate, all fiery-red,
Opening on Neptune, with fair blessed beams
Turns into yellow gold his salt green streams.

56

BERNARDO

It was about to speak when the cock crew.

HORATIO

And then it started like a guilty thing
Upon a fearful summons. I have heard,
The cock, that is the trumpet to the morn,
Doth with his lofty and shrill-sounding throat
Awake the god of day; and at his warning,
Whether in sea or fire, in earth or air,
Th' extravagant and erring spirit hies
To his confine: and of the truth herein
This present object made probation.

MARCELLUS

It faded on the crowing of the cock.
Some say, that ever 'gainst that season comes
Wherein our Saviour's birth is celebrated,
The bird of dawning singeth all night long:
And then, they say, no spirit dare stir abroad;
The nights are wholesome; then no planets strike,
No fairy takes, nor witch hath power to charm;
So hallow'd and so gracious is the time.

PUCK

Now the hungry lion roars,
  And the wolf behowls the moon;
Whilst the heavy ploughman snores,
  All with weary task fordone.
Now the wasted brands do glow,
  Whilst the screech-owl, screeching loud
Puts the wretch that lies in woe
  In remembrance of a shroud.
Now it is the time of night,
  That the graves, all gaping wide,
Every one lets forth his sprite,
  In the church-way paths to glide:
And we fairies, that do run
  By the triple Hecate's team
From the presence of the sun,
  Following darkness like a dream,
Now are frolic: not a mouse
Shall disturb this hallow'd house:
I am sent, with broom, before,
To sweep the dust behind the door.

OBERON

Through the house give glimmering light,
  By the dead and drowsy fire;
Every elf and fairy sprite
  Hop as light as bird from brier;
And this ditty, after me,
Sing, and dance it trippingly.

TITANIA

First, rehearse your song by rote,
To each word a warbling note:
Hand in hand, with fairy grace,
Will we sing, and bless this place.

58   How use doth breed a habit in a man!
This shadowy desert, unfrequented woods,
I better brook than flourishing peopled towns:
Here can I sit alone, unseen of any,
And to the nightingale's complaining notes
Tune my distresses and record my woes.
O thou that dost inhabit in my breast,
Leave not the mansion so long tenantless,
Lest, growing ruinous, the building fall,
And leave no memory of what it was!

59   Now, my co-mates and brothers in exile,
Hath not old custom made this life more sweet
Than that of painted pomp? Are not these words
More free from peril than the envious court?
Here feel we but the penalty of Adam,
The seasons' difference; as the icy fang
And churlish chiding of the winter's wind,
Which, when it bites and blows upon my body,
Even till I shrink with cold, I smile, and say
'This is no flattery; these are counsellors
That feelingly persuade me what I am.'
Sweet are the uses of adversity;
Which, like the toad, ugly and venomous,
Wears yet a precious jewel in his head;
And this our life, exempt from public haunt,
Finds tongues in trees, books in the running brooks,
Sermons in stones, and good in every thing.

60   BELARIUS
                       O, this life
Is nobler than attending for a check,
Richer than doing nothing for a bauble,
Prouder than rustling in unpaid-for silk:
Such gain the cap of him that makes 'em fine,
Yet keeps his book uncrost: no life to ours.

GUIDERIUS

Out of your proof you speak: we, poor unfledged,
Have never wing'd from view o'the nest, nor know not
What air's from home. Haply this life is best,
If quiet life be best; sweeter to you
That have a sharper known; well corresponding
With your stiff age: but unto us it is
A cell of ignorance; travelling a-bed;
A prison for a debtor, that not dares
To stride a limit.

ARVIRAGUS

What should we speak of
When we are old as you? when we shall hear
The rain and wind beat dark December, how,
In this our pinching cave, shall we discourse
The freezing hours away? We have seen nothing:
We are beastly; subtle as the fox for prey;
Like warlike as the wolf for what we eat:
Our valour is to chase what flies; our cage
We make a quire, as doth the prison'd bird,
And sing our bondage freely.

61

Under the greenwood tree
Who loves to lie with me,
And turn his merry note
Unto the sweet bird's throat,
Come hither, come hither, come hither:
Here shall he see
No enemy
But winter and rough weather.

Who doth ambition shun
And loves to live i'th'sun,
Seeking the food he eats
And pleased with what he gets.

Come hither, come hither, come hither:
Here shall he see
No enemy
But winter and rough weather.

62   No, rather I abjure all roofs, and choose
To wage against the enmity o' the air;
To be a comrade with the wolf and owl,--
Necessity's sharp pinch!

63   But whate'er you are,
That in this desert inaccessible,
Under the shade of melancholy boughs,
Lose and neglect the creeping hours of time;
If ever you have lookt on better days,
If ever been where bells have knoll'd to church,
If ever sat at any good man's feast,
If ever from your eyelids wiped a tear,
And know what 'tis to pity and be pitied,—
Let gentleness my strong enforcement be:
In the which hope I blush, and hide my sword.

64   No, no, no, no! Come, let's away to prison:
We two alone will sing like birds i' the cage:
When thou dost ask me blessing, I'll kneel down,
And ask of thee forgiveness: so we'll live,
And pray, and sing, and tell old tales, and laugh
At gilded butterflies, and hear poor rogues
Talk of court news; and we'll talk with them too,—
Who loses and who wins; who's in, who's out;—
And take upon's the mystery of things,
As if we were God's spies: and we'll wear out,
In a wall'd prison, packs and sects of great ones,
That ebb and flow by th'moon.

65 These your unusual weeds to each part of you
Do give a life: no shepherdess; but Flora
Peering in April's front. This your sheep-shearing
Is as a meeting of the petty gods,
And you the queen on't.

PERDITA
66 Give me those flowers there, Dorcas.—Reverend sirs,
For you there's rosemary and rue; these keep
Seeming and savour all the winter long:
Grace and remembrance be to you both,
And welcome to our shearing!
POLIXENES
                    Shepherdess,—
A fair one are you,—well you fit our ages
With flowers of winter.
PERDITA
            Sir, the year growing ancient,—
Not yet on summer's death, nor on the birth
Of trembling winter,—the fairest flowers o'the season
Are our carnations, and streakt gillyvors,
Which some call nature's bastards: of that kind
Our rustic garden's barren; and I care not
To get slips of them.
POLIXENES
            Wherefore, gentle maiden,
Do you neglect them?
PERDITA
            For I have heard it said,
There is an art which, in their piedness, shares
With great creating nature.
POLIXENES
                    Say there be;
Yet nature is made better by no mean,
But nature makes that mean: so, over that art

Which you say adds to nature, is an art
That nature makes. You see, sweet maid, we marry
A gentler scion to the wildest stock,
And make conceive a bark of baser kind
By bud of nobler race: this is an art
Which does mend nature,—change it rather; but
The art itself is nature.

PERDITA

So it is.

POLIXENES

Then make your garden rich in gillyvors,
And do not call them bastards.

PERDITA

I'll not put
The dibble in earth to set one slip of them;
No more than, were I painted, I would wish
This youth should say, 'twere well, and only therefore
Desire to breed by me.—Here's flowers for you;
Hot lavender, mints, savory, marjoram;
The marigold, that goes to bed wi' the sun,
And with him rises weeping: these are flowers
Of middle summer, and, I think, they are given
To men of middle age. Y'are very welcome.

CAMILLO

I should leave grazing, were I of your flock,
And only live by gazing.

PERDITA

Out, alas!
You'ld be so lean, that blasts of January
Would blow you through and through.—Now, my
fair'st friend,
I would I had some flowers o'the spring that might
Become your time of day;—and yours, and yours,
That wear upon your virgin branches yet
Your maidenheads growing:—O Proserpina,
For the flowers now, that, frighted, thou lett'st fall
From Dis's wagon! daffodils,

That come before the swallow dares, and take
The winds of March with beauty; violets dim,
But sweeter than the lids of Juno's eyes
Or Cytherea's breath; pale primroses,
That die unmarried, ere they can behold
Bright Phœbus in his strength,—a malady
Most incident to maids; bold oxlips and
The crown-imperial; lilies of all kinds,
The flower-de-luce being one! O, these I lack,
To make you garlands of; and my sweet friend,
To strew him o'er and o'er!

FLORIZEL
What, like a corse?

PERDITA
No, like a bank for love to lie and play on;
Not like a corse; or if,—not to be buried,
But quick, and in mine arms.—Come, take your
    flowers:
Methinks I play as I have seen them do
In Whitsun pastorals: sure, this robe of mine
Does change my disposition.

67   This side is Hiems, Winter, this Ver, the Spring; the
one maintain'd by the owl, the other by the cuckoo.
Ver, begin.

SPRING
When daisies pied and violets blue,
    And lady-smocks all silver-white,
And cuckoo-buds of yellow hue
    Do paint the meadows with delight,
The cuckoo then on every tree
Mocks married men; for thus sings he,
            Cuckoo;
Cuckoo, cuckoo: O word of fear,
Unpleasing to a married ear!

When shepherds pipe on oaten straws
   And merry larks are ploughmen's clocks,
When turtles tread, and rooks, and daws,
   And maidens bleach their summer smocks,
The cuckoo then on every tree
Mocks married men; for thus sings he,
           Cuckoo;
Cuckoo, cuckoo: O word of fear,
Unpleasing to a married ear!

WINTER

When icicles hang by the wall,
   And Dick the shepherd blows his nail,
And Tom bears logs into the hall,
   And milk comes frozen home in pail,
When blood is nipt and ways be foul,
Then nightly sings the staring owl,
           Tu-whit;
Tu-who, a merry note,
While greasy Joan doth keel the pot.

When all aloud the wind doth blow,
   And coughing drowns the parson's saw,
And birds sit brooding in the snow,
   And Marian's nose looks red and raw,
When roasted crabs hiss in the bowl,
Then nightly sings the staring owl,
           Tu-whit;
Tu-who, a merry note,
While greasy Joan doth keel the pot.

68   Look how a bird lies tangled in a net,
So fasten'd in her arms Adonis lies.

69
The ousel-cock so black of hue,
  With orange-tawny bill,
The throstle with his note so true,
  The wren with little quill:
The finch, the sparrow, and the lark,
  The plain-song cuckoo gray,
Whose note full many a man doth mark,
  And dares not answer nay.

70
Lo, here the gentle lark, weary of rest,
From his moist cabinet mounts up on high,
And wakes the morning, from whose silver breast
The sun ariseth in his majesty;
  Who doth the world so gloriously behold,
  That cedar-tops and hills seem burnisht gold.

71
Like a dive-dapper peering through a wave,
Who, being lookt on, ducks as quickly in.

72
As wild geese that the creeping fowler eye,
Or russet-pated choughs, many in sort,
Rising and cawing at the gun's report,
Sever themselves, and madly sweep the sky.

73
Hark, hark! the lark at heaven's gate sings,
  And Phœbus gins arise,
His steeds to water at those springs
On chaliced flowers that lies;
And winking Mary-buds begin
  To ope their golden eyes:
With every thing that pretty is,
  My lady sweet, arise;
    Arise, arise!

74   Come on, sir; here's the place:—stand still.—How
      fearful
And dizzy 'tis to cast one's eyes so low!
The crows and choughs that wing the midway air
Show scarce so gross as beetles: half way down
Hangs one that gathers samphire,—dreadful trade!
Methinks he seems no bigger than his head:
The fishermen, that walk upon the beach,
Appear like mice; and yond tall anchoring bark,
Diminisht to her cock,—her cock, a buoy
Almost too small for sight: the murmuring surge,
That on the unnumber'd idle pebbles chafes,
Cannot be heard so high.—I'll look no more;
Lest my brain turn, and the deficient sight
Topple down headlong.

75   This guest of summer,
The temple-haunting martlet, does approve,
By his lov'd mansionry, that the heavens' breath
Smells wooingly here: no jutty, frieze,
Buttress, nor coign of vantage, but this bird
Hath made his pendent bed and procreant cradle:
Where they most breed and haunt, I have observed
The air is delicate.

76   Between two hawks, which flies the higher pitch;
Between two dogs, which hath the deeper mouth;
Between two blades, which bears the better temper;
Between two horses, which doth bear him best;
Between two girls, which hath the merriest eye;—
I have, perhaps, some shallow spirit of judgement:
But in these nice sharp quillets of the law,
    Good faith, I am no wiser than a daw.

77   My falcon now is sharp, and passing empty;
     And, till she stoop, she must not be full-gorged,
     For then she never looks upon her lure.
     Another way I have to man my haggard,
     To make her come, and know her keeper's call,
     That is, to watch her, as we watch these kites
     That bate, and beat, and will not be obedient.

78   If I do prove her haggard,
     Though that her jesses were my dear heartstrings,
     I'ld whistle her off, and let her down the wind,
     To prey at fortune.

79   The pleasant'st angling is to see the fish
     Cut with her golden oars the silver stream,
     And greedily devour the treacherous bait.

80   DAUPHIN
     My Lord of Orleans, and my lord high-Constable,
     you talk of horse and armour?
                       DUKE OF ORLEANS
     You are as well provided of both as any prince in the
     world.
                       DAUPHIN
     What a long night is this!—I will not change my
     horse with any that treads but on four pasterns.
     Ça, ha! he bounds from the earth, as if his entrails
     were hairs; le cheval volant, the Pegasus, qui a les
     narines de feu! When I bestride him, I soar, I am a
     hawk: he trots the air; the earth sings when he
     touches it; the basest horn of his hoof is more musical
     than the pipe of Hermes.

THE AGES OF MAN

DUKE OF ORLEANS

He's of the colour of the nutmeg.

DAUPHIN

And of the heat of the ginger. It is a beast for Perseus: he is pure air and fire; and the dull elements of earth and water never appear in him, but only in patient stillness while his rider mounts him: he is, indeed, a horse; and all other jades you may call beasts.

THE CONSTABLE OF FRANCE

Indeed, my lord, it is a most absolute and excellent horse.

DAUPHIN

It is the prince of palfreys; his neigh is like the bidding of a monarch, and his countenance enforces homage.

DUKE OF ORLEANS

No more, cousin.

DAUPHIN

Nay, the man hath no wit that cannot, from the rising of the lark to the lodging of the lamb, vary deserved praise on my palfrey: it is a theme as fluent as the sea; turns the sands into eloquent tongues, and my horse is argument for them all: 'tis a subject for a sovereign to reason on, and for a sovereign's sovereign to ride on; and for the world, familiar to us and unknown, to lay apart their particular functions, and wonder at him. I once writ a sonnet in his praise, and began thus 'Wonder of nature,'—

DUKE OF ORLEANS

I have heard a sonnet begin so to one's mistress.

DAUPHIN

Then did they imitate that which I composed to my courser; for my horse is my mistress.

81   But, lo, from forth a copse that neighbours by,
A breeding jennet, lusty, young, and proud,
Adonis' trampling courser doth espy,
And forth she rushes, snorts, and neighs aloud:
   The strong neckt steed, being tied unto a tree,
   Breaketh his rein, and to her straight goes he.

Imperiously he leaps, he neighs, he bounds,
And now his woven girths he breaks asunder;
The bearing earth with his hard hoof he wounds,
Whose hollow womb resounds like heaven's thunder;
   The iron bit he crusheth 'tween his teeth,
   Controlling what he was controlled with.

His ears up-prickt; his braided hanging mane
Upon his compast crest now stand on end;
His nostrils drink the air, and forth again,
As from a furnace, vapours doth he send;
   His eye, which scornfully glisters like fire,
   Shows his hot courage and his high desire.

Sometimes he trots, as if he told the steps,
With gentle majesty and modest pride;
Anon he rears upright, curvets and leaps,
As who should say, 'Lo, thus my strength is tried;
   And this I do to captivate the eye
   Of the fair breeder that is atanding by.'

What recketh he his rider's angry stir,
His flattering 'Holla' or his 'Stand, I say'?
What cares he now for curb or pricking spur?
For rich caparisons or trapping gay?
   He sees his love, and nothing else he sees,
   For nothing else with his proud sight agrees.

THE AGES OF MAN

Look, when a painter would surpass the life
In limning out a well-proportion'd steed,
His art with nature's workmanship at strife,
As if the dead the living should exceed;
  So did this horse excel a common one
  In shape, in courage, colour, pace, and bone.

Round-hooft, short-jointed, fetlocks shag and long,
Broad breast, full eye, small head, and nostril wide,
High crest, short ears, straight legs, and passing
    strong,
Thin mane, thick tail, broad buttock, tender hide:
  Look, what a horse should have he did not lack,
  Save a proud rider on so proud a back.

Sometime he scuds far off, and there he stares;
Anon he starts at stirring of a feather;
To bid the wind a base he now prepares,
And whe'r he run or fly they know not whether;
  For through his mane and tail the high wind sings,
  Fanning the hairs, who wave like feather'd wings.

He looks upon his love, and neighs unto her;
She answers him, as if she knew his mind:
Being proud, as females are, to see him woo her,
She puts on outward strangeness, seems unkind;
  Spurns at his love, and scorns the heat he feels,
  Beating his kind embracements with her heels.

82   Two months since,
Here was a gentleman of Normandy,—
I've seen myself, and served against, the French,
And they can well on horseback: but this gallant
Had witchcraft in't; he grew unto his seat;

And to such wondrous doing brought his horse,
As he had been incorpsed and demi-natured
With the brave beast: so far he topt my thought,
That I, in forgery of shapes and tricks,
Come short of what he did.

83 Why, Petruchio is coming, in a new hat and an old
jerkin; a pair of old breeches, thrice turn'd; a pair of
boots that have been candle-cases, one buckled,
another laced; an old rusty sword ta'en out of the
town-armoury, with a broken hilt, and chapeless;
with two broken points: his horse hipt with an old
mothy saddle, and stirrups of no kindred; besides,
possest with the glanders, and like to mose in the
chine; troubled with the lampass, infected with the
fashions, full of windgalls, sped with spavins, ray'd
with the yellows, past cure of the fives, stark spoil'd
with the staggers, begnawn with the bots; sway'd in
the back, and shoulder-shotten; near-legg'd before,
and with a half-cheekt bit, and a headstall of sheep's
leather, which, being restrain'd to keep him from
stumbling, hath been often burst, and new-repair'd
with knots; one girth six times pieced, and a woman's
crupper of velure, which hath two letters for her
name fairly set down in studs, and here and there
pieced with packthread.

84   HIPPOLYTA
I was with Hercules and Cadmus once,
When in a wood of Crete they bay'd the bear
With hounds of Sparta: never did I hear
Such gallant chiding; for, besides the groves,
The skies, the fountains, every region near
Seem all one mutual cry: I never heard
So musical a discord, such sweet thunder.

THESEUS

My hounds are bred out of the Spartan kind,
So flew'd, so sanded; and their heads are hung
With ears that sweep away the morning dew;
Crook-knee'd, and dew-lapt like Thessalian bulls
Slow in pursuit, but matcht in mouth like bells,
Each under each. A cry more tuneable
Was never holla'd to, nor cheer'd with horn,
In Crete, in Sparta, nor in Thessaly:
Judge when you hear.

85

LORD

Huntsman, I charge thee, tender well my hounds:
Brach Merriman, the poor cur is imbost;
And couple Clowder with the deep-mouth'd brach.
Saw'st thou not, boy, how Silver made it good
At the hedge-corner, in the coldest fault?
I would not lose the dog for twenty pound.

FIRST HUNTSMAN

Why, Belman is as good as he, my lord;
He cried upon it at the merest loss,
And twice to-day pickt out the dullest scent:
Trust me, I take him for the better dog.

LORD

Thou art a fool: if Echo were as fleet,
I would esteem him worth a dozen such.
But sup them well, and look unto them all:
To-morrow I intend to hunt again.

86

MURDERER

                We are men, my liege.

MACBETH

Ay, in the catalogue ye go for men;
As hounds, and greyhounds, mongrels, spaniels, curs,
Shoughs, water-rugs, and demi-wolves, are clept

A HUNTED HARE

All by the name of dogs: the valued file
Distinguishes the swift, the slow, the subtle,
The housekeeper, the hunter, every one
According to the gift which bounteous nature
Hath in him closed; whereby he does receive
Particular addition, from the bill
That writes them all alike: and so of men.

87   I think Crab my dog be the sourest-natured dog that
lives: my mother weeping, my father wailing, my
sister crying, our maid howling, our cat wringing
her hands, and all our house in a great perplexity,
yet did not this cruel-hearted cur shed one tear:
he is a stone, a very pebble-stone, and has no more
pity in him than a dog: a Jew would have wept to
have seen our parting; why, my grandam, having no
eyes, look you, wept herself blind at my parting.

88   But if thou needs wilt hunt, be ruled by me;
Uncouple at the timorous flying hare,
Or at the fox which lives by subtlety,
Or at the roe which no encounter dare:
   Pursue these fearful creatures o'er the downs,
   And on thy well-breathed horse keep with thy
     hounds.

And when thou hast on foot the purblind hare,
Mark the poor wretch, to overshoot his troubles
How he outruns the wind, and with what care
He cranks and crosses with a thousand doubles:
   The many musets through the which he goes
   Are like a labyrinth to amaze his foes.

Sometime he runs among a flock of sheep,
To make the cunning hounds mistake their smell,
And sometime where earth-delving conies keep,
To stop the loud pursuers in their yell;
    And sometime sorteth with a herd of deer:
    Danger deviseth shifts; wit waits on fear:

For there his smell with others being mingled,
The hot scent-snuffing hounds are driven to doubt,
Ceasing their clamorous cry till they have singled
With much ado the cold fault cleanly out;
    Then do they spend their mouths: Echo replies,
    As if another chase were in the skies.

By this, poor Wat, far off upon a hill,
Stands on his hinder legs with list'ning ear,
To hearken if his foes pursue him still:
Anon their loud alarums he doth hear;
    And now his grief may be compared well
    To one sore sick that hears the passing-bell.

Then shalt thou see the dew-bedabbled wretch
Turn, and return, indenting with the way;
Each envious brier his weary legs doth scratch,
Each shadow makes him stop, each murmur stay;
    For misery is trodden on by many,
    And being low never relieved by any.

89

    Tell me where is fancy bred,
    Or in the heart or in the head?
    How begot, how nourished?
        Reply, reply.
    It is engender'd in the eyes,
    With gazing fed; and fancy dies
    In the cradle where it lies.
        Let us all ring fancy's knell;
        I'll begin it,—Ding, dong, bell.

90
    But love, first learned in a lady's eyes,
    Lives not alone immured in the brain;
    But, with the motion of all elements,
    Courses as swift as thought in every power,
    And gives to every power a double power,
    Above their functions and their offices.
    It adds a precious seeing to the eye;
    A lover's eyes will gaze an eagle blind;
    A lover's ear will hear the lowest sound,
    When the suspicious head of theft is stopt:
    Love's feeling is more soft and sensible
    Than are the tender horns of cockled snails;
    Love's tongue proves dainty Bacchus gross in taste
    For valour, is not Love a Hercules,
    Still climbing trees in the Hesperides?
    Subtle as Sphinx; as sweet and musical
    As bright Apollo's lute, strung with his hair:
    And when Love speaks, the voice of all the gods
    Make heaven drowsy with the harmony.
    Never durst poet touch a pen to write
    Until his ink were temper'd with Love's sighs;
    O, then his lines would ravish savage ears
    And plant in tyrants mild humility.
    From women's eyes this doctrine I derive:
    They sparkle still the right Promethean fire;
    They are the books, the arts, the academes,
    That show, contain and nourish all the world:
    Else none at all in aught proves excellent.

91
    Or as the snail, whose tender horns being hit,
    Shrinks backward in his shelly cave with pain,
    And there, all smother'd up, in shade doth sit,
    Long after fearing to creep forth again.

92 Our poesy is as a gum, which oozes
From whence 'tis nourisht: the fire i'the flint
Shows not till it be struck; our gentle flame
Provokes itself, and, like the current, flies
Each bound it chafes.

93 The lunatic, the lover, and the poet
Are of imagination all compact:—
One sees more devils than vast hell can hold,—
That is, the madman: the lover, all as frantic,
Sees Helen's beauty in a brow of Egypt:
The poet's eye, in a fine frenzy rolling,
Doth glance from heaven to earth, from earth to
  heaven;
And, as imagination bodies forth
The forms of things unknown, the poet's pen
Turns them to shapes, and gives to airy nothing
A local habitation and a name.

94   TOUCHSTONE
Truly, I would the gods had made thee poetical.
      AUDREY
I do not know what 'poetical' is: is it honest in deed
and word? is it a true thing?
      TOUCHSTONE
No, truly; for the truest poetry is the most feigning;
and lovers are given to poetry; and what they swear
in poetry may be said as lovers they do feign.

95 When in the chronicle of wasted time
I see descriptions of the fairest wights,
And beauty making beautiful old rime
In praise of ladies dead and lovely knights,

Then, in the blazon of sweet beauty's best,
Of hand, of foot, of lip, of eye, of brow,
I see their antique pen would have exprest
Even such a beauty as you master now.
So all their praises are but prophecies
Of this our time, all you prefiguring;
And, for they lookt but with divining eyes,
They had not skill enough your worth to sing:
    For we, which now behold these present days,
    Have eyes to wonder, but lack tongues to praise.

96 I had rather be a kitten, and cry mew,
Than one of these same metre ballet-mongers;
I had rather hear a brazen canstick turn'd,
Or a dry wheel grate on the axletree;
And that would set my teeth nothing on edge,
Nothing so much as mincing poetry:—
'Tis like the forced gait of a shuffling nag.

97   PHEBE
Good shepherd, tell this youth what 'tis to love.
                    SILVIUS
It is to be all made of sighs and tears;—
And so am I for Phebe.
                    PHEBE
And I for Ganymede.
                    ORLANDO
And I for Rosalind.
                    ROSALIND
And I for no woman.
                    SILVIUS
It is to be all made of faith and service;—
And so am I for Phebe.

PHEBE
And I for Ganymede.

ORLANDO
And I for Rosalind.

ROSALIND
And I for no woman.

SILVIUS
It is to be all made of fantasy,
All made of passion, and all made of wishes;
All adoration, duty, and observance,
All humbleness, all patience, and impatience,
All purity, all trial, all deservings;—
And so am I for Phebe.

PHEBE
And so am I for Ganymede.

ORLANDO
And so am I for Rosalind.

ROSALIND
And so am I for no woman.

98 Ay me! for aught that I could ever read,
Could ever hear by tale or history,
The course of true love never did run smooth;
But, either it was different in blood,—
Or, if there were a sympathy in choice,
War, death, or sickness did lay siege to it,
Making it momentary as a sound,
Swift as a shadow, short as any dream;
Brief as the lightning in the collied night,
That, in a spleen, unfolds both heaven and earth,
And ere a man hath power to say, 'Behold!'
The jaws of darkness do devour it up:
So quick bright things come to confusion.

99   Lovers and madmen have such seething brains,
      Such shaping fantasies, that apprehend
      More than cool reason ever comprehends.

100   O, how this spring of love resembleth
           The uncertain glory of an April day,
           Which now shows all the beauty of the sun,
           And by and by a cloud takes all away!

101   I remember, when I was in love I broke my
      sword upon a stone, and bid him take that for
      coming a-night to Jane Smile: and I remember the
      kissing of her batlet, and the cow's dugs that her
      pretty chopt hands had milkt: and I remember the
      wooing of a peascod instead of her; from whom I took
      two cods, and, giving her them again, said with weep-
      ing tears, 'Wear these for my sake.' We that are true
      lovers run into strange capers; but as all is mortal in
      nature, so is all nature in love mortal in folly.

102   I have not seen
      So likely an ambassador of love:
      A day in April never came so sweet,
      To show how costly summer was at hand,
      As this fore-spurrer comes before his lord.

103   She shall be dignified with this high honour,—
      To bear my lady's train, lest the base earth
      Should from her vesture chance to steal a kiss,
      And, of so great a favour growing proud,
      Disdain to root the summer-swelling flower,
      And make rough winter everlastingly.

104   O, she is lame! love's heralds should be thoughts,
Which ten times faster glide than the sun's beams,
Driving back shadows over louring hills:
Therefore do nimble-pinion'd doves draw love,
And therefore hath the wind-swift Cupid wings.
Now is the sun upon the highmost hill
Of this day's journey; and from nine till twelve
Is three long hours,—yet she is not come.
Had she affections and warm youthful blood,
She'ld be as swift in motion as a ball;
My words would bandy her to my sweet love,
And his to me.

105   Madam, an hour before the worshipt sun
Peer'd forth the golden window of the east,
A troubled mind drave me to walk abroad;
Where—underneath the grove of sycamore
That westward rooteth from the city's side—
So early walking did I see your son:
Towards him I made; but he was ware of me,
And stole into the covert of the wood:
I, measuring his affections by my own,
Which then most sought where most might not be
    found,
Being one too many by my weary self,
Pursued my humour, not pursuing his,
And gladly shunn'd who gladly fled from me.

Many a morning hath he there been seen,
With tears augmenting the fresh morning's dew,
Adding to clouds more clouds with his deep sighs:
But all so soon as the all-cheering sun
Should in the farthest east begin to draw
The shady curtains from Aurora's bed,
Away from light steals home my heavy son.

And private in his chamber pens himself;
Shuts up his windows, locks fair daylight out,
And makes himself an artificial night:
Black and portentous must this humour prove,
Unless good counsel may the cause remove.

But he, his own affections' counsellor,
Is to himself,—I will not say how true,—
But to himself so secret and so close,
So far from sounding and discovery,
As is the bud bit with an envious worm,
Ere he can spread his sweet leaves to the air,
Or dedicate his beauty to the sun.

106   O,—and I, forsooth, in love! I, that have been love's
     whip;
A very beadle to a humorous sigh;
A critic, nay, a night-watch constable;
A domineering pedant o'er the boy,
Than whom no mortal so magnificent!
This wimpled, whining, purblind, wayward boy;
This signior-junior, giant-dwarf, Dan Cupid;
Regent of love-rimes, lord of folded arms,
Th' anointed sovereign of sighs and groans,
Liege of all loiterers and malecontents,
Dread prince of plackets, king of codpieces,
Sole imperator and great general
Of trotting paritors:—O my little heart!—
And I to be a corporal of his field,
And wear his colours like a tumbler's hoop!
What! I love! I sue! I seek a wife!
A woman, that is like a German clock,
Still a-repairing; ever out of frame;
And never going aright, being a watch,
But being watcht that it may still go right!

Nay, to be perjured, which is worst of all;
And, among three, to love the worst of all;
A whitely wanton with a velvet brow,
With two pitch-balls stuck in her face for eyes;
Ay, and, by heaven, one that will do the deed,
Though Argus were her eunuch and her guard:
And I to sigh for her! to watch for her!
To pray for her! Go to; it is a plague
That Cupid will impose for my neglect
Of his almighty dreadful little might.
Well, I will love, write, sigh, pray, sue, and groan:
Some men must love my lady, and some Joan.

107

SILVIUS

O Corin, that thou knew'st how I do love her!

CORIN

I partly guess; for I have loved ere now.

SILVIUS

No, Corin, being old, thou canst not guess;
Though in thy youth thou wast as true a lover
As ever sigh'd upon a midnight pillow:
But if thy love were ever like to mine,—
As sure I think did never man love so,—
How many actions most ridiculous
Hast thou been drawn to by thy fantasy?

CORIN

Into a thousand that I have forgotten.

SILVIUS

O, thou didst then never love so heartily!
If thou remember'st not the slightest folly
That ever love did make thee run into,
Thou hast not loved:
Or if thou hast not sat as I do now,
Wearing thy hearer in thy mistress' praise,

Thou hast not loved:
Or if thou hast not broke from company
Abruptly, as my passion now makes me,
Thou hast not loved.
O Phebe, Phebe, Phebe!

108   O, never will I trust to speeches penn'd,
     Nor to the motion of a schoolboy's tongue,
Nor never come in visard to my friend,
     Nor woo in rime, like a blind harper's song!
Taffeta phrases, silken terms precise,
     Three-piled hyperboles, spruce affectation,
Figures pedantical; these summer-flies
     Have blown me full of maggot ostentation:
I do forswear them; and I here protest,
     By this white glove,—how white the hand, God
      knows!—
Henceforth my wooing mind shall be exprest
     In russet yeas and honest kersey noes.

109

ROSALIND

There is none of my uncle's marks upon you: he
taught me how to know a man in love; in which cage
of rushes I am sure you are not prisoner.

ORLANDO

What were his marks?

ROSALIND

A lean cheek,—which you have not; a blue eye and
sunken,—which you have not; an unquestionable
spirit,—which you have not; a beard neglected,—
which you have not;—but I pardon you for that; for
simply your having in beard is a younger brother's
revenue:—then your hose should be ungarter'd, your

bonnet unbanded, your sleeve unbutton'd, your shoe untied, and every thing about you demonstrating a careless desolation;—but you are no such a man,— you are rather point-devise in your accoutrements, as loving yourself than seeming the lover of any other.

110   If he be not in love with some woman, there is no believing old signs: a' brushes his hat o' mornings; what should that bode?

111   VALENTINE
Why, how know you that I am in love?
                         SPEED
Marry, by these special marks: first, you have learn'd, like Sir Proteus, to wreathe your arms, like a malecontent; to relish a love-song, like a robin-redbreast; to walk alone, like one that had the pestilence; to sigh, like a school-boy that had lost his A B C ; to weep, like a young wench that had buried her grandam; to fast, like one that takes diet; to watch, like one that fears robbing; to speak puling, like a beggar at Hallowmas. You were wont, when you laugh'd, to crow like a cock; when you walk'd, to walk like one of the lions; when you fasted, it was presently after dinner; when you look'd sadly, it was for want of money: and now you are metamorphosed with a mistress, that, when I look on you, I can hardly think you my master.

112   My lord, as I was sewing in my chamber,
Lord Hamlet,—with his doublet all unbraced;
No hat upon his head; his stockings foul'd,
Ungarter'd, and down-gyved to his ancle;

WOOING

Pale as his shirt; his knees knocking each other;
And with a look so piteous in purport
As if he had been loosed out of hell
To speak of horrors,—he comes before me . .

He took me by the wrist, and held me hard;
Then goes he to the length of all his arm;
And, with his other hand thus o'er his brow,
He falls to such perusal of my face
As he would draw it. Long stay'd he so;
At last,—a little shaking of mine arm,
And thrice his head thus waving up and down,—
He raised a sigh so piteous and profound,
That it did seem to shatter all his bulk,
And end his being: that done, he lets me go:
And, with his head over his shoulder turn'd,
He seem'd to find his way without his eyes;
For out o' doors he went without their help,
And, to the last, bended their light on me.

13   Come, woo me, woo me; for now I am in a holiday
      humour, and like enough to consent.

14   Say, that upon the altar of her beauty
      You sacrifice your tears, your sighs, your heart:
      Write till your ink be dry, and with your tears
      Moist it again, and frame some feeling line
      That may discover such integrity:
      For Orpheus' lute was strung with poets' sinews;
      Whose golden touch could soften steel and stones,
      Make tigers tame, and huge leviathans
      Forsake unsounded deeps to dance on sands.

115
VIOLA
If I did love you in my master's flame,
With such a suffering, such a deadly life,
In your denial I would find no sense;
I would not understand it.
OLIVIA
Why, what would you?
VIOLA
Make me a willow cabin at your gate,
And call upon my soul within the house;
Write loyal cantons of contemned love,
And sing them loud even in the dead of night;
Holla your name to the reverberate hills,
And make the babbling gossip of the air
Cry out, 'Olivia!' O, you should not rest
Between the elements of air and earth,
But you should pity me!

116
Tell me, Apollo, for thy Daphne's love,
What Cressid is, what Pandar, and what we?
Her bed is India; there she lies, a pearl:
Between our Ilium and where she resides,
Let it be call'd the wild and wandering flood.
Ourself the merchant; and this sailing Pandar,
Our doubtful hope, our convoy, and our bark.

117
He says he loves my daughter:
I think so too; for never gazed the moon
Upon the water, as he'll stand, and read,
As 'twere, my daughter's eyes: and, to be plain,
I think there is not half a kiss to choose
Who loves another best.

118   This is the deadly spite that angers me,—
My wife can speak no English, I no Welsh.
I understand thy looks: that pretty Welsh
Which thou pour'st down from these swelling heavens
I am too perfect in; and, but for shame,
In such a parley should I answer thee.
I understand thy kisses, and thou mine,
And that's a feeling disputation:
But I will never be a truant, love,
Till I have learn'd thy language; for thy tongue
Makes Welsh as sweet as ditties highly penn'd,
Sung by a fair queen in a summer's bower,
With ravishing division, to her lute.

119   She bids you on the wanton rushes lay you down,
And rest your gentle head upon her lap,
And she will sing the song that pleaseth you,
And on your eyelids crown the god of sleep,
Charming your blood with pleasing heaviness,
Making such difference 'twixt wake and sleep,
As is the difference betwixt day and night,
The hour before the heavenly-harness'd team
Begins his golden progress in the east.

120   Let thy song be love: this love will undo us all.
O Cupid, Cupid, Cupid!

121   Give me some music,—music, moody food
Of as that trade in love.

122   If music be the food of love, play on;
Give me excess of it, that, surfeiting,
The appetite may sicken, and so die.—
That strain again!—it had a dying fall:
O, it came o'er my ear like the sweet sound,
That breathes upon a bank of violets,
Stealing and giving odour!—Enough; no more;
'Tis not so sweet now as it was before.
O spirit of love, how quick and fresh art thou!
That, notwithstanding thy capacity
Receiveth as the sea, naught enters there,
Of what validity and pitch so'er,
But falls into abatement and low price,
Even in a minute! so full of shapes is fancy,
That it alone is high-fantastical.

123   ORSINO
Come hither, boy: if ever thou shalt love,
In the sweet pangs of it remember me;
For such as I am all true lovers are,
Unstaid and skittish in all motions else,
Save in the constant image of the creature
That is beloved.—How dost thou like this tune?
               VIOLA
It gives a very echo to the seat
Where Love is throned.

124   How sweet the moonlight sleeps upon this bank!
Here will we sit, and let the sounds of music
Creep in our ears: soft stillness and the night
Become the touches of sweet harmony.
Sit, Jessica. Look, how the floor of heaven
Is thick inlaid with patines of bright gold:

GIFTS

There's not the smallest orb which thou behold'st
But in his motion like an angel sings,
Still quiring to the young-eyed cherubins,—
Such harmony is in immortal souls;
But whilst this muddy vesture of decay
Doth grossly close it in, we cannot hear it.

125 Since once I sat upon a promontory,
And heard a mermaid, on a dolphin's back,
Uttering such dulcet and harmonious breath,
That the rude sea grew civil at her song,
And certain stars shot madly from their spheres,
To hear the sea-maid's music.

126 Our love was new, and then but in the spring,
When I was wont to greet it with my lays;
As Philomel in summer's front doth sing,
And stops her pipe in growth of riper days:
Not that the summer is less pleasant now
Than when her mournful hymns did hush the night,
But that wild music burdens every bough,
And sweets grown common lose their dear delight.

127 Lawn as white as driven snow;
Cyprus black as e'er was crow;
Gloves as sweet as damask roses;
Masks for faces and for noses;
Bugle-bracelet, necklace-amber,
Perfume for a lady's chamber;
Golden quoifs and stomachers,
For my lads to give their dears;

Pins and poking-sticks of steel,
What maids lack from head to heel:
Come buy of me, come; come buy, come buy;
Buy, lads, or else your lasses cry:
Come buy.

128   Look here, what tributes wounded fancies sent me,
Of paled pearls and rubies red as blood;
Figuring that they their passions likewise lent me
Of grief and blushes, aptly understood
In bloodless white and the encrimson'd mood;
Effects of terror and dear modesty,
Encampt in hearts, but fighting outwardly.

And, lo, behold these talents of their hair,
With twisted metal amorously impleacht,
I have received from many a several fair—,
Their kind acceptance weepingly beseecht,—
With the annexions of fair gems enricht,
And deep-brain'd sonnets that did amplify
Each stone's dear nature, worth, and quality.

129   OPHELIA
My lord, I have remembrances of yours,
That I have longed long to re-deliver;
I pray you, now receive them.
                  HAMLET
                         No, not I;
I never gave you aught.
                  OPHELIA
My honour'd lord, you know right well you did;
And with them, words of so sweet breath composed
As made the things more rich: their perfume lost,
Take these again; for to the noble mind
Rich gifts wax poor when givers prove unkind.

130   I do much wonder that one man, seeing how much another man is a fool when he dedicates his behaviours to love, will, after he hath laught at such shallow follies in others, become the argument of his own scorn by falling in love: and such a man is Claudio. I have known when there was no music with him but the drum and the fife; and now had he rather hear the tabor and the pipe: I have known when he would have walkt ten mile a-foot to see a good armour; and now will he lie ten nights awake, carving the fashion of a new doublet. He was wont to speak plain and to the purpose, like an honest man and a soldier; and now is he turn'd orthography; his words are a very fantastical banquet,—just so many strange dishes.

131   O mistress mine, where are you roaming?
O, stay and hear; your true-love's coming,
    That can sing both high and low:
Trip no further, pretty sweeting;
Journeys end in lovers' meeting,
    Every wise man's son doth know.

What is love? 'tis not hereafter;
Present mirth hath present laughter;
    What's to come is still unsure:
In delay there lies no plenty;
Then come kiss me, sweet-and-twenty,
    Youth's a stuff will not endure.

132   'Tis beauty truly blent, whose red and white
Nature's own sweet and cunning hand laid on:
Lady, you are the cruell'st she alive,
If you will lead these graces to the grave,
And leave the world no copy

133

Who is Silvia? what is she,
    That all our swains commend her?
Holy, fair, and wise is she;
    The heaven such grace did lend her,
That she might admired be.

Is she kind as she is fair,—
    For beauty lives with kindness?
Love doth to her eyes repair,
    To help him of his blindness;
And, being help'd, inhabits there.

Then to Silvia let us sing,
    That Silvia is excelling;
She excels each mortal thing
    Upon the dull earth dwelling:
To her let us garlands bring.

134

What is your substance, whereof are you made,
That millions of strange shadows on you tend?
Since every one hath, every one, one shade,
And you, but one, can every shadow lend.
Describe Adonis, and the counterfeit
Is poorly imitated after you;
On Helen's cheek all art of beauty set,
And you in Grecian tires are painted new:
Speak of the spring, and foison of the year;
The one doth shadow of your beauty show,
The other as your bounty doth appear,
And you in every blessed shape we know.
    In all external grace you have some part,
    But you like none, none you, for constant heart.

135 Why is my verse so barren of new pride,
So far from variation or quick change?
Why, with the time, do I not glance aside
To new-found methods and to compounds strange?
Why write I still all one, ever the same,
And keep invention in a noted weed,
That every word doth almost tell my name,
Showing their birth, and where they did proceed?
O, know, sweet love, I always write of you,
And you and love are still my argument;
So all my best is dressing old words new,
Spending again what is already spent:
  For as the sun is daily new and old,
  So is my love still telling what is told

136   O, hear me breathe my life
Before this ancient sir, who, it should seem,
Hath sometime loved! I take thy hand,—this hand,
As soft as dove's down and as white as it,
Or Ethiopian's tooth, or the fann'd snow
That's bolted by the northern blasts twice o'er.

137 O, she doth teach the torches to burn bright!
Her beauty hangs upon the cheek of night
Like a rich jewel in an Ethiop's ear.

138   Here are sever'd lips,
Parted with sugar breath: so sweet a bar
Should sunder such sweet friends.

139
O, that her hand,
In whose comparison all whites are ink,
Writing their own reproach; to whose soft seizure
The cygnet's down is harsh, and spirit of sense
Hard as the palm of ploughman!

140
Here comes the lady:—O, so light a foot
Will ne'er wear out the everlasting flint:
A lover may bestride the gossamer
That idles in the wanton summer air,
And yet not fall; so light is vanity.

141
O happy fair!
Your eyes are lode-stars; and your tongue's sweet air
More tuneable than lark to shepherd's ear,
When wheat is green, when hawthorn buds appear.

142
My dearest wife was like this maid, and such a one
My daughter might have been: my queen's square
brows;
Her stature to an inch; as wand-like straight;
As silver-voiced; her eyes as jewel-like,
And cased as richly; in pace another Juno;
Who starves the ears she feeds, and makes them
hungry,
The more she gives them speech.

143
JAQUES
What stature is she of?
ORLANDO
Just as high as my heart

144
 Her lily hand her rosy cheek lies under,
 Cozening the pillow of a lawful kiss.

145
 Full gently now she takes him by the hand,
 A lily prison'd in a goal of snow,
 Or ivory in an alabaster band;
 So white a friend engirts so white a foe:
  This beauteous combat, wilful and unwilling,
  Show'd like two silver doves that sit a-billing.

146
 Without the bed her other fair hand was,
 On the green coverlet; whose perfect white
 Show'd like an April daisy on the grass,
 With pearly sweat, resembling dew of night.
 Her eyes, like marigolds, had sheathed their light,
  And canopied in darkness sweetly lay,
  Till they might open to adorn the day.

147
      Cytherea,
 How bravely thou becomest thy bed! fresh lily!
 And whiter than the sheets! That I might touch!
 But kiss; one kiss!—Rubies unparagon'd,
 How dearly they do't!—'Tis her breathing that
 Perfumes the chamber thus: the flame o'the taper
 Bows towards her; and would under-peep her lids,
 To see the enclosed lights, now canopied
 Under these windows, white and azure, laced
 With blue of heaven's own tinct. . . .
      On her left breast
 A mole cinque-spotted, like the crimson drops
 I'the bottom of a cowslip.

148   Her breasts, like ivory globes circled with blue,
       A pair of maiden worlds unconquered.

149   Chaste as the icicle,
       That's curdied by the frost from purest snow,
       And hangs on Dian's temple.

150   Things base and vile, holding no quantity,
       Love can transpose to form and dignity:
       Love looks not with the eyes, but with the mind;
       And therefore is wing'd Cupid painted blind:
       Nor hath love's mind of any judgement taste;
       Wings, and no eyes, figure unheedy haste:
       And therefore is Love said to be a child,
       Because in choice he is so oft beguiled.
       As waggish boys in game themselves forswear,
       So the boy Love is perjured every where.

151   Methought I was enamour'd of an ass.

152   A poor virgin, sir, an ill-favour'd thing, sir,
       but mine own; a poor humour of mine, sir, to take
       that that no man else will.

153   My mistress' eyes are nothing like the sun;
       Coral is far more red than her lips' red:
       If snow be white, why then her breasts are dun;
       If hairs be wires, black wires grow on her head.
       I have seen roses damaskt, red and white,
       But no such roses see I in her cheeks;
       And in some perfumes is there more delight
       Than in the breath that from my mistress reeks

I love to hear her speak, yet well I know
That music hath a far more pleasing sound:
I grant I never saw a goddess go;
My mistress when she walks treads on the ground.
  And yet, by heaven, I think my love as rare
  As any she belied with false compare.

154   Why, what means this? Why do you look on me?
I see no more in you than in the ordinary
Of nature's sale-work:—'Od's my little life,
I think she means to tangle my eyes too!—
No, faith, proud mistress, hope not after it:
'Tis not your inky brows, your black-silk hair,
Your bugle eyeballs, nor your cheek of cream,
That can entame my spirits to your worship.—
You foolish shepherd, wherefore do you follow her,
Like foggy south, puffing with wind and rain?
You are a thousand times a properer man
Than she a woman: 'tis such fools as you
That makes the world full of ill-favour'd children:
'Tis not her glass, but you, that flatters her;
And out of you she sees herself more proper
Than any of her lineaments can show her.

155   The master, the swabber, the boatswain, and I,
     The gunner, and his mate,
Loved Mall, Meg, and Marian, and Margery,
     But none of us cared for Kate;
     For she had a tongue with a tang,
     Would cry to a sailor, Go hang!
She loved not the savour of tar nor of pitch;
Yet a tailor might scratch her where'er she did itch.
     Then, to sea, boys, and let her go hang!

156   O, what a deal of scorn looks beautiful
        In the contempt and anger of his lip!

157   Disdain and scorn ride sparkling in her eyes.

158   When he speaks,
        The air, a charter'd libertine, is still,
        And the mute wonder lurketh in men's ears,
        To steal his sweet and honey'd sentences.

159   Once more the ruby-colour'd portal open'd,
        Which to his speech did honey passage yield;
        Like a red morn, that ever yet betoken'd
        Wrack to the seaman, tempest to the field,
            Sorrow to shepherds, woe unto the birds,
            Gusts and foul flaws to herdmen and to herds.

160   If love have lent you twenty thousand tongues,
        And every tongue more moving than your own,
        Bewitching like the wanton mermaid's songs,
        Yet from mine ear the tempting tune is blown;
            For know, my heart stands armed in mine ear,
            And will not let a false sound enter there;

        Lest the deceiving harmony should run
        Into the quiet closure of my breast;
        And then my little heart were quite undone,
        In his bedchamber to be barr'd of rest.
            No, lady, no; my heart longs not to groan,
            But soundly sleeps, while now it sleeps alone.

161   Beauty itself doth of itself persuade
        The eyes of men without an orator

162   It was a lover and his lass,
           With a hey, and a ho, and a hey nonino,
       That o'er the green corn-field did pass
           In spring-time, the only pretty ring-time,
     When birds do sing, hey ding a ding, ding:
     Sweet lovers love the spring.

     Between the acres of the rye,
           With a hey, and a ho, and a hey nonino,
     These pretty country-folks would lie
           In spring-time, &c.

     This carol they began that hour,
           With a hey, and a ho, and a hey nonino,
     How that a life was but a flower
           In spring-time, &c.

     And therefore take the present time,
           With a hey, and a ho, and a hey nonino;
     For love is crowned with the prime
           In spring-time, the only pretty ring-time,
     When birds do sing, hey ding a ding, ding:
     Sweet lovers love the spring.

163   On a day, alack the day!
     Love, whose month is ever May,
     Spied a blossom passing fair,
     Playing in the wanton air:
     Through the velvet leaves the wind
     All unseen gan passage find;
     That the lover, sick to death,

Wisht himself the heaven's breath,
'Air,' quoth he, 'thy cheeks may blow;
Air, would I might triumph so!
But, alas! my hand hath sworn
Ne'er to pluck thee from thy thorn:
Vow, alack! for youth unmeet:
Youth, so apt to pluck a sweet.
Do not call it sin in me
That I am forsworn for thee;
Thou for whom e'en Jove would swear
Juno but an Ethiope were;
And deny himself for Jove,
Turning mortal for thy love.'

164   What you do
Still betters what is done. When you speak, sweet,
I'ld have you do it ever: when you sing,
I'ld have you buy and sell so; so give alms;
Pray so; and, for the ord'ring your affairs,
To sing them too: when you do dance, I wish you
A wave o'the sea, that you might ever do
Nothing but that; move still, still so,
And own no other function: each your doing,
So singular in each particular,
Crowns what you are doing in the present deeds,
That all your acts are queens.

165 Her tongue will not obey her heart, nor can
Her heart inform her tongue,—the swan's down-
   feather,
That stands upon the swell at full of tide,
And neither way inclines.

166   O, how her fear did make her colour rise!
       First red as roses that on lawn we lay,
       Then white as lawn, the roses took away

167   O, speak again, bright angel! for thou art
       As glorious to this night, being o'er my head,
       As is a winged messenger of heaven
       Unto the white-upturned wondering eyes
       Of mortals that fall back to gaze on him
       When he bestrides the lazy-pacing clouds
       And sails upon the bosom of the air.

168   It is my lady; O, it is my love!
            O, that she knew she were!

169   ENOBARBUS
    I will tell you.
    The barge she sat in, like a burnisht throne,
    Burnt on the water: the poop was beaten gold;
    Purple the sails, and so perfumed that
    The winds were love-sick with them; the oars were
        silver,
    Which to the tune of flutes kept stroke, and made
    The water which they beat to follow faster,
    As amorous of their strokes. For her own person,
    It beggar'd all description: she did lie
    In her pavilion—cloth-of-gold of tissue—
    O'er-picturing that Venus where we see
    The fancy outwork nature: on each side her
    Stood pretty dimpled boys, like smiling Cupids,
    With divers-colour'd fans, whose wind did seem
    To glow the delicate cheeks which they did cool,
    And what they undid did.

AGRIPPA
   O, rare for Antony!

ENOBARBUS

Her gentlewomen, like the Nereides,
So many mermaids, tended her i'the eyes,
And made their bends adornings: at the helm
A seeming mermaid steers: the silken tackle
Swell with the touches of those flower-soft hands,
That yarely frame the office. From the barge
A strange invisible perfume hits the sense
Of the adjacent wharfs. The city cast
Her people out upon her; and Antony,
Enthroned i'the market-place, did sit alone,
Whistling to the air; which, but for vacancy,
Had gone to gaze on Cleopatra too,
And made a gap in nature.

AGRIPPA
    Rare Egyptian!

ENOBARBUS

Upon her landing, Antony sent to her,
Invited her to supper: she replied,
It should be better he became her guest;
Which she entreated: our courteous Antony,
Whom ne'er the word of 'No' woman heard speak,
Being barber'd ten times o'er, goes to the feast,
And for his ordinary pays his heart
For what his eyes eat only.

AGRIPPA
   Royal wench!

She made great Cæsar lay his sword to bed:
He plough'd her, and she cropt.

ENOBARBUS
    I saw her once

Hop forty paces through the public street;
And having lost her breath, she spoke, and panted,
That she did make defect perfection,
And, breathless, power breathe forth.

HOLY LOVE

MAECENAS
Now Antony must leave her utterly.
ENOBARBUS
Never; he will not:
Age cannot wither her, nor custom stale
Her infinite variety: other women cloy
The appetites they feed; but she makes hungry
Where most she satisfies: for vilest things
Become themselves in her; that the holy priests
Bless her when she is riggish.

170   O, she that hath a heart of that fine frame
To pay this debt of love but to a brother,
How will she love, when the rich golden shaft
Hath kill'd the flock of all affections else
That live in her; when liver, brain, and heart,
These sovereign thrones, are all supplied, and fill'd
Her sweet perfections with one self king!—
Away before me to sweet beds of flowers:
Love-thoughts lie rich when canopied with bowers.

171   Proceed, sweet Cupid: thou hast thumpt him
with thy bird-bolt under the left pap.

172   So holy and so perfect is my love,
And I in such a poverty of grace,
That I shall think it a most plenteous crop
To glean the broken ears after the man
That the main harvest reaps: loose now and then
A scatter'd smile, and that I'll live upon.

173
                Then, I confess,
Here on my knee, before high heaven and you,
That before you, and next unto high heaven,
I love your son:—
My friends were poor, but honest; so's my love:
Be not offended; for it hurts not him,
That he is loved of me: I follow him not
By any token of presumptuous suit;
Nor would I have him till I do deserve him;
Yet never know how that desert should be.
I know I love in vain, strive against hope;
Yet in this captious intenible sieve
I still pour in the waters of my love,
And lack not to lose still: thus, Indian-like,
Religious in mine error, I adore
The sun, that looks upon his worshipper,
But knows of him no more.

174
I am no pilot; yet, wert thou as far
As that vast shore washt with the furthest sea,
I would adventure for such merchandise.

175
                ROMEO
Lady, by yonder blessed moon I swear,
That tips with silver all these fruit-tree tops,—
                JULIET
O, swear not by the moon, th'inconstant moon,
That monthly changes in her circled orb,
Lest that thy love prove likewise variable.
                ROMEO
What shall I swear by?
                JULIET
                Do not swear at all;
Or, if thou wilt, swear by thy gracious self,
Which is the god of my idolatry,
And I'll believe thee.

176 My bounty is as boundless as the sea,
My love as deep; the more I give to thee,
The more I have, for both are infinite.

177
JULIET
'Tis almost morning; I would have thee gone,—
And yet no further than a wanton's bird,
Who lets it hop a little from her hand,
Like a poor prisoner in his twisted gyves,
And with a silk thread plucks it back again,
So loving-jealous of his liberty.
ROMEO
I would I were thy bird.
JULIET
                    Sweet, so would I:
Yet I should kill thee with much cherishing.
Good night, good night! parting is such sweet sorrow
That I shall say good night till it be morrow.

178
TROILUS
Dear, trouble not yourself: the morn is cold.
CRESSIDA
Then, sweet my lord, I'll call mine uncle down;
He shall unbolt the gates.
TROILUS
              Trouble him not;
To bed, to bed; sleep kill those pretty eyes,
And give as soft attachment to thy senses
As infants' empty of all thought!
CRESSIDA
              Good morrow, then.
TROILUS
I prithee now, to bed.
CRESSIDA
              Are you a-weary of me?

TROILUS

O Cressida! but that the busy day,
Waked by the lark, hath roused the ribald crows,
And dreaming night will hide our joys no longer,
I would not from thee.

CRESSIDA

   Night hath been too brief.

TROILUS

Beshrew the witch! with venomous wights she stays
As tediously as hell; but flies the grasps of love
With wings more momentary-swift than thought.
You will catch cold, and curse me.

CRESSIDA

    Prithee, tarry;—
You men will never tarry.—
O foolish Cressid!—I might have still held off,
And then you would have tarried.

79

LORENZO

The moon shines bright:—in such a night as this,
When the sweet wind did gently kiss the trees,
And they did make no noise,—in such a night
Troilus methinks mounted the Troyan walls,
And sigh'd his soul toward the Grecian tents,
Where Cressid lay that night.

JESSICA

     In such a night
Did Thisbe fearfully o'ertrip the dew,
And saw the lion's shadow ere himself,
And ran dismay'd away.

LORENZO

     In such a night
Stood Dido with a willow in her hand
Upon the wild sea-banks, and waft her love
To come again to Carthage.

JESSICA

In such a night
Medea gather'd the enchanted herbs
That did renew old Aeson

LORENZO

In such a night
Did Jessica steal from the wealthy Jew,
And with an unthrift love did run from Venice
As far as Belmont.

JESSICA

In such a night
Did young Lorenzo swear he loved her well,
Stealing her soul with many vows of faith,
And ne'er a true one.

LORENZO

In such a night
Did pretty Jessica, like a little shrew,
Slander her love, and he forgave it her.

JESSICA

I would out-night you, did no body come:
But, hark, I hear the footing of a man.

180

VIOLA

Say that some lady—as, perhaps, there is—
Hath for your love as great a pang of heart
As you have for Olivia: you cannot love her;
You tell her so; must she not, then, be answer'd?

ORSINO

There is no woman's sides
Can bide the beating of so strong a passion
As love doth give my heart; no woman's heart
So big, to hold so much; they lack retention.
Alas, their love may be call'd appetite,—
No motion of the liver, but the palate,—
That suffer surfeit, cloyment, and revolt;
But mine is all as hungry as the sea,

And can digest as much: make no compare
Between that love a woman can bear me
And that I owe Olivia.

VIOLA

                Ay, but I know,—

ORSINO

What dost thou know?

VIOLA

Too well what love women to men may owe:
In faith, they are as true of heart as we.
My father had a daughter loved a man,
As it might be, perhaps, were I a woman,
I should your lordship.

ORSINO

                And what's her history?

VIOLA

A blank, my lord. She never told her love,
But let concealment, like a worm i'th'bud,
Feed on her damask cheek: she pined in thought;
And, with a green and yellow melancholy,
She sat like Patience on a monument,
Smiling at grief. Was not this love indeed?
We men may say more, swear more: but, indeed,
Our shows are more than will; for still we prove
Much in our vows, but little in our love.

181
                    Yet thou dost look
Like Patience gazing on kings' graves, and smiling
Extremity out of act.

182
ARIEL

Come unto these yellow sands,
   And then take hands:
Court'sied when you have and kist,—
   The wild waves whist,—

Foot it featly here and there;
And, sweet sprites, the burden bear.
   Hark, hark!
      [*Burden, dispersedly, within.* Bow, wow.]
   The watch-dogs bark:
      [*Burden, dispersedly, within.* Bow, wow.]
   Hark, hark! I hear
   The strain of strutting chanticleer.
      [*Cry:* Cock-a-diddle-dow.]

FERDINAND

Where should this music be? i'the air or the earth?
It sounds no more:—and, sure, it waits upon
Some god o'the island. Sitting on a bank,
Weeping again the king my father's wrack,
This music crept by me upon the waters,
Allaying both their fury and my passion
With its sweet air: thence I have follow'd it,
Or it hath drawn me rather:—but 'tis gone.
No, it begins again.

ARIEL

Full fadom five thy father lies;
   Of his bones are coral made;
Those are pearls that were his eyes;
   Nothing of him that doth fade
But doth suffer a sea-change
Into something rich and strange.
Sea-nymphs hourly ring his knell:
      [*Burden within.* Ding-dong.]
Hark! now I hear them,—Ding-dong, bell.

FERDINAND

The ditty does remember my drown'd father:—
This is no mortal business, nor no sound
That the earth owes:—I hear it now above me.

PROSPERO

The fringed curtains of thine eye advance,
And say what thou see'st yond

THE AGES OF MAN

MIRANDA

What is't? a spirit?
Lord, how it looks about! Believe me, sir,
It carries a brave form:—but 'tis a spirit.

PROSPERO

No, wench; it eats, and sleeps, and hath such senses
As we have, such. This gallant which thou see'st
Was in the wrack; and, but he's something stain'd
With grief, that's beauty's canker, thou mightst call
      him
A goodly person: he hath lost his fellows,
And strays about to find 'em.

MIRANDA

I might call him
A thing divine; for nothing natural
I ever saw so noble.

PROSPERO

It goes on, I see,
As my soul prompts it.—Spirit, fine spirit! I'll free
      thee
Within two days for this.

FERDINAND

Most sure, the goddess
On whom these airs attend!—Vouchsafe my prayer
May know if you remain upon this island;
And that you will some good instruction give
How I may bear me here: my prime request,
Which I do last pronounce, is, O you wonder!
If you be maid or no?

MIRANDA

No wonder, sir;
But certainly a maid.

FERDINAND

My language! heavens!
I am the best of them that speak this speech,
Were I but where 'tis spoken.

183   My spirits, as in a dream, are all bound up.
My father's loss, the weakness which I feel,
The wrack of all my friends, nor this man's threats
To whom I am subdued, are but light to me,
Might I but through my prison once a day
Behold this maid: all corners else o'the earth
Let liberty make use of; space enough
Have I in such a prison.

184

FERDINAND
I do beseech you,—
Chiefly that I might set it in my prayers,—
What is your name?

MIRANDA
Miranda:—O my father,
I've broke your hest to say so!

FERDINAND
Admired Miranda!
Indeed the top of admiration; worth
What's dearest to the world! Full many a lady
I have eyed with best regard; and many a time
The harmony of their tongues hath into bondage
Brought my too diligent ear: for several virtues
Have I liked several women; never any
With so full soul, but some defect in her
Did quarrel with the noblest grace she owed,
And put it to the foil: but you, O you,
So perfect and so peerless, are created
Of every creature's best!

MIRANDA
I do not know
One of my sex; no woman's face remember,
Save, from my glass, mine own; nor have I seen
More that I may call men, than you, good friend,
And my dear father: how features are abroad,

I'm skilless of; but, by my modesty,—
The jewel in my dower,—I would not wish
Any companion in the world but you;
Nor can imagination form a shape,
Besides yourself, to like of. But I prattle
Something too wildly, and my father's precepts
I therein do forget.

FERDINAND
                        I am, in my condition,
A prince, Miranda; I do think, a king,—
I would not so!—and would no more endure
This wooden slavery than to suffer
The flesh-fly blow my mouth. Hear my soul speak:
The very instant that I saw you, did
My heart fly to your service; there resides
To make me slave to it; and for your sake
Am I this patient log-man.

MIRANDA
                        Do you love me?

FERDINAND
O heaven, O earth, bear witness to this sound,
And crown what I profess with kind event,
If I speak true! if hollowly, invert
What best is boded me to mischief! I,
Beyond all limit of what else i'the world,
Do love, prize, honour you.

MIRANDA
                        I am a fool
To weep at what I am glad of.

PROSPERO
                        Fair encounter
Of two most rare affections! Heavens rain grace
On that which breeds between 'em!

FERDINAND
                        Wherefore weep you?

MIRANDA

At mine unworthiness, that dare not offer
What I desire to give; and much less take
What I shall die to want. But this is trifling;
All and the more it seeks to hide itself,
The bigger bulk it shows. Hence, bashful cunning!
And prompt me, plain and holy innocence!
I am your wife, if you will marry me;
If not, I'll die your maid: to be your fellow
You may deny me; but I'll be your servant,
Whether you will or no.

FERDINAND

My mistress, dearest;
And I thus humble ever.

MIRANDA

My husband, then?

FERDINAND

Ay, with a heart as willing
As bondage e'er of freedom: here's my hand.

MIRANDA

And mine, with my heart in't.

185   Dead shepherd, now I find thy saw of might,—
'Who ever loved that loved not at first sight?'

186   I have inly wept,
Or should have spoke ere this.—Look down, you
   gods,
And on this couple drop a blessed crown!
For it is you that have chalk'd forth the way
Which brought us hither.

187　Touch but my lips with those fair lips of thine,—
Though mine be not so fair, yet are they red,—
The kiss shall be thine own as well as mine:—
What see'st thou in the ground? hold up thy head:
　　Look in mine eyeballs, there thy beauty lies;
　　Then why not lips on lips, since eyes in eyes?

The tender spring upon thy tempting lip
Shows thee unripe; yet mayst thou well be tasted:
Make use of time, let not advantage slip;
Beauty within itself should not be wasted:
　　Fair flowers that are not gather'd in their prime
　　Rot and consume themselves in little time.

Thou canst not see one wrinkle in my brow;
Mine eyes are gray, and bright, and quick in
　　turning;
My beauty as the spring doth yearly grow,
My flesh is soft and plump, my marrow burning;
　　My smooth moist hand, were it with thy hand felt,
　　Would in thy palm dissolve, or seem to melt.

Bid me discourse, I will enchant thine ear,
Or, like a fairy, trip upon the green,
Or, like a nymph, with long dishevell'd hair,
Dance on the sands, and yet no footing seen:
　　Love is a spirit all compact of fire,
　　Not gross to sink, but light, and will aspire.

Torches are made to light, jewels to wear,
Dainties to taste, fresh beauty for the use,
Herbs for their smell, and sappy plants to bear;
Things growing to themselves are growth's abuse:
　　Seeds spring from seeds, and beauty breedeth
　　　beauty;
　　Thou wast begot; to get it is thy duty.

188 From fairest creatures we desire increase,
That thereby beauty's Rose might never die, . . .

Thou that art now the world's fresh ornament,
And only herald to the gaudy spring,
Within thine own bud buriest thy content,
And, tender churl, makest waste in niggarding.

189 With this, he breaketh from the sweet embrace
Of those fair arms which bound him to her breast,
And homeward through the dark laund runs apace;
Leaves Love upon her back deeply distrest.
    Look, how a bright star shooteth from the sky,
    So glides he in the night from Venus' eye;

Which after him she darts, as one on shore
Gazing upon a late-embarked friend,
Till the wild waves will have him see no more,
Whose ridges with the meeting clouds contend:
    So did the merciless and pitchy night
    Fold-in the object that did feed her sight.

Whereat amazed, as one that unaware
Hath dropt a precious jewel in the flood,
Or stonisht as night-wanderers often are,
Their light blown out in some mistrustful wood;
    Even so confounded in the dark she lay,
    Having lost the fair discovery of her way.

190   O, a kiss
Long as my exile, sweet as my revenge!
Now, by the jealous queen of heaven, that kiss
I carried from thee, dear; and my true lip
Hath virgin'd it e'er since.

191

ROSALIND

And his kissing is as full of sanctity as the touch of holy bread.

CELIA

He hath bought a pair of cast lips of Diana: a nun of winter's sisterhood kisses not more religiously; the very ice of chastity is in them.

192

Pure lips, sweet seals in my soft lips imprinted,
What bargains may I make, still to be sealing?
To sell myself I can be well contented,
So thou wilt buy, and pay, and use good dealing;
    Which purchase if thou make, for fear of slips
    Set thy seal-manual on my wax-red lips.

193

CLEOPATRA

Give me mine angle,—we'll to the river: there,
My music playing far off, I will betray
Tawny-finn'd fishes; my bended hook shall pierce
Their slimy jaws; and, as I draw them up,
I'll think them every one an Antony,
And say, 'Ah, ha! y'are caught.'

CHARMIAN

                          'Twas merry when
You wager'd on your angling; when your diver
Did hang a salt-fish on his hook, which he
With fervency drew up.

CLEOPATRA

                          That time,—O times!—
I laught him out of patience; and that night
I laught him into patience: and next morn,
Ere the ninth hour, I drunk him to his bed;
Then put my tires and mantles on him, whilst
I wore his sword Philippan.

194 Sweet Helen, I must woo you
To help unarm our Hector: his stubborn buckles,
With these your white enchanting fingers toucht,
Shall more obey than to the edge of steel
Or force of Greekish sinews; you shall do more
Than all the island kings,—disarm great Hector.

195 My mother told me just how he would woo,
As if she sat in's heart; she says all men
Have the like oaths.

196 In faith, I'll break thy little finger, Harry,
An if thou wilt not tell me all things true.

197 Let me not to the marriage of true minds
Admit impediments. Love is not love
Which alters when it alteration finds,
Or bends with the remover to remove:
O, no! it is an ever-fixed mark,
That looks on tempests, and is never shaken,
It is the star to every wandering bark,
Whose worth's unknown, although his height be
 taken.
Love's not Time's fool, though rosy lips and cheek
Within his bending sickle's compass come;
Love alters not with his brief hours and weeks,
But bears it out even to the edge of doom.
 If this be error, and upon me proved,
 I never writ, nor no man ever loved.

198 But, mistress, know yourself: down on your knees,
And thank heaven, fasting, for a good man's love.

199 Ay, but hearken, sir; though the chameleon Love
can feed on the air, I am one that am nourish'd by
my victuals, and would fain have meat.

200

ROSALINE

Oft have I heard of you, my Lord Berowne,
Before I saw you; and the world's large tongue
Proclaims you for a man replete with mocks,
Full of comparisons and wounding flouts,
Which you on all estates will execute
That lie within the mercy of your wit.
To weed this wormwood from your fruitful brain,
And therewithal to win me, if you please,
Without the which I am not to be won,
You shall this twelvemonth term from day to day
Visit the speechless sick and still converse
With groaning wretches; and your task shall be,
With all the fierce endeavour of your wit
To enforce the pained impotent to smile.

BEROWNE

To move wild laughter in the throat of death?
It cannot be; it is impossible:
Mirth cannot move a soul in agony.

ROSALINE

Why, that's the way to choke a gibing spirit,
Whose influence is begot of that loose grace
Which shallow laughing hearers give to fools:
A jest's prosperity lies in the ear
Of him that hears it, never in the tongue
Of him that makes it: then, if sickly ears,
Deaf'd with the clamours of their own dear groans,
Will hear your idle scorns, continue then,
And I will have you and that fault withal;
But if they will not, throw away that spirit,
And I shall find you empty of that fault,
Right joyful of your reformation.

201   Mislike me not for my complexion,
The shadow'd livery of the burnisht sun,
To whom I am a neighbour and near bred.
Bring me the fairest creature northward born,
Where Phœbus' fire scarce thaws the icicles,
And let us make incision for your love,
To prove whose blood is reddest, his or mine.
I tell thee, lady, this aspect of mine
Hath fear'd the valiant: by my love, I swear
The best-regarded virgins of our clime
Hath loved it too: I would not change this hue,
Except to steal your thoughts, my gentle queen.
                      By this scimitar,
That slew the Sophy and a Persian prince
That won three fields of Sultan Solyman,
I would outstare the sternest eyes that look,
Outbrave the heart most daring on the earth,
Pluck the young sucking-cubs from the she-bear,
Yea, mock the lion when he roars for prey,
To win thee, lady. But, alas the while!
If Hercules and Lichas play at dice
Which is the better man, the greater throw
May turn by fortune from the weaker hand:
So is Alcides beaten by his page;
And so may I, blind Fortune leading me,
Miss that which one unworthier may attain,
And die with grieving.

202   Her father loved me; oft invited me;
Still question'd me the story of my life,
From year to year,—the battles, sieges, fortunes,
That I have past.
I ran it through, even from my boyish days

THE AGES OF MAN

To the very moment that he bade me tell it:
Wherein I spake of most disastrous chances,
Of moving accidents by flood and field;
Of hair-breadth scapes i'th'imminent deadly breach;
Of being taken by the insolent foe,
And sold to slavery; of my redemption thence,
And portance in my travel's history:
Wherein of antres vast and deserts idle,
Rough quarries, rocks, and hills whose heads touch
    heaven,
It was my hint to speak,—such was the process;
And of the Cannibals that each other eat,
The Anthropophagi, and men whose heads
Do grow beneath their shoulders. This to hear
Would Desdemona seriously incline:
But still the house-affairs would draw her thence;
Which ever as she could with haste dispatch,
She'd come again, and with a greedy ear
Devour up my discourse:—which I observing,
Took once a pliant hour; and found good means
To draw from her a prayer of earnest heart
That I would all my pilgrimage dilate,
Whereof by parcels she had something heard,
But not intentively: I did consent;
And often did beguile her of her tears,
When I did speak of some distressful stroke
That my youth suffer'd. My story being done,
She gave me for my pains a world of sighs:
She swore,—in faith, 'twas strange, 'twas passing
    strange;
'Twas pitiful, 'twas wondrous pitiful:
She wisht she had not heard it: yet she wisht
That heaven had made her such a man: she thankt
    me;
And bade me, if I had a friend that loved her,
I should but teach him how to tell my story,
And that would woo her. Upon this hint I spake:

A SOLDIER'S PROPOSAL

She loved me for the dangers I had past;
And I loved her that she did pity them.
This only is the witchcraft I have used:—
Here comes the lady; let her witness it.

203 If I could win a lady at leap-frog, or by vaulting into
my saddle with my armour on my back, under the
correction of bragging be it spoken, I should quickly
leap into a wife. Or if I might buffet for my love, or
bound my horse for her favours, I could lay on like
a butcher, and sit like a jack-an-apes, never off. But,
before God, Kate, I cannot look greenly, nor gasp
out my eloquence, nor I have no cunning in protesta-
tion; only downright oaths, which I never use till
urged, nor never break for urging. If thou canst love
a fellow of this temper, Kate, whose face is not worth
sun-burning, that never looks in his glass for love of
any thing he sees there,—let thine eye be thy cook.
I speak to thee plain soldier: if thou canst love me for
this, take me; if not, to say to thee that I shall die,
is true,—but for thy love, by the Lord, no; yet I
love thee too. And while thou livest, dear Kate, take
a fellow of plain and uncoin'd constancy; for he perforce must do thee right, because he hath not the
gift to woo in other places: for these fellows of infinite
tongue, that can rime themselves into ladies' favours,
they do always reason themselves out again. What!
a speaker is but a prater; a rime is but a ballad. A
good leg will fall; a straight back will stoop; a black
beard will turn white; a curl'd pate will grow bald;
a fair face will wither; a full eye will wax hollow: but
a good heart, Kate, is the sun and the moon; or,
rather, the sun, and not the moon,—for it shines
bright, and never changes, but keeps his course truly.

If thou would have such a one, take me: and take
me, take a soldier; take a soldier, take a king: and
what say'st thou, then, to my love? speak, my fair,
and fairly, I pray thee.

204

PORTIA

You see me, Lord Bassanio, where I stand,
Such as I am: though for myself alone
I would not be ambitious in my wish,
To wish myself much better; yet for you
I would be trebled twenty times myself;
A thousand times more fair, ten thousand times
   more rich;
That, only to stand high in your account,
I might in virtues, beauties, livings, friends,
Exceed account: but the full sum of me
Is sum of nothing; which, to term in gross,
Is an unlesson'd girl, unschool'd, unpractised:
Happy in this, she is not yet so old
But she may learn; happier than this,
She is not bred so dull but she can learn;
Happiest of all is that her gentle spirit
Commits itself to yours to be directed,
As from her lord, her governor, her king.
Myself and what is mine to you and yours
Is now converted: but now I was the lord
Of this fair mansion, master of my servants,
Queen o'er myself; and even now, but now,
This house, these servants, and this same myself,
Are yours, my lord: I give them with this ring:
Which when you part from, lose, or give away,
Let it presage the ruin of your love,
And be my vantage to exclaim on you.

BASSANIO

Madam, you have bereft me of all words,
Only my blood speaks to you in my veins:
And there is such confusion in my powers,
As, after some oration fairly spoke
By a beloved prince, there doth appear
Among the buzzing pleased multitude;
Where every something, being blent together,
Turns to a wild of nothing, save of joy,
Exprest and not exprest. But when this ring
Parts from this finger, then parts life from hence:
O, then be bold to say Bassanio's dead!

205   Gallop apace, you fiery-footed steeds,
Towards Phœbus' lodging: such a wagoner
As Phaethon would whip you to the west,
And bring in cloudy night immediately.
Spread thy close curtain, love-performing night,
That runaway's eyes may wink, and Romeo
Leap to these arms untalkt-of and unseen.
Lovers can see to do their amorous rites
By their own beauties; or, if love be blind,
It best agrees with night.—Come, civil night,
Thou sober-suited matron, all in black,
And learn me how to lose a winning match,
Play'd for a pair of stainless maidenhoods:
Hood my unmann'd blood, bating in my cheeks,
With thy black mantle; till strange love, grown bold
Think true love acted simple modesty.
O, I have bought the mansion of a love,
But not possest it; and, though I am sold,
Not yet enjoy'd: so tedious is this day,
As is the night before some festival
To an impatient child that hath new robes
And may not wear them.

206   Now is he come unto the chamber-door
That shuts him from the heaven of his thought,
Which with a yielding latch, and with no more,
Hat h barr'd him from the blessed thing he sought.

207   First, her bedchamber,—
Where, I confess, I slept not; but profess
Had that was well worth watching,—it was hang'd
With tapestry of silk and silver; the story
Proud Cleopatra, when she met her Roman,
And Cydnus swell'd above the banks, or for
The press of boats or pride: a piece of work
So bravely done, so rich, that it did strive
In workmanship and value; . . .
                  The chimney
Is south the chamber; and the chimney-piece
Chaste Dian bathing: never saw I figures
So lively to report themselves: the cutter
Was as another nature, dumb; outwent her,
Motion and breath left out. . . .
                  The roof o'the chamber
With golden cherubins is fretted: her andirons—
I had forgot them—were two winking Cupids
Of silver, each on one foot standing, nicely
Depending on their brands

208   I stalk about her door
Like a strange soul upon the Stygian banks,
Staying for waftage.

209   I have no joy of this contract to-night:
It is too rash, too unadvised, too sudden;
Too like the lightning, which doth cease to be
Ere one can say 'It lightens.' Sweet, good night!

This bud of love, by summer's ripening breath,
May prove a beauteous flower when next we meet.
Good night, good night! as sweet repose and rest
Come to thy heart as that within my breast!

210   How all the other passions fleet to air,—
As doubtful thoughts, and rash-embraced despair,
And shuddering fear, and green-eyed jealousy!
O love, be moderate; allay thy ecstasy;
In measure rain thy joy; scant this excess!
I feel too much thy blessing: make it less,
For fear I surfeit!

211   TROILUS
I am giddy; expectation whirls me round.
Th'imaginary relish is so sweet
That it enchants my sense: what will it be,
When that the watery palate tastes indeed
Love's thrice-repured nectar? death, I fear me;
Swooning destruction; or some joy too fine,
Too subtle-potent, tuned too sharp in sweetness,
For the capacity of my ruder powers:
I fear it much; and I do fear besides,
That I shall lose distinction in my joys;
As doth a battle, when they charge on heaps
The enemy flying.
             PANDARUS
She's making her ready, she'll come straight: you
must be witty now. She does so blush, and fetches
her wind so short, as if she were fray'd with a sprite:
I'll fetch her. It is the prettiest villain: she fetches
her breath as short as a new-ta'en sparrow.

THE AGES OF MAN

Even such a passion doth embrace my bosom:
My heart beats thicker than a feverous pulse;
And all my powers do their bestowing lose,
Like vassalage at unawares encountering
The eye of majesty.

212   Not mine own fears, nor the prophetic soul
       Of the wide world dreaming on things to come,
       Can yet the lease of my true love control,
       Supposed as forfeit to a confined doom.

213   If I may trust the flattering eye of sleep,
       My dreams presage some joyful news at hand:
       My bosom's lord sits lightly in his throne;
       And all this day an unaccustom'd spirit
       Lifts me above the ground with cheerful thoughts.
       I dreamt my lady came and found me dead,—
       Strange dream, that gives a dead man leave to
            think!—
       And breathed such life with kisses in my lips,
       That I revived, and was an emperor.
       Ah me! how sweet is love itself possest,
       When but love's shadows are so rich in joy!

214   This is the very ecstasy of love;
       Whose violent property fordoes itself,
       And leads the will to desperate undertakings,
       As oft as any passion under heaven
       That does afflict our natures.

215   O my soul's joy!
If after every tempest come such calms,
May the winds blow till they have waken'd death!
And let the labouring bark climb hills of seas
Olympus-high, and duck again as low
As hell's from heaven! If it were now to die,
'Twere now to be most happy; for, I fear,
My soul hath her content so absolute,
That not another comfort like to this
Succeeds in unknown fate.

216   Give me a gash, put me to present pain,
Lest this great sea of joys rushing upon me
O'erbear the shores of my mortality,
And drown me with their sweetness.

217   O coz, coz, coz, my pretty little coz, that thou didst
know how many fathom deep I am in love! But it
cannot be sounded: my affection hath an unknown
bottom, like the bay of Portugal.

218   TROILUS
Cressid, I love thee in so strain'd a purity,
That the blest gods, as angry with my fancy,
More bright in zeal than the devotion which
Cold lips blow to their deities, take thee from me.
             CRESSIDA
Have the gods envy?
             PANDARUS
Ay, ay, ay, ay; 'tis too plain a case.
             CRESSIDA
And is it true that I must go from Troy?

TROILUS
A hateful truth.

CRESSIDA
What, and from Troilus too?

TROILUS
From Troy and Troilus.

CRESSIDA
Is it possible?

TROILUS
And suddenly; where injury of chance
Puts back leave-taking, justles roughly by
All time of pause, rudely beguiles our lips
Of all rejoindure, forcibly prevents
Our lockt embrasures, strangles our dear vows
Even in the birth of our own labouring breath:
We two, that with so many thousand sighs
Did buy each other, must poorly sell ourselves
With the rude brevity and discharge of one.
Injurious time now, with a robber's haste,
Crams his rich thievery up, he knows not how:
As many farewells as be stars in heaven,
With distinct breath and consign'd kisses to them,
He fumbles up into a loose adieu;
And scants us with a single famisht kiss,
Distasted with the salt of broken tears.

219

JULIET
Wilt thou be gone? it is not yet near day:
It was the nightingale, and not the lark,
That pierced the fearful hollow of thine ear;
Nightly she sings on yond pomegranate-tree:
Believe me, love, it was the nightingale.

ROMEO
It was the lark, the herald of the morn,
No nightingale: look, love, what envious streaks

FAREWELL

Do lace the severing clouds in yonder east:
Night's candles are burnt out, and jocund day
Stands tiptoe on the misty mountain tops.
I must be gone and live, or stay and die.

220   Farewell! thou art too dear for my possessing,
And like enough thou know'st thy estimate:
The charter of thy worth gives thee releasing;
My bonds in thee are all determinate.

221

CLEOPATRA
Nay, pray you, seek no colour for your going,
But bid farewell, and go: when you sued staying,
Then was the time for words: no going then;—
Eternity was in our lips and eyes,
Bliss in our brows' bent; none our parts so poor,
But was a race of heaven: they are so still,
Or thou, the greatest soldier of the world,
Art turn'd the greatest liar.

MARK ANTONY
      How now, lady!

CLEOPATRA
I would I had thy inches; thou shouldst know
There were a heart in Egypt.

MARK ANTONY
I'll leave you, lady.

CLEOPATRA
    Courteous lord, one word.
Sir, you and I must part,—but that's not it:
Sir, you and I have loved,—but there's not it;
That you know well: something it is I would,—
O, my oblivion is a very Antony,
And I am all forgotten.

MARK ANTONY

But that your royalty
Holds idleness your subject, I should take you
For idleness itself.

CLEOPATRA

'Tis sweating labour.
To bear such idleness so near the heart
As Cleopatra this. But, sir, forgive me;
Since my becomings kill me, when they do not
Eye well to you: your honour calls you hence;
Therefore be deaf to my unpitied folly,
And all the gods go with you! upon your sword
Sit laurel victory! and smooth success
Be strew'd before your feet!

MARK ANTONY

Let us go. Come;
Our separation so abides, and flies,
That thou, residing here, go'st yet with me,
And I, hence fleeting, here remain with thee.
Away!

222   From you have I been absent in the spring,
When proud-pied April, drest in all his trim,
Hath put a spirit of youth in every thing,
That heavy Saturn laught and leapt with him.
Yet nor the lays of birds, nor the sweet smell
Of different flowers in odour and in hue,
Could make me any summer's story tell,
Or from their proud lap pluck them where they grew:
Nor did I wonder at the lily's white,
Nor praise the deep vermilion in the rose;
They were but sweet, but figures of delight,
Drawn after you,—you pattern of all those.
    Yet seem'd it winter still, and, you away,
    As with your shadow I with these did play

223   The forward violet thus did I chide:
Sweet thief, whence didst thou steal thy sweet that
  smells,
If not from my love's breath? The purple pride
Which on thy soft cheek for complexion dwells
In my love's veins thou hast too grossly dyed.
The lily I condemned for thy hand;
And buds of marjoram had stoln thy hair:
The roses fearfully on thorns did stand,
One blushing shame, another white despair;
A third, nor red nor white, had stoln of both,
And to his robbery had annext thy breath;
But, for his theft, in pride of all his growth
A vengeful canker eat him up to death.
   More flowers I noted, yet I none could see
   But sweet or colour it had stoln from thee.

224   'Twas pretty, though a plague,
To see him every hour; to sit and draw
His arched brows, his hawking eye, his curls,
In our heart's table,—heart too capable
Of every line and trick of his sweet favour:
But now he's gone, and my idolatrous fancy
Must sanctify his reliques.

225   That god forbid that made me first your slave,
I should in thought control your times of pleasure,
Or at your hand the account of hours to crave,
Being your vassal, bound to stay your leisure!
O, let me suffer, being at your beck,
The imprison'd absence of your liberty;
And patience, tame to sufferance, bide each check,
Without accusing you of injury.

Be where you list, your charter is so strong,
That you yourself may privilege your time
To what you will; to you it doth belong
Yourself to pardon of self-doing crime.
    I am to wait, though waiting so be hell;
    Not blame your pleasure, be it ill or well.

226   How like a winter hath my absence been
From thee, the pleasure of the fleeting year!
What freezings have I felt, what dark days seen!
What old December's bareness every where!

227

CLEOPATRA

Give me to drink mandragora.

CHARMIAN

              Why, madam?

CLEOPATRA

That I might sleep out this great gap of time
My Antony is away. O Charmian,
Where think'st thou he is now? Stands he, or sits
    he?
Or does he walk? or is he on his horse?
O happy horse, to bear the weight of Antony!
Do bravely, horse! for wott'st thou whom thou
    movest?
The demi-Atlas of this earth, the arm
And burgonet of men.—He's speaking now,
Or murmuring, 'Where's my serpent of old Nile?'
For so he calls me:—now I feed myself
With most delicious poison:—think on me,
That am with Phœbus' amorous pinches black,
And wrinkled deep in time? Broad-fronted Cæsar,
When thou wast here above the ground, I was

A morsel for a monarch; and great Pompey
Would stand, and make his eyes grow in my brow;
There would he anchor his aspect, and die
With looking on his life.

ALEXAS

Sovereign of Egypt, hail!

CLEOPATRA

How much unlike art thou Mark Antony!
Yet, coming from him, that great medicine hath
With his tinct gilded thee.—
How goes it with my brave Mark Antony?

ALEXAS

Last thing he did, dear queen,
He kist—the last of many doubled kisses—
This orient pearl:—his speech sticks in my heart.

CLEOPATRA

Mine ear must pluck it thence.

ALEXAS

'Good friend,' quoth he,
'Say, the firm Roman to great Egypt sends
This treasure of an oyster; at whose foot,
To mend the petty present, I will piece
Her opulent throne with kingdoms; all the east,
Say thou, shall call her mistress.' So he nodded,
And soberly did mount an arm-gaunt steed,
Who neigh'd so high, that what I would have spoke
Was beastly dumb'd by him.

CLEOPATRA

What, was he sad or merry?

ALEXAS

Like to the time o'the year between the extremes
Of hot and cold, he was nor sad nor merry.

CLEOPATRA

O well-divided disposition!—Note him,
Note him, good Charmian, 'tis the man; but note him:
He was not sad,—for he would shine on those
That make their looks by his; he was not merry,—

Which seem'd to tell them his remembrance lay
In Egypt with his joy; but between both:
O heavenly mingle!—Be'st thou sad or merry,
The violence of either thee becomes,
So does it no man else.

228 Being your slave, what should I do but tend
Upon the hours and times of your desire?
I have no precious time at all to spend,
Nor services to do, till you require.
Nor dare I chide the world-without-end hour
Whilst I, my sovereign, watch the clock for you,
Nor think the bitterness of absence sour
When you have bid your servant once adieu;
Nor dare I question with my jealous thought
Where you may be, or your affairs suppose,
But, like a sad slave, stay and think of nought
Save, where you are how happy you make those.
 So true a fool is love, that in your Will,
 Though you do any thing, he thinks no ill.

229 No longer mourn for me when I am dead
Than you shall hear the surly sullen bell
Give warning to the world that I am fled
From this vile world, with vilest worms to dwell:
Nay, if you read this line, remember not
The hand that writ it; for I love you so,
That I in your sweet thoughts would be forgot,
If thinking on me then should make you woe.
O, if, I say, you look upon this verse
When I perhaps compounded am with clay,
Do not so much as my poor name rehearse;
But let your love even with my life decay;
 Lest the wise world should look into your moan,
 And mock you with me after I am gone.

230   For it so falls out,
That what we have we prize not to the worth
Whiles we enjoy it; but being lackt and lost,
Why, then we rack the value, then we find
The virtue that possession would not show us
Whiles it was ours. So will it fare with Claudio:
When he shall hear she died upon his words,
Th'idea of her life shall sweetly creep
Into his study of imagination;
And every lovely organ of her life
Shall come apparell'd in more precious habit,
More moving-delicate and full of life,
Into the eye and prospect of his soul,
Than when she lived indeed.

231 That thou didst love her, strikes some scores away
From the great compt: but love that comes too late,
Like a remorseful pardon slowly carried,
To the great sender turns a sour offence,
Crying, 'That's good that's gone.' Our rasher faults
Make trivial price of serious things we have,
Not knowing them until we know their grave:
Oft our displeasures, to ourselves unjust,
Destroy our friends, and after weep their dust:
Our old love waking cries to see what's done,
While shameful hate sleeps out the afternoon.

232 Men are April when they woo, December when they
wed: maids are May when they are maids, but the
sky changes when they are wives. I will be more
jealous of thee than a Barbary cock-pigeon over his
hen; more clamorous than a parrot against rain;
more new-fangled than an ape; more giddy in my

desires than a monkey: I will weep for nothing, like
Diana in the fountain, and I will do that when you
are disposed to be merry; I will laugh like a hyen,
and that when thou art inclined to weep.

233   I take to-day a wife, and my election
Is led on in the conduct of my will;
My will enkindled by mine eyes and ears,
Two traded pilots 'twixt the dangerous shores
Of will and judgement: how may I avoid,
Although my will distaste what it elected,
The wife I chose? there can be no evasion
To blench from this, and to stand firm by honour:
We turn not back the silks upon the merchant
When we have soil'd them; nor the remainder viands
We do not throw in unrespective sieve
Because we now are full.

234   O, my good lord, why are you thus alone?
For what offence have I this fortnight been
A banisht woman from my Harry's bed?
Tell me, sweet lord, what is't that takes from thee
Thy stomach, pleasure, and thy golden sleep?
Why dost thou bend thine eyes upon the earth,
And start so often when thou sitt'st alone?
Why hast thou lost the fresh blood in thy cheeks;
And given my treasures and my rights of thee
To thick-eyed musing and curst melancholy?
In thy faint slumbers I by thee have watcht,
And heard thee murmur tales of iron wars;
Speak terms of manage to thy bounding steed;
Cry, 'Courage! to the field!'—and thou hast talkt
Of sallies and retires, of trenches, tents,

Of palisadoes, frontiers, parapets,
Of basilisks, of cannon, culverin,
Of prisoners' ransom, and of soldiers slain,
And all the currents of a heady fight.
Thy spirit within thee hath been so at war,
And thus hath so bestirr'd thee in thy sleep,
That beads of sweat have stood upon thy brow,
Like bubbles in a late-disturbed stream;
And in thy face strange motions have appear'd,
Such as we see when men restrain their breath
On some great sudden hest. O, what portents are
    these?
Some heavy business hath my lord in hand,
And I must know it, else he loves me not.

235

PORTIA
                Dear my lord,
Make me acquainted with your cause of grief.
BRUTUS
I am not well in health, and that is all.
PORTIA
Brutus is wise, and, were he not in health,
He would embrace the means to come by it.
BRUTUS
Why, so I do.—Good Portia, go to bed.
PORTIA
Is Brutus sick,—and is it physical
To walk unbraced, and suck up the humours
Of the dank morning? What, is Brutus sick,—
And will he steal out of his wholesome bed,
To dare the vile contagion of the night,
And tempt the rheumy and unpurged air
To add unto his sickness? No, my Brutus;
You have some sick offence within your mind,
Which, by the right and virtue of my place,

I ought to know of: and, upon my knees,
I charm you, by my once-commended beauty,
By all your vows of love, and that great vow
Which did incorporate and make us one,
That you unfold to me, yourself, your half,
Why you are heavy; and what men to-night
Have had resort to you,—for here have been
Some six or seven, who did hide their faces
Even from darkness.

BRUTUS

Kneel not, gentle Portia.

PORTIA

I should not need, if you were gentle Brutus.
Within the bond of marriage, tell me, Brutus,
Is it excepted I should know no secrets
That appertain to you? Am I yourself
But, as it were, in sort or limitation,—
To keep with you at meals, comfort your bed,
And talk to you sometimes? Dwell I but in the
    suburbs
Of your good pleasure? If it be no more,
Portia is Brutus' harlot, not his wife.

BRUTUS

You are my true and honourable wife;
As dear to me as are the ruddy drops
That visit my sad heart.

PORTIA

If this were true, then should I know this secret.
I grant I am a woman; but withal
A woman that Lord Brutus took to wife:
I grant I am a woman; but withal
A woman well-reputed,—Cato's daughter.
Think you I am no stronger than my sex,
Being so father'd and so husbanded?
Tell me your counsels; I will not disclose 'em:
I have made strong proof of my constancy,
Giving myself a voluntary wound

Here, in the thigh: can I bear that with patience,
And not my husband's secrets?
BRUTUS
O ye gods,
Render me worthy of this noble wife!
Hark, hark! one knocks: Portia, go in awhile;
And by and by thy bosom shall partake
The secrets of my heart:
All my engagements I will construe to thee,
All the charactery of my sad brows.

236   TROILUS
O, that I thought it could be in a woman—
As, if it can, I will presume in you—
To feed for aye her lamp and flames of love;
To keep her constancy in plight and youth,
Outliving beauty's outward, with a mind
That doth renew swifter than blood decays!
Or, that persuasion could but thus convince me,—
That my integrity and truth to you
Might be affronted with the match and weight
Of such a winnow'd purity in love;
How were I then uplifted! but, alas!
I am as true as truth's simplicity,
And simpler than the infancy of truth.
CRESSIDA
In that I'll war with you.
TROILUS
O virtuous fight,
When right with right wars who shall be most right!
True swains in love shall, in the world to come,
Approve their truths by Troilus: when their rimes,
Full of protest, of oath, and big compare,
Want similes, truth tired with iteration,—
As true as steel, as plantage to the moon,

As sun to day, as turtle to her mate,
As iron to adamant, as earth to th'centre,—
Yet, after all comparisons of truth,
As truth's authentic author to be cited,
'As true as Troilus' shall crown up the verse,
And sanctify the numbers.

CRESSIDA
        Prophet may you be!
If I be false, or swerve a hair from truth,
When time is old and hath forgot itself,
When waterdrops have worn the stones of Troy,
And blind oblivion swallow'd cities up,
And mighty states characterless are grated
To dusty nothing; yet let memory,
From false to false, among false maids in love,
Upbraid my falsehood! when they've said 'as false
As air, as water, wind, or sandy earth,
As fox to lamb, or wolf to heifer's calf,
Pard to the hind, or stepdame to her son,'—
'Yea,' let them say, to stick the heart of falsehood
'As false as Cressid.'

237   The chariest maid is prodigal enough,
       If she unmask her beauty to the moon:
       Virtue itself scapes not calumnious strokes:
       The canker galls the infants of the spring,
       Too oft before their buttons be disclosed;
       And in the morn and liquid dew of youth
       Contagious blastments are most imminent.
       Be wary, then; best safety lies in fear:
       Youth to itself rebels, though none else near.

238   Nature craves
       All dues be render'd to their owners: now,
       What nearer debt in all humanity

Than wife is to the husband? If this law
Of nature be corrupted through affection,
And that great minds, of partial indulgence
To their benumbed wills, resist the same,
There is a law in each well-order'd nation
To curb those raging appetites that are
Most disobedient and refractory.

239   Fie, fie! unknit that threatening unkind brow:
And dart not scornful glances from those eyes,
To wound thy lord, thy king, thy governor:
It blots thy beauty, as frosts do bite the meads;
Confounds thy fame, as whirlwinds shake fair buds;
And in no sense is meet or amiable.
A woman moved is like a fountain troubled,
Muddy, ill-seeming, thick, bereft of beauty;
And while it is so, none so dry or thirsty
Will deign to sip, or touch one drop of it.
Thy husband is thy lord, thy life, thy keeper,
Thy head, thy sovereign; one that cares for thee,
And for thy maintenance commits his body
To painful labour both by sea and land,
To watch the night in storms, the day in cold,
Whilst thou liest warm at home, secure and safe;
And craves no other tribute at thy hands
But love, fair looks, and true obedience,—
Too little payment for so great a debt.
Such duty as the subject owes the prince,
Even such a woman oweth to her husband;
And when she is froward, peevish, sullen, sour,
And not obedient to his honest will,
What is she but a foul contending rebel,
And graceless traitor to her loving lord?

240   The time was once when thou unurged wouldst vow
That never words were music to thine ear,
That never object pleasing in thine eye,
That never touch well-welcome to thy hand,
That never meat sweet-savour'd in thy taste,
Unless I spake, or look'd, or touch'd, or carved to
     thee.
How comes it now, my husband, O, how comes it,
That thou art then estranged from thyself?
Thyself I call it, being strange to me,
That, undividable, incorporate,
Am better than thy dear self's better part.
Ah, do not tear away thyself from me!
For know, my love, as easy mayst thou fall
A drop of water in the breaking gulf,
And take unmingled thence that drop again,
Without addition or diminishing,
As take from me thyself, and not me too.

241
               IAGO
   O, beware my lord, of jealousy;
It is the green-eyed monster, which doth mock
The meat it feeds on: that cuckold lives in bliss
Who, certain of his fate, loves not his wronger;
But, O, what damned minutes tells he o'er
Who dotes, yet doubts, suspects, yet strongly loves!
            OTHELLO
O misery!
               IAGO
Poor and content is rich, and rich enough;
But riches fineless is as poor as winter
To him that ever fears he shall be poor:—
Good heaven, the souls of all my tribe defend
From jealousy!

JEALOUSY

Why, why is this?
Think'st thou I'ld make a life of jealousy,
To follow still the changes of the moon
With fresh suspicions? No; to be once in doubt
Is once to be resolved: exchange me for a goat,
When I shall turn the business of my soul
To such exsufflicate and blown surmises,
Matching thy inference. 'Tis not to make me
    jealous
To say my wife is fair, feeds well, loves company,
Is free of speech, sings, plays, and dances well;
Where virtue is, these are more virtuous:
Nor from mine own weak merits will I draw
The smallest fear or doubt of her revolt;
For she had eyes, and chose me. No, Iago;
I'll see before I doubt; when I doubt, prove;
And, on the proof, there is no more but this,—
Away at once with love or jealousy!

242
For where Love reigns, disturbing Jealousy
Doth call himself Affection's sentinel;
Gives false alarms, suggesteth mutiny,
And in a peaceful hour doth cry "Kill, kill!"
    Distemp'ring gentle Love in his desire,
    As air and water do abate the fire.

This sour informer, this bate-breeding spy,
This canker that eats up Love's tender spring,
This carry-tale, dissentious Jealousy,
That sometime true news, sometime false doth bring,
    Knocks at my heart, and whispers in mine ear,
    That if I love thee, I thy death should fear.

243   But jealous souls will not be answer'd so;
      They are not ever jealous for the cause,
      But jealous for they're jealous: it is a monster
      Begot upon itself, born on itself.

244   Trifles light as air
      Are to the jealous confirmations strong
      As proofs of holy writ: this may do something . .
      Dangerous conceits are, in their natures, poisons,
      Which at the first are scarce found to distaste,
      But, with a little act upon the blood,
      Burn like the mines of sulphur.

245   This jealousy
      Is for a precious creature: as she's rare,
      Must it be great; and, as his person's mighty,
      Must it be violent; and as he does conceive
      He is dishonour'd by a man which ever
      Profest to him, why, his revenges must
      In that be made more bitter.

246   Too hot, too hot!
      To mingle friendship far, is mingling bloods.
      I have *tremor cordis* on me,—my heart dances;
      But not for joy,—not joy.—This entertainment
      May a free face put on; derive a liberty
      From heartiness, from bounty's fertile bosom,
      And well become the agent; 't may, I grant:
      But to be paddling palms and pinching fingers,
      As now they are; and making practised smiles,
      As in a looking-glass; and then to sigh, as 'twere
      The mort o'the deer; O, that is entertainment
      My bosom likes not, nor my brows!

247   Lest Jealousy, that sour unwelcome guest,
Should, by his stealing in, disturb the feast.

248   O curse of marriage,
That we can call these delicate creatures ours,
And not their appetites! I had rather be a toad,
And live upon the vapour of a dungeon,
Than keep a corner in the thing I love
For others' uses.

249   If thou dost marry, I'll give thee this plague for thy
dowry,—be thou as chaste as ice, as pure as snow
thou shalt not escape calumny.

250   Is whispering nothing?
Is leaning cheek to cheek? is meeting noses?
Kissing with inside lip? stopping the career
Of laughter with a sigh?—a note infallible
Of breaking honesty;—horsing foot on foot?
Skulking in corners? wishing clocks more swift?
Hours, minutes? noon, midnight? and all eyes
Blind with the pin-and-web, but theirs, theirs only,
That would unseen be wicked? is this nothing?
Why, then the world and all that's in't is nothing;
The covering sky is nothing; Bohemia nothing;
My wife is nothing; nor nothing have these nothings,
If this be nothing.

251   For I the ballad will repeat,
                Which men full true shall find;
            Your marriage comes by destiny,
                Your cuckoo sings by kind.

252   But I do think it is their husband's faults
       If wives do fall: say that they slack their duties,
       And pour our treasures into foreign laps;
       Or else break out in peevish jealousies,
       Throwing restraint upon us; or say they strike us,
       Or scant our former having in despite;
       Why, we have galls; and though we have some grace
       Yet have we some revenge. Let husbands know
       Their wives have sense like them: they see, and smell
       And have their palates both for sweet and sour,
       As husbands have. What is it that they do
       When they change us for others? Is it sport?
       I think it is: and doth affection breed it?
       I think it doth: is't frailty that thus errs?
       It is so too:—and have not we affections,
       Desires for sport, and frailty, as men have?
       Then let them use us well: else let them know,
       The ills we do, their ills instruct us so.

253   Sigh no more, ladies, sigh no more,
                   Men were deceivers ever;
                One foot in sea, and one on shore;
                   To one thing constant never:
                      Then sigh not so,
                      But let them go,
                   And be you blithe and bonny;
                Converting all your sounds of woe
                   Into Hey nonny, nonny.

                Sing no more ditties, sing no moe
                   Of dumps so dull and heavy;
                The fraud of men was ever so,
                   Since summer first was leavy.

Then sigh not so,
But let them go,
And be you blithe and bonny;
Converting all your sounds of woe
Into Hey nonny, nonny.

254   Thou didst swear to me upon a parcel-gilt
goblet, sitting in my Dolphin-chamber, at the round
table, by a sea-coal fire, upon Wednesday in
Wheeson-week, when the prince broke thy head for
liking his father to a singing-man of Windsor, thou
didst swear to me then, as I was washing thy wound,
to marry me, and make me my lady thy wife. Canst
thou deny it? Did not goodwife Keech, the butcher's
wife, come in then, and call me gossip Quickly?
coming in to borrow a mess of vinegar; telling us she
had a good dish of prawns; whereby thou didst desire
to eat some; whereby I told thee they were ill for
a green wound? And didst thou not, when she was
gone down stairs, desire me to be no more so
familiarity with such poor people; saying that ere
long they should call me madam? And didst thou
not kiss me, and bid me fetch thee thirty shillings?
I put thee now to thy book-oath: deny it, if thou
canst.

255   From off a hill whose concave womb re-worded
A plaintful story from a sistering vale,
My spirits t'attend this double voice accorded,
And down I laid to list the sad-tuned tale;
Ere long espied a fickle maid full pale,
Tearing of papers, breaking rings a-twain,
Storming her world with sorrow's wind and rain.

Upon her head a platted hive of straw,
Which fortified her visage from the sun,
Whereon the thought might think sometime it saw
The carcass of a beauty spent and done:
Time had not scythed all that youth begun,
Nor youth all quit; but, spite of heaven's fell rage,
Some beauty peept through lattice of sear'd age.

Her hair, nor loose nor tied in formal plat,
Proclaim'd in her a careless hand of pride;
For some, untuckt, descended her sheaved hat,
Hanging her pale and pined cheek beside;
Some in her threaden fillet still did bide,
And, true to bondage, would not break from thence,
Though slackly braided in loose negligence.

A thousand favours from a maund she drew
Of amber, crystal, and of beaded jet,
Which one by one she in a river threw,
Upon whose weeping margent she was set;
Like usury, applying wet to wet,
Or monarch's hands that lets not bounty fall
Where want cries some, but where excess begs all.

Of folded schedules had she many a one,
Which she perused, sigh'd, tore, and gave the flood;
Crackt many a ring of posied gold and bone,
Bidding them find their sepulchres in mud;
Found yet moe letters sadly penn'd in blood,
With sleided silk feat and affectedly
Enswathed, and seal'd to curious secrecy.

256   If she be false, O, then heaven mocks itself!—
I'll not believe't.

257   False to his bed! What is it to be false?
To lie in watch there, and to think on him?
To weep 'twixt clock and clock? if sleep charge
    nature,
To break it with a fearful dream of him,
And cry myself awake! that's false to's bed, is it?

258   O thou weed,
Who art so lovely fair, and smell'st so sweet,
That the sense aches at thee,—would thou hadst
    ne'er been born!

259   Take, O take those lips away.
    That so sweetly were forsworn;
And those eyes, the break of day,
    Lights that do mislead the morn:
But my kisses bring again, bring again;
Seals of love, but seal'd in vain, seal'd in vain.

260   Fie, fie upon her!
There's language in her eye, her cheek, her lip,
Nay, her foot speaks; her wanton spirits look out
At every joint and motive of her body.
O, these encounterers, so glib of tongue,
That give a coasting welcome ere it comes,
And wide unclasp the tables of their thoughts
To every ticklish reader! set them down
For sluttish spoils of opportunity
And daughters of the game.

261   He brought a Grecian queen, whose youth and
        freshness
    Wrinkles Apollo's, and makes stale the morning:
    Is she worth keeping? why, she is a pearl,
    Whose price hath launcht above a thousand ships,
    And turn'd crown'd kings to merchants.

262   She's bitter to her country: hear me, Paris:—
    For every false drop in her bawdy veins
    A Grecian's life hath sunk; for every scruple
    Of her contaminated carrion weight
    A Trojan hath been slain; since she could speak,
    She hath not given so many good words breath
    As for her Greeks and Trojans suffer'd death.

263   She is a theme of honour and renown;
    A spur to valiant and magnanimous deeds;
    Whose present courage may beat down our foes,
    And fame in time to come canonize us.

264   Show me the strumpet that began this stir,
    That with my nails her beauty I may tear.
    Thy heat of lust, fond Paris, did incur
    This load of wrath that burning Troy doth bear:
    Thy eye kindled the fire that burneth here;
        And here in Troy, for trespass of thine eye,
        The sire, the son, the dame, and daughter die.

    'Why should the private pleasure of some one
    Become the public plague of many moe?
    Let sin, alone committed, light alone

Upon his head that hath transgressed so;
Let guiltless souls be freed from guilty woe:
  For one's offence why should so many fall,
  To plague a private sin in general?

Lo, here weeps Hecuba, here Priam dies,
Here manly Hector faints, here Troilus swounds,
Here friend by friend in bloody channel lies,
And friend to friend gives unadvised wounds,
And one man's lust these many lives confounds:
  Had doting Priam checkt his son's desire,
  Troy had been bright with fame, and not with fire

265   Let it not be believed for womanhood!
Think, we had mothers; do not give advantage
To stubborn critics,—apt, without a theme,
For depravation,—to square the general sex
By Cressid's rule: rather think this not Cressid.

This she? no, this is Diomed's Cressida:
If beauty have a soul, this is not she;
If souls guide vows, if vows be sanctimonies,
If sanctimony be the gods' delight,
If there be rule in unity itself,
This is not she. O madness of discourse,
That cause sets up with and against itself!
Bi-fold authority! where reason can revolt
Without perdition, and loss assume all reason
Without revolt: this is, and is not, Cressid!
Within my soul there doth conduce a fight
Of this strange nature, that a thing inseparate
Divides more wider than the sky and earth;
And yet the spacious breadth of this division
Admits no orifex for a point, as subtle
As Ariachne's broken woof, to enter.

Instance, O instance! strong as Pluto's gates;
Cressid is mine, tied with the bonds of heaven:
Instance, O instance! strong as heaven itself;
The bonds of heaven are slipt, dissolved, and loosed;
And with another knot, five-finger-tied,
The fractions of her faith, orts of her love,
The fragments, scraps, the bits and greasy relics
Of her o'er-eaten faith, are bound to Diomed.

O Cressid! O false Cressid! false, false, false!
Let all untruths stand by thy stained name,
And they'll seem glorious.

266   My thoughts and my discourse as madmen's are,
At random from the truth vainly exprest;
    For I have sworn thee fair, and thought thee bright,
    Who art as black as hell, as dark as night.

267   O constancy, be strong upon my side,
Set a huge mountain 'tween my heart and tongue!
I have a man's mind, but a woman's might.
How hard it is for women to keep counsel!

268   All my merry jigs are quite forgot,
All my lady's love is lost, God wot:
Where her faith was firmly fixt in love,
There a nay is placed without remove.
      One silly cross
      Wrought all my loss;
O frowning Fortune, cursed, fickle dame!
      For now I see
      Inconstancy

More in women than in men remain.
Clear wells spring not,
Sweet birds sing not,
Green plants bring not
Forth their dye;
Herds stand weeping,
Flocks all sleeping,
Nymphs back peeping
Fearfully:
All our pleasure known to us poor swains,
All our merry meetings on the plains,
All our evening sport from us is fled,
All our love is lost, for Love is dead.
Farewell, sweet lass,
Thy like ne'er was
For a sweet content, the cause of all my moan;
Poor Corydon
Must live alone;
Other help for him I see that there is none.

269   When my love swears that she is made of truth,
I do believe her, though I know she lies,
That she might think me some untutor'd youth,
Unlearned in the world's false subtleties.

270   It is the cause, it is the cause, my soul,—
Let me not name it to you, you chaste stars!
It is the cause.—Yet I'll not shed her blood;
Nor scar that whiter skin of hers than snow,
And smooth as monumental alabaster.
Yet she must die, else she'll betray more men.—
Put out the light, and then put out the light:
If I quench thee, thou flaming minister,

I can again thy former light restore,
Should I repent me:—but once put out thy light,
Thou cunning'st pattern of excelling nature,
I know not where is that Promethean heat
That can thy light relume. When I have pluckt the
    rose,
I cannot give it vital growth again,
It needs must wither:—I'll smell it on the tree.—
O balmy breath, that dost almost persuade
Justice to break her sword!—One more, one more:—
Be thus when thou art dead, and I will kill thee,
And love thee after:—one more, and this the last:
So sweet was ne'er so fatal. I must weep,
But they are cruel tears: this sorrow's heavenly;
It strikes where it doth love.

271   Frailty, thy name is woman!

272   Ha! have you eyes?
You cannot call it love; for at your age
The hey-day in the blood is tame, it's humble,
And waits upon the judgement: and what judgement
Would step from this to this? Sense, sure, you have,
Else could you not have motion: but, sure, that sense
Is apoplext: for madness would not err;
Nor sense to ecstasy was ne'er so thrall'd
But it reserved some quantity of choice,
To serve in such a difference. What devil was't
That thus hath cozen'd you at hoodman-blind?

273   This is the monstruosity in love, lady,—that
the will is infinite, and the execution confined; that
the desire is boundless, and the act a slave to limit.

274
Call it not love, for Love to heaven is fled,
Since sweating Lust on earth usurpt his name;
Under whose simple semblance he hath fed
Upon fresh beauty, blotting it with blame;
   Which the hot tyrant stains and soon bereaves,
   As caterpillars do the tender leaves.

Love comforteth like sunshine after rain,
But Lust's effect is temptest after sun;
Love's gentle spring doth always fresh remain,
Lust's winter comes ere summer half be done;
   Love surfeits not, Lust like a glutton dies;
   Love is all truth, Lust full of forged lies.

275
COUNTESS
Tell me thy reason why thou wilt marry.
CLOWN
My poor body, madam, requires it: I am driven on
by the flesh; and he must needs go that the devil
drives.

276
The expense of spirit in a waste of shame
Is lust in action; and till action, lust
Is perjured, murd'rous, bloody, full of blame,
Savage, extreme, rude, cruel, not to trust;
Enjoy'd no sooner but despised straight;
Past reason hunted; and no sooner had,
Past reason hated, as a swallow'd bait,
On purpose laid to make the taker mad:
Mad in pursuit, and in possession so;
Had, having, and in quest to have, extreme;
A bliss in proof, and proved, a very woe;
Before, a joy proposed; behind, a dream.
   All this the world well knows; yet none knows well
   To shun the heaven that leads men to this hell.

277   What win I, if I gain the thing I seek?
A dream, a breath, a froth of fleeting joy.
Who buys a minute's mirth to wail a week?
Or sells eternity to get a toy?
For one sweet grape who will the vine destroy?

278   'But, woe is me! too early I attended
A youthful suit—it was to gain my grace—
Of one by nature's outwards so commended,
That maidens' eyes stuck over all his face:
Love lackt a dwelling, and made him her place;
And when in his fair parts she did abide,
She was new lodged, and newly deified.

'His browny locks did hang in crooked curls;
And every light occasion of the wind
Upon his lips their silken parcels hurls.
What's sweet to do, to do will aptly find:
Each eye that saw him did enchant the mind;
For on his visage was in little drawn
What largeness thinks in Paradise was sawn.

'Small show of man was yet upon his chin;
His phœnix down began but to appear,
Like unshorn velvet, on that termless skin,
Whose bare out-bragg'd the web it seem'd to wear:
Yet show'd his visage by that cost more dear;
And nice affections wavering stood in doubt
If best were as it was, or best without.

'O father, what a hell of witchcraft lies
In the small orb of one particular tear!
But with the inundation of the eyes
What rocky heart to water will not wear?
What breast so cold that is not warmed here?
O cleft effect! cold modesty, hot wrath,
Both fire from hence and chill extincture hath

'For, lo, his passion, but an art of craft,
Even there resolved my reason into tears;
There my white stole of chastity I daft,
Shook off my sober guards and civil fears;
Appear to him, as he to me appears,
All melting; though our drops this difference bore,
His poison'd me, and mine did him restore.

'Thus merely with the garment of a Grace
The naked and concealed fiend he cover'd;
That th' unexperient gave the tempter place,
Which, like a cherubin, above them hover'd.
Who, young and simple, would not be so lover'd?
Ay me! I fell; and yet do question make
What I should do again for such a sake.

'O, that infected moisture of his eye,
O, that false fire which in his cheek so glow'd,
O, that forced thunder from his heart did fly,
O, that sad breath his spongy lungs bestow'd,
O, all that borrow'd motion seeming ow'd,
Would yet again betray the fore-betray'd,
And new pervert a reconciled maid!'

279   DESDEMONA
My mother had a maid call'd Barbara:
She was in love; and he she loved proved mad,
And did forsake her: she had a song of 'willow;'
An old thing 'twas, but it exprest her fortune,
And she died singing it: that song to-night
Will not go from my mind; I have much to do,
But to go hang my head all at one side,
And sing it like poor Barbara.—Prithee, dispatch.
                        EMILIA
Shall I go fetch your night-gown?

DESDEMONA
No, unpin me here.—
This Lodovico is a proper man.

EMILIA
A very handsome man.

DESDEMONA
He speaks well.

EMILIA
I know a lady in Venice would have walkt bare-foot to Palestine for a touch of his nether lip.

DESDEMONA
The poor soul sat sighing by a sycamore tree,
    Sing all a green willow;
Her hand on her bosom, her head on her knee,
    Sing willow, willow, willow:
The fresh streams ran by her, and murmur'd
    her moans;
    Sing willow, willow, willow;
Her salt tears fell from her, and soften'd the
    stones;—
Lay by these:—
    Sing willow, willow, willow;
Prithee, hie thee; he'll come anon:—
    Sing all a green willow must be my garland.
    Let nobody blame him; his scorn I approve,—
Nay, that's not next.—Hark! who is't that knocks?

EMILIA
It is the wind

DESDEMONA
I call'd my love false love; but what said he then?
    Sing willow, willow, willow;
If I court moe women, you'll couch with moe men.—
So, get thee gone; good night.

Finish, good lady; the bright day is done,
And we are for the dark.

281   The spinsters and the knitters in the sun,
And the free maids that weave their thread with
    bones,
Do use to chant it: it is silly sooth,
And dallies with the innocence of love,
Like the old age.

    Come away, come away, death,
      And in sad cypress let me be laid;
    Fly away, fly away, breath;
      I am slain by a fair cruel maid.
    My shroud of white, stuck all with yew,
        O, prepare it!
    My part of death, no one so true
        Did share it.
    Not a flower, not a flower sweet,
      On my black coffin let there be strown;
    Not a friend, not a friend greet
      My poor corpse, where my bones shall be
        thrown:
    A thousand thousand sighs to save,
        Lay me, O, where
    Sad true lover never find my grave,
        To weep there!

282   Leander the good swimmer, Troilus the first employer
of Pandars, and a whole book full of these quondam
carpet-mongers, whose names yet run smoothly in
the even road of a blank verse, why they were never
so truly turned over and over as my poor self in love.

283   The poor world is almost six thousand years old,
and in all this time there was not any man died
in his own person, *videlicet*, in a love-cause. Troilus
had his brains dasht out with a Grecian club; yet he

THE AGES OF MAN

did what he could to die before; and he is one of the
patterns of love. Leander, he would have lived many
a fair year, though Hero had turn'd nun, if it had not
been for a hot midsummer night; for, good youth,
he went but forth to wash him in the Hellespont,
and, being taken with the cramp, was drown'd: and
the foolish chroniclers of that age found it was—
Hero of Sestos. But these are all lies: men have died
from time to time, and worms have eaten them, but
not for love.

284

CLEOPATRA
    Come, come, Antony,—
Help me, my women,—we must draw thee up;—
Assist, good friends.

MARK ANTONY
    O, quick, or I am gone.

CLEOPATRA
Here's sport indeed!—How heavy weighs my lord!
Our strength is all gone into heaviness;
That makes the weight: had I great Juno's power,
The strong-wing'd Mercury should fetch thee up,
And set thee by Jove's side. Yet come a little,—
Wishers were ever fools,—O, come, come, come;
And welcome, welcome! die where thou hast lived:
Quicken with kissing: had my lips that power,
Thus would I wear them out.

ALL
A heavy sight!

MARK ANTONY
I am dying, Egypt, dying:
Give me some wine, and let me speak a little.

CLEOPATRA
No, let me speak; and let me rail so high,
That the false housewife Fortune break her wheel,
Provoked by my offence.

THE AGES OF MAN

CHARMIAN
Lady!

IRAS
Madam!

CHARMIAN
O madam, madam, madam!

IRAS
Royal Egypt, Empress!

CHARMIAN
Peace, peace, Iras!

CLEOPATRA
No more, but e'en a woman, and commanded
By such poor passion as the maid that milks
And does the meanest chares.—It were for me
To throw my sceptre at the injurious gods;
To tell them that this world did equal theirs
Till they had stoln our jewel. All's but naught;
Patience is sottish, and impatience does
Becomes a dog that's mad; then is it sin
To rush into the secret house of death,
Ere death dare come to us?—How do you, women?
What, what! good cheer! Why, how now, Charmian!
My noble girls! Ah, women, women, look,
Our lamp is spent, it's out! Good sirs, take heart:—
We'll bury him; and then, what's brave, what's noble,
Let's do it after the high Roman fashion,
And make death proud to take us. Come, away:
This case of that huge spirit now is cold:
Ah, women, women! come; we have no friend
But resolution, and the briefest end.

285

CLEOPATRA
I dreamt there was an emperor Antony:—
O, such another sleep, that I might see
But such another man!

MARK ANTONY
One word, sweet queen:
Of Cæsar seek your honour, with your safety.—O!

CLEOPATRA
They do not go together.

MARK ANTONY
Gentle, hear me:
None about Cæsar trust but Proculeius.

CLEOPATRA
My resolution and my hands I'll trust;
None about Cæsar.

MARK ANTONY
The miserable change now at my end
Lament nor sorrow at; but please your thoughts
In feeding them with those my former fortunes,
Wherein I lived the greatest prince o'the world,
The noblest; and do now not basely die,
Not cowardly put off my helmet to
My countryman,—a Roman by a Roman
Valiantly vanquisht. Now my spirit is going;
I can no more.

CLEOPATRA
Noblest of men, woo't die?
Hast thou no care of me? shall I abide
In this dull world, which in thy absence is
No better than a sty?—O, see, my women,
The crown o'the earth doth melt.—My lord!
O, wither'd is the garland of the war,
The soldiers' pole is fall'n: young boys and girls
Are level now with men; the odds is gone,
And there is nothing left remarkable
Beneath the visiting moon.

CHARMIAN
O, quietness, lady!

IRAS
She is dead too, our sovereign.

Let the bird of loudest lay,
On the sole Arabian tree,
Herald sad and trumpet be,
To whose sound chaste wings obey.

But thou shrieking harbinger,
Foul precurrer of the fiend,
Augur of the fever's end,
To this troop come thou not near!

From this session interdict
Every fowl of tyrant wing,
Save the eagle, feather'd king:
Keep the obsequy so strict.

Let the priest in surplice white,
That defunctive music can,
Be the death-divining swan,
Lest the requiem lack his right.

And thou treble-dated crow,
That thy sable gender makest
With the breath thou givest and takest,
'Mongst our mourners shalt thou go.

Here the anthem doth commence:
Love and constancy is dead;
Phœnix and the turtle fled
In a mutual flame from hence.

So they loved, as love in twain
Had the essence but in one;
Two distincts, division none:
Number there in love was slain.

DOLABELLA

    If it might please ye,—

CLEOPATRA

His face was as the heavens; and therein stuck
A sun and moon, which kept their course, and lighted
The little O, the earth.

DOLABELLA

    Most sovereign creature,—

CLEOPATRA

His legs bestrid the ocean: his rear'd arm
Crested the world; his voice was propertied
As all the tuned spheres, and that to friends;
But when he meant to quail and shake the orb,
He was as rattling thunder. For his bounty,
There was no winter in't; an autumn 'twas
That grew the more by reaping: his delights
Were dolphin-like; they show'd his back above
The element they lived in: in his livery
Walkt crowns and crownets; realms and islands were
As plates dropt from his pocket.

DOLABELLA

    Cleopatra,—

CLEOPATRA

Think you there was, or might be, such a man
As this I dreamt of?

DOLABELLA

    Gentle madam, no.

CLEOPATRA

You lie, up to the hearing of the gods.
But, if there be, or ever were, one such,
It's past the size of dreaming: nature wants stuff
To vie strange forms with fancy; yet, t'imagine
An Antony, were nature's piece 'gainst fancy,
Condemning shadows quite.

Hearts remote, yet not asunder;
Distance, and no space was seen
'Twixt the turtle and his queen:
But in them it were a wonder.

So between them love did shine,
That the turtle saw his right
Flaming in the phœnix' sight;
Either was the other's mine.

Property was thus appalled,
That the self was not the same;
Single nature's double name
Neither two nor one was called.

Reason, in itself confounded,
Saw division grow together,
To themselves yet either neither,
Simple were so well compounded,

That it cried, How true a twain
Seemeth this concordant one!
Love hath reason, reason none,
If what parts can so remain.

Whereupon it made this threne
To the phœnix and the dove,
Co-supremes and stars of love,
As chorus to their tragic scene.

THRENOS

Beauty, truth, and rarity,
Grace in all simplicity,
Here enclosed in cinders lie.

THE AGES OF MAN

Death is now the phœnix' nest;
And the turtle's loyal breast
To eternity doth rest,

Leaving no posterity:
'Twas not their infirmity,
It was married chastity.

Truth may seem, but cannot be;
Beauty brag, but 'tis not she;
Truth and beauty buried be.

To this urn let those repair
That are either true or fair;
For these dead birds sigh a prayer

Book II ★ Manhood

WAR

CIVIL STRIFE

KINGSHIP

GOVERNMENT AND SOCIETY

PASSION AND CHARACTER

287 O for a Muse of fire, that would ascend
     The brightest heaven of invention,—
     A kingdom for a stage, princes to act,
     And monarchs to behold the swelling scene!
     Then should the warlike Harry, like himself,
     Assume the port of Mars; and at his heels,
     Leasht-in like hounds, should famine, sword, and fire,
     Crouch for employment.

288 In Troy, there lies the scene. From isles of Greece
     The princes orgulous, their high blood chafed,
     Have to the port of Athens sent their ships,
     Fraught with the ministers and instruments
     Of cruel war: sixty and nine, that wore
     Their crownets regal, from th'Athenian bay
     Put forth toward Phrygia: and their vow is made
     To ransack Troy; within whose strong immures
     The ravisht Helen, Menelaus' queen,
     With wanton Paris sleeps; and that's the quarrel.
     To Tenedos they come;
     And the deep-drawing barks do there disgorge
     Their warlike fraughtage: now on Dardan plains
     The fresh and yet unbruised Greeks do pitch
     Their brave pavilions: Priam's six-gated city,
     Dardan, and Tymbria, Helias, Chetas, Troien,
     And Antenorides, with massy staples,
     And corresponsive and fulfilling bolts,
     Sperr up the sons of Troy.
     Now expectation, tickling skittish spirits,
     On one and other side, Trojan and Greek,
     Sets all on hazard: and hither am I come
     A prologue arm'd.

289

SECOND SERVING-MAN

Why, then we shall have a stirring world again. This peace is nothing, but to rust iron, increase tailors, and breed ballad-makers.

FIRST SERVING-MAN

Let me have war, say I; it exceeds peace as far as day does night; it's spritely, waking, audible, and full of vent. Peace is a very apoplexy, lethargy; mull'd, deaf, sleepy, insensible; a getter of more bastard children than war's a destroyer of men.

SECOND SERVING-MAN

'Tis so: and as war, in some sort, may be said to be a ravisher, so it cannot be denied but peace is a great maker of cuckolds.

FIRST SERVING-MAN

Ay, and it makes men hate one another.

THIRD SERVING-MAN

Reason; because they then less need one another. The wars for my money.

290

Will you tell me, Master Shallow, how to choose a man? Care I for the limb, the thews, the stature, bulk, and big assemblance of a man! Give me the spirit, Master Shallow.—Here's Wart;—you see what a ragged appearance it is: a' shall charge you, and discharge you, with the motion of a pewterer's hammer; come off, and on, swifter than he that gibbets-on the brewer's bucket. And this same half-faced fellow, Shadow,—give me this man: he presents no mark to the enemy,—the foeman may with as great aim level at the edge of a penknife. And, for a retreat,—how swiftly will this Feeble, the woman's tailor, run off! O, give me the spare men, and spare me the great ones.

291 Now all the youth of England are on fire,
And silken dalliance in the wardrobe lies:
Now thrive the armourers, and honour's thought
Reigns solely in the breast of every man:
They sell the pasture now to buy the horse;
Following the mirror of all Christian kings,
With winged heels, as English Mercuries.
For now sits Expectation in the air,
And hides a sword from hilts unto the point
With crowns imperial, crowns, and coronets,
Promised to Harry and his followers.

292   Suppose that you have seen
The well-appointed king at Hampton pier
Embark his royalty; and his brave fleet
With silken streamers the young Phœbus fanning:
Play with your fancies; and in them behold
Upon the hempen tackle ship-boys climbing;
Hear the shrill whistle which doth order give
To sounds confused; behold the threaden sails,
Borne with th'invisible and creeping wind,
Draw the huge bottoms through the furrow'd sea,
Breasting the lofty surge: O, do but think
You stand upon the rivage, and behold
A city on th'inconstant billows dancing;
For so appears this fleet majestical,
Holding due course to Harfleur. Follow, follow!
Grapple your minds to sternage of this navy;
And leave your England, as dead midnight still,
Guarded with grandsires, babies, and old women,
Either past, or not arrived to, pith and puissance;
For who is he, whose chin is but enricht
With one appearing hair, that will not follow
These cull'd and choice-drawn cavaliers to France?
Work, work your thoughts, and therein see a siege;
Behold the ordnance on their carriages,
With fatal mouths gaping on girded Harfleur.

GOWER

How now, Captain Macmorris! have you quit the
mines? have the pioners given o'er?

MACMORRIS

By Chrish, la, tish ill done; the work ish give over,
the trompet sound the retreat. By my hand, I swear,
and my father's soul, the work ish ill done; it ish give
over: I would have blow'd up the town, so Chrish save
me, la, in an hour: O, tish ill done, tish ill done; by my
hand, tish ill done!

FLUELLEN

Captain Macmorris, I peseech you now, will you
voutsafe me, look you, a few disputations with you, as
partly touching or concerning the disciplines of the
war, the Roman wars, in the way of argument, look
you, and friendly communication; partly to satisfy
my opinion, and partly for the satisfaction, look you,
of my mind, as touching the direction of the military
discipline; that is the point.

JAMY

It shall be vary gude, gude feith, gude captains baith:
and I sall quit you with gude leve, as I may pick
occasion; that sall I, marry.

MACMORRIS

It is no time to discourse, so Chrish save me: the day
is hot, and the weather, and the wars, and the king,
and the dukes: it is no time to discourse. The town is
beseecht, and the trompet call us to the breach; and
we talk, and, be Chrish, do nothing: 'tis shame for us
all: so God sa' me, 'tis shame to stand still; it is
shame, by my hand: and there is throats to be cut,
and works to be done; and there ish nothing done, so
Chrish sa' me, la.

All furnisht, all in arms;
All plumed like estridges that wing the wind;
Bated like eagles having lately bathed;

Glittering in golden coats, like images;
As full of spirit as the month of May,
And gorgeous as the sun at midsummer;
Wanton as youthful goats, wild as young bulls
I saw young Harry,—with his beaver on,
His cuisses on his thighs, gallantly arm'd,—
Rise from the ground like feather'd Mercury,
And vaulted with such ease into his seat,
As if an angel dropt down from the clouds,
To turn and wind a fiery Pegasus,
And witch the world with noble horsemanship.

295   They come like sacrifices in their trim,
And to the fire-eyed maid of smoky war,
All hot and bleeding, will we offer them:
The mailed Mars shall on his altar sit
Up to the ears in blood. I am on fire
To hear this rich reprisal is so nigh,
And yet not ours.

296

PRINCE HENRY
But tell me, Jack,
whose fellows are these that come after?

SIR JOHN FALSTAFF
Mine, Hal, mine.

PRINCE HENRY
I did never see such pitiful rascals.

SIR JOHN FALSTAFF
Tut, tut; good enough to toss; food for powder, food
for powder; they'll fill a pit as well as better: tush.
man, mortal men, mortal men.

297   Now entertain conjecture of a time
        When creeping murmur and the poring dark
        Fills the wide vessel of the universe.
        From camp to camp, through the foul womb of night,
        The hum of either army stilly sounds,
        That the fixt sentinels almost receive
        The secret whispers of each other's watch:
        Fire answers fire; and through their paly flames
        Each battle sees the other's umber'd face:
        Steed threatens steed, in high and boastful neighs
        Piercing the night's dull ear; and from the tents,
        The armourers, accomplishing the knights,
        With busy hammers closing rivets up,
        Give dreadful note of preparation:
        The country cocks do crow, the clocks do toll,
        And the third hour of drowsy morning name.
        Proud of their numbers, and secure in soul,
        The confident and over-lusty French
        Do the low-rated English play at dice;
        And chide the cripple tardy-gaited night,
        Who, like a foul and ugly witch, doth limp
        So tediously away. The poor condemned English,
        Like sacrifices, by their watchful fires
        Sit patiently, and inly ruminate
        The morning's danger; and their gesture sad
        Investing lank-lean cheeks, and war-worn coats,
        Presenteth them unto the gazing moon
        So many horrid ghosts. O, now, who will behold
        The royal captain of this ruin'd band
        Walking from watch to watch, from tent to tent,
        Let him cry, 'Praise and glory on his head!'
        For forth he goes and visits all his host;
        Bids them good morrow with a modest smile,
        And calls them brothers, friends and countrymen.
        Upon his royal face there is no note
        How dread an army hath enrounded him;
        Nor doth he dedicate one jot of colour

Unto the weary and all-watched night;
But freshly looks, and over-bears attaint
With cheerful semblance and sweet majesty;
That every wretch, pining and pale before,
Beholding him, plucks comfort from his looks:
A largess universal, like the sun,
His liberal eye doth give to every one,
Thawing cold fear. Then, mean and gentle all,
Behold, as may unworthiness define,
A little touch of Harry in the night.

298   Once more unto the breach, dear friends, once more;
Or close the wall up with our English dead!
In peace there's nothing so becomes a man
As modest stillness and humility:
But when the blast of war blows in our ears,
Then imitate the action of the tiger;
Stiffen the sinews, summon up the blood,
Disguise fair nature with hard-favour'd rage:
Then lend the eye a terrible aspect;
Let it pry through the portage of the head
Like the brass cannon; let the brow o'erwhelm it
As fearfully as doth a galled rock
O'erhang and jutty his confounded base,
Swill'd with the wild and wasteful ocean.
Now set the teeth, and stretch the nostril wide;
Hold hard the breath, and bend up every spirit
To his full height!—On, on, you noble English,
Whose blood is fet from fathers of war-proof!—
Fathers that, like so many Alexanders,
Have in these parts from morn till even fought,
And sheathed their swords for lack of argument:—
Dishonour not your mothers; now attest
That those whom you call'd fathers did beget you!

Be copy now to men of grosser blood,
And teach them how to war!—And you, good
    yeomen,
Whose limbs were made in England, show us here
The mettle of your pasture; let us swear
That you are worth your breeding: which I doubt not;
For there is none of you so mean and base,
That hath not noble lustre in your eyes.
I see you stand like greyhounds in the slips,
Straining upon the start. The game's afoot:
Follow your spirit; and, upon this charge,
Cry 'God for Harry, England, and Saint George!'

299

FLUELLEN

Your grandfather of famous memory, an't please
your majesty, and your great-uncle Edward the
Plack Prince of Wales, as I have read in the chronicles,
fought a most prave pattle here in France.

KING HENRY

They did, Fluellen.

FLUELLEN

Your majesty says very true: if your majesties is
remember'd of it, the Welshmen did goot service in a
garden where leeks did grow, wearing leeks in their
Monmouth caps; which, your majesty knows, to this
hour is an honourable padge of the service; and I do
pelieve your majesty takes no scorn to wear the leek
upon Saint Tavy's day.

KING HENRY

I wear it for a memorable honour;
For I am Welsh, you know, good countryman

FLUELLEN

All the water in Wye cannot wash your majesty's
Welsh plood out of your pody, I can tell you that:

HONOUR

Got pless it, and preserve it, as long as it pleases his
grace, and his majesty too!
                    KING HENRY
Thanks, good my countryman.
                    FLUELLEN
By Cheshu, I am your majesty's countryman, I care
not who know it; I will confess it to all the 'orld: I
need not to be ashamed of your majesty, praised be
Got, so long as your majesty is an honest man.

0   WORCESTER
And now I will unclasp a secret book,
And to your quick-conceiving discontents
I'll read you matter deep and dangerous,
As full of peril and adventurous spirit
As to o'er-walk a current roaring loud
On the unsteadfast footing of a spear.
                    HOTSPUR
If he fall in, good night!—or sink or swim:—
Send danger from the east unto the west,
So honour cross it from the north to south,
And let them grapple:—O, the blood more stirs
To rouse a lion than to start a hare!
                    NORTHUMBERLAND
Imagination of some great exploit
Drives him beyond the bounds of patience.
                    HOTSPUR
By heaven, methinks it were an easy leap,
To pluck bright honour from the pale-faced moon;
Or dive into the bottom of the deep,
Where fadom-line could never touch the ground,
And pluck up drowned honour by the locks;
So he that doth redeem her thence might wear
Without corrival all her dignities.

301   But wherefore do you hold me here so long?
        What is it that you would impart to me?
        If it be aught toward the general good,
        Set honour in one eye, and death i'th'other,
        And I will look on both indifferently;
        For, let the gods so speed me as I love
        The name of honour more than I fear death.

302   SIR JOHN FALSTAFF
        Hal, if thou see me down in the battle, and bestride
        me, so; 'tis a point of friendship.
                       PRINCE HENRY
        Nothing but a colossus can do thee that friendship.
        Say thy prayers, and farewell.
                       SIR JOHN FALSTAFF
        I would 'twere bedtime, Hal, and all well.
                       PRINCE HENRY
        Why, thou owest God a death.
                       SIR JOHN FALSTAFF
        'Tis not due yet; I would be loth to pay him before his
        day. What need I be so forward with him that calls
        not on me? Well, 'tis no matter; honour pricks me on.
        Yea, but how if honour prick me off when I come on?
        how then? Can honour set to a leg? no: or an arm? no:
        or take away the grief of a wound? no. Honour hath
        no skill in surgery, then? no. What is honour? a
        word. What is that word honour? air. A trim
        reckoning!—Who hath it? he that died o' Wednes-
        day. Doth he feel it? no. Doth he hear it? no. 'Tis
        insensible, then? yea, to the dead. But will it not live
        with the living? no. Why? detraction will not suffer it.
        Therefore I'll none of it: honour is a mere scutcheon:
        —and so ends my catechism.

303   O, that a man might know
The end of this day's business ere it come!
But it sufficeth that the day will end,
And then the end is known.

304   What is a man
If his chief good and market of his time
Be but to sleep and feed? a beast, no more.
Sure, he that made us with such large discourse,
Looking before and after, gave us not
That capability and godlike reason
To fust in us unused. Now, whether it be
Bestial oblivion, or some craven scruple
Of thinking too precisely on th'event,—
A thought which, quarter'd, hath but one part wisdom
And ever three parts coward,—I do not know
Why yet I live to say 'This thing's to do;'
Sith I have cause, and will, and strength, and means
To do't. Examples, gross as earth, exhort me:
Witness this army, of such mass and charge,
Led by a delicate and tender prince;
Whose spirit, with divine ambition puft,
Makes mouths at the invisible event;
Exposing what is mortal and unsure
To all that fortune, death, and danger dare,
Even for an egg-shell. Rightly to be great
Is not to stir without great argument,
But greatly to find quarrel in a straw
When honour's at the stake.

305   We have, great Agamemnon, here in Troy
A prince call'd Hector,—Priam is his father,—
Who in this dull and long-continued truce
Is rusty grown: he bade me take a trumpet,

And to this purpose speak. Kings, princes, lords!
If there be one among the fair'st of Greece
That holds his honour higher than his ease;
That seeks his praise more than he fears his peril;
That knows his valour, and knows not his fear;
That loves his mistress more than in confession
With truant vows to her own lips he loves,
And dare avow her beauty and her worth
In other arms than hers,—to him this challenge.
Hector, in view of Trojans and of Greeks,
Shall make it good, or do his best to do it,
He hath a lady, wiser, fairer, truer,
Than ever Greek did compass in his arms;
And will to-morrow with his trumpet call
Midway between your tents and walls of Troy,
To rouse a Grecian that is true in love:
If any come, Hector shall honour him;
If none, he'll say in Troy when he retires,
The Grecian dames are sunburnt, and not worth
The splinter of a lance. Even so much.

306   See, what a grace was seated on this brow;
Hyperion's curls; the front of Jove himself;
An eye like Mars, to threaten and command;
A station like the herald Mercury
New-lighted on a heaven-kissing hill;
A combination and a form indeed,
Where every god did seem to set his seal,
To give the world assurance of a man.

307   It is held
That valour is the chiefest virtue, and
Most dignifies the haver: if it be,
The man I speak of cannot in the world
Be singly counterpoised. At sixteen years,

VALOUR

When Tarquin made a head for Rome, he fought
Beyond the mark of others: our then dictator,
Whom with all praise I point at, saw him fight,
When with his Amazonian chin he drove
The bristled lips before him: he bestrid
An o'er-prest Roman, and i'the consul's view
Slew three opposers: Tarquin's self he met,
And struck him on his knee: in that day's feats,
When he might act the woman in the scene,
He proved best man i'the field, and for his meed
Was brow-bound with the oak. His pupil age
Man-enter'd thus, he waxed like a sea;
And, in the brunt of seventeen battles since,
He lurcht all swords of the garland. For this last,
Before and in Corioli, let me say,
I cannot speak him home: he stopt the fliers;
And by his rare example made the coward
Turn terror into sport: as weeds before
A vessel under sail, so men obey'd,
And fell below his stem: his sword, death's stamp
Where it did mark, it took; from face to foot
He was a thing of blood, whose every motion
Was timed with dying cries: alone he enter'd
The mortal gate of the city, which he painted
With shunless destiny; aidless came off,
And with a sudden re-enforcement struck
Corioli like a planet: now all's his:
When, by and by, the din of war gan pierce
His ready sense; then straight his doubled spirit
Re-quicken'd what in flesh was fatigate,
And to the battle came he; where he did
Run reeking o'er the lives of men, as if
'Twere a perpetual spoil: and till we call'd
Both field and city ours, he never stood
To ease his breast with panting.
                  Our spoils he kick'd at;
And lookt upon things precious as they were

The common muck of the world: he covets less
Than misery itself would give; rewards
His deeds with doing them; and is content
To spend the time to end it.

308

VOLUMNIA

When yet he was but tender-bodied, and the only
son of my womb; when youth with comeliness pluckt
all gaze his way; when, for a day of kings' entreaties,
a mother should not sell him an hour from her
beholding; I—considering how honour would become
such a person; that it was no better than picture-like
to hang by the wall, if renown made it not stir—was
pleased to let him seek danger where he was like
to find fame. To a cruel war I sent him: from whence
he return'd, his brows bound with oak. I tell thee,
daughter, I sprang not more in joy at first hearing
he was a man-child than now in first seeing he had
proved himself a man.

VIRGILIA

But had he died in the business, madam,—how then?

VOLUMNIA

Then his good report should have been my son; I
therein would have found issue.

309

Ha, majesty! how high thy glory towers,
When the rich blood of kings is set on fire!
O, now doth Death line his dead chaps with steel;
The swords of soldiers are his teeth, his fangs;
And now he feasts, mousing the flesh of men,
In undetermined differences of kings.

310   Come, I'll be friends with thee, Jack: thou art going
to the wars; and whether I shall ever see thee again
or no, there is nobody cares.

311

VOLUMNIA

Methinks I hear hither your husband's drum;
See him pluck Aufidius down by the hair;
As children from a bear, the Volsces shunning him:
Methinks I see him stamp thus, and call thus,—
'Come on, you cowards! you were got in fear,
Though you were born in Rome:' his bloody brow
With his mail'd hand then wiping, forth he goes,
Like to a harvest-man, that's taskt to mow
Or all, or lose his hire.

VIRGILIA

His bloody brow! O Jupiter, no blood!

VOLUMNIA

Away, you fool! it more becomes a man
Than gilt his trophy: the breasts of Hecuba,
When she did suckle Hector, lookt not lovelier
Than Hector's forehead when it spit forth blood
At Grecian sword, contemning.

312   I am not yet of Percy's mind, the Hotspur of the
north; he that kills me some six or seven dozen of
Scots at a breakfast, washes his hands, and says to
his wife, 'Fie upon this quiet life! I want work.'
'O my sweet Harry,' says she, 'how many hast thou
kill'd to-day?' 'Give my roan horse a drench,' says
he; and answers, 'Some fourteen,' an hour after,—
'a trifle, a trifle.'

313   There's no man in the world
       More bound to's mother; yet here he lets me prate
       Like one i'the stocks.—Thou hast never in thy life
       Show'd thy dear mother any courtesy;
       When she, poor hen, fond of no second brood,
       Has cluckt thee to the wars, and safely home,
       Loaden with honour.

314   If we are markt to die, we are enow
       To do our country loss; and if to live,
       The fewer men, the greater share of honour.
       God's will! I pray thee, wish not one man more.
       By Jove, I am not covetous for gold;
       Nor care I who doth feed upon my cost;
       It yearns me not if men my garments wear;
       Such outward things dwell not in my desires:
       But if it be a sin to covet honour,
       I am the most offending soul alive.
       No, faith, my coz, wish not a man from England:
       God's peace! I would not lose so great an honour,
       As one man more, methinks, would share from me,
       For the best hope I have. O, do not wish one more!
       Rather proclaim it, Westmoreland, through my host,
       That he which hath no stomach to this fight,
       Let him depart; his passport shall be made,
       And crowns for convoy put into his purse:
       We would not die in that man's company
       That fears his fellowship to die with us.
       This day is call'd the feast of Crispian:
       He that outlives this day, and comes safe home,
       Will stand a tip-toe when this day is named,
       And rouse him at the name of Crispian.
       He that shall live this day, and see old age,
       Will yearly on the vigil feast his neighbours,
       And say, 'To-morrow is Saint Crispian:'

Then will he strip his sleeve and show his scars,
And say, 'These wounds I had on Crispin's day.'
Old men forget; yet all shall be forgot,
But he'll remember with advantages
What feats he did that day: then shall our names,
Familiar in their mouths as household words,—
Harry the king, Bedford and Exeter,
Warwick and Talbot, Salisbury and Gloster,—
Be in their flowing cups freshly remember'd.
This story shall the good man teach his son;
And Crispin Crispian shall ne'er go by,
From this day to the ending of the word,
But we in it shall be remembered,—
We few, we happy few, we band of brothers;
For he to-day that sheds his blood with me
Shall be my brother; be he ne'er so vile,
This day shall gentle his condition:
And gentlemen in England now a-bed
Shall think themselves accurst they were not here;
And hold their manhoods cheap whiles any speaks
That fought with us upon Saint Crispin's day.

315   MARK ANTONY

We have beat him to his camp:—run one before,
And let the queen know of our gests.—To-morrow,
Before the sun shall see's, we'll spill the blood
That has to-day escaped. I thank you all;
For doughty-handed are you, and have fought
Not as you served the cause, but as't had been
Each man's like mine; you have shown all Hectors.
Enter the city, clip your wives, your friends,
Tell them your feats; whilst they with joyful tears
Wash the congealment from your wounds, and kiss
The honour'd gashes whole.—Give me thy hand;

To this great fairy I'll commend thy acts,
Make her thanks bless thee. O thou day o'the
world,
Chain mine arm'd neck; leap thou, attire and all,
Through proof of harness to my heart, and there
Ride on the pants triumphing!

CLEOPATRA
Lord of lords!
O infinite virtue, comest thou smiling from
The world's great snare uncaught?

MARK ANTONY
My nightingale.
We have beat them to their beds. What, girl! though
gray
Do something mingle with our younger brown, yet
ha' we
A brain that nourishes our nerves, and can
Get goal for goal of youth. Behold this man;
Commend unto his lips thy favouring hand:—
Kiss it, my warrior:—he hath fought to-day
As if a god, in hate of mankind, had
Destroy'd in such a shape.

316

PANDARUS
That's Hector, that, that, look you, that; there's a
fellow!—Go thy way, Hector!—There's a brave man,
niece.—O brave Hector!—Look how he looks! there's
a countenance! is't not a brave man?

CRESSIDA
O, a brave man!

PANDARUS
Is a' not? it does a man's heart good:—look you what
hacks are on his helmet! look you yonder, do you
see? look you there: there's no jesting; there's laying
on, take't off who will, as they say: there be hacks!

CRESSIDA

Be those with swords?

PANDARUS

Swords! any thing, he cares not; an the devil come
to him, it's all one: by God's lid, it does one's heart
good.

317   And from the walls of strong-besieged Troy
When their brave hope, bold Hector, marcht to field,
Stood many Trojan mothers, sharing joy
To see their youthful sons bright weapons wield;
And to their hope they such odd action yield,
    That through their light joy seemed to appear,
    Like bright things stain'd, a kind of heavy fear.

And from the strond of Dardan, where they fought,
To Simois' reedy banks the red blood ran,
Whose waves to imitate the battle sought
With swelling ridges; and their ranks began
To break upon the galled shore, and than
    Retire again, till meeting greater ranks,
    They join, and shoot their foam at Simois' banks

318   I have, thou gallant Trojan, seen thee oft,
Labouring for destiny, make cruel way
Through ranks of Greekish youth; and I have seen
    thee,
As hot as Perseus, spur thy Phrygian steed,
Despising many forfeits and subduements,
When thou hast hung thy advanced sword i'th'air,
Not letting it decline on the declined;
That I have said to some my standers-by,

'Lo, Jupiter is yonder, dealing life!'
And I have seen thee pause and take thy breath,
When that a ring of Greeks have hemm'd thee in,
Like an Olympian wrestling: this have I seen;
But this thy countenance, still lockt in steel,
I never saw till now. I knew thy grandsire,
And once fought with him: he was a soldier good;
But, by great Mars, the captain of us all,
Never like thee. Let an old man embrace thee;
And, worthy warrior, welcome to our tents.

319

COSTARD

I Pompey am, Pompey surnamed the Big,—
                    DUMAINE

The Great.

COSTARD

It is 'Great,' sir:—
                    Pompey surnamed the Great;
That oft in field, with targe and shield, did make my
    foe to sweat:
And travelling along this coast, I here am come by
    chance,
And lay my arms before the legs of this sweet lass
    of France.
If your ladyship would say, 'Thanks, Pompey,' I
    had done.

PRINCESS

Great thanks, great Pompey.

COSTARD

'Tis not so much worth; but I hope I was perfect:
I made a little fault in 'Great.'

BEROWNE

My hat to a halfpenny, Pompey proves the best
Worthy.

SIR NATHANIEL

When in the world I lived, I was the world's commander;

By east, west, north, and south, I spread my conquering might:

My scutcheon plain declares that I am Alisander,—

PRINCESS

The conqueror is dismay'd. Proceed, good Alexander.

SIR NATHANIEL

When in the world I lived, I was the world's commander.

BOYET

Most true, 'tis right; you were so, Alisander.

BEROWNE

Pompey the Great,—

COSTARD

Your servant, and Costard.

BEROWNE

Take away the conqueror, take away Alisander.

COSTARD

O, sir, you have overthrown Alisander the conqueror! You will be scraped out of the painted cloth for this: your lion, that holds his poll-axe sitting on a close-stool, will be given to Ajax: he will be the ninth Worthy. A conqueror, and afeard to speak! run away for shame, Alisander. There, an't shall please you; a foolish mild man; an honest man, look you, and soon dasht. He is a marvellous good neighbour, faith, and a very good bowler: but, for Alisander,—alas, you see how 'tis,—a little o'erparted.

320   The sweet war-man is dead and rotten; sweet chucks, beat not the bones of the buried: when he breathed, he was a man.

321

GOWER

O, 'tis a gallant king!

FLUELLEN

Ay, he was porn at Monmouth, Captain Gower. What call you the town's name where Alexander the Pig was porn?

GOWER

Alexander the Great.

FLUELLEN

Why, I pray you, is not pig great? the pig, or the great, or the mighty, or the huge, or the magnanimous, are all one reckonings, save the phrase is a little variations.

GOWER

I think Alexander the Great was born in Macedon: his father was call'd Philip of Macedon, as I take it.

FLUELLEN

I think it is in Macedon where Alexander is porn. I tell you, captain, if you look in the maps of the 'orld, I warrant you sall find, in the comparisons between Macedon and Monmouth, that the situations, look you, is both alike. There is a river in Macedon; and there is also moreover a river at Monmouth: it is called Wye at Monmouth; but it is out of my prains what is the name of the other river; but 'tis all one, 'tis alike as my fingers is to my fingers, and there is salmons in both.

322

HAMLET

To what base uses we may return, Horatio! Why may not imagination trace the noble dust of Alexander till he find it stopping a bung-hole?

HORATIO

'Twere to consider too curiously, to consider so.

HAMLET

No, faith, not a jot; but to follow him thither with
modesty enough, and likelihood to lead it: as thus;
Alexander died, Alexander was buried, Alexander
returneth into dust; the dust is earth: of earth we
make loam; and why of that loam whereto he was
converted might they not stop a beer-barrel?
    Imperious Cæsar, dead and turn'd to clay,
    Might stop a hole to keep the wind away.

323   Why, 'tis a gull, a fool, a rogue, that now and then
goes to the wars, to grace himself, at his return into
London, under the form of a soldier. And such
fellows are perfect in the great commanders' names:
and they will learn you by rote where services were
done;—at such and such a sconce, at such a breach,
at such a convoy; who came off bravely, who was
shot, who disgraced, what terms the enemy stood
on; and this they con perfectly in the phrase of war,
which they trick up with new-turn'd oaths: and what
a beard of the general's cut, and a horrid suit of the
camp, will do among foaming bottles and ale-washt
wits, is wonderful to be thought on. But you must
learn to know such slanders of the age, or else you
may be marvellously mistook.

324   I have seen the dumb men throng to see him, and
The blind to hear him speak: matrons flung gloves,
Ladies and maids their scarfs and handkerchers,
Upon him as he past: the nobles bended
As to Jove's statue; and the commons made
A shower and thunder with their caps and shouts:
I never saw the like.

325   Behold, the English beach
Pales in the flood with men, with wives, and boys,
Whose shouts and claps out-voice the deep-mouth'd
    sea,
Which, like a mighty whiffler 'fore the king,
Seems to prepare his way: so let him land;
And solemnly see him set on to London.
So swift a pace hath thought, that even now
You may imagine him upon Blackheath;
Where that his lords desire him to have borne
His bruised helmet and his bended sword
Before him through the city: he forbids it,
Being free from vainness and self-glorious pride;
Giving full trophy, signal, and ostent,
Quite from himself to God. But now behold,
In the quick forge and working-house of thought,
How London doth pour out her citizens!
The mayor, and all his brethren, in best sort,—
Like to the senators of th'antique Rome,
With the plebeians swarming at their heels,—
Go forth, and fetch their conquering Cæsar in:
As, by a lower but loving likelihood,
Were now the general of our gracious empress—
As in good time he may—from Ireland coming,
Bringing rebellion broached on his sword,
How many would the peaceful city quit,
To welcome him! much more, and much more cause,
Did they this Harry.

326   I do not know what witchcraft's in him, but
Your soldiers use him as the grace 'fore meat.
Their talk at table, and their thanks at end.

327   O you hard hearts, you cruel men of Rome,
Knew you not Pompey? Many a time and oft

Have you climb'd up to walls and battlements,
To towers and windows, yea, to chimney-tops,
Your infants in your arms, and there have sat
The live-long day, with patient expectation,
To see great Pompey pass the streets of Rome:
And when you saw his chariot but appear,
Have you not made an universal shout,
That Tiber trembled underneath her banks,
To hear the replication of your sounds
Made in her concave shores?
And do you now put on your best attire?
And do you now cull out a holiday?
And do you now strew flowers in his way
That comes in triumph over Pompey's blood?

328   All tongues speak of him, and the bleared sights
Are spectacled to see him: your prattling nurse
Into a rapture lets her baby cry
While she chats him: the kitchen malkin pins
Her richest lockram 'bout her reechy neck,
Clamb'ring the walls to eye him: stalls, bulks,
    windows,
Are smother'd up, leads fill'd, and ridges horsed
With variable complexions; all agreeing
In earnestness to see him: seld-shown flamens
Do press among the popular throngs, and puff
To win a vulgar station: our veil'd dames
Commit the war of white and damask in
Their nicely-gawded cheeks to the wanton spoil
Of Phœbus' burning kisses: such a pother,
As if that whatsoever god who leads him
Were slily crept into his human powers,
And gave him graceful posture.

329

ROSS

Your son, my lord, has paid a soldier's debt:
He only lived but till he was a man,
The which no sooner had his prowess confirm'd
In the unshrinking station where he fought,
But like a man he died.

SIWARD

Then he is dead?

ROSS

Ay, and brought off the field: your cause of sorrow
Must not be measured by his worth, for then
It hath no end.

SIWARD

Had he his hurts before?

ROSS

Ay, on the front.

SIWARD

Why then, God's soldier be he!
Had I as many sons as I have hairs,
I would not wish them to a fairer death.

330

Many a time hath banisht Norfolk fought
For Jesu Christ in glorious Christian field,
Streaming the ensign of the Christian cross
Against black pagans, Turks, and Saracens;
And toil'd with works of war, retired himself
To Italy; and there, at Venice, gave
His body to that pleasant country's earth,
And his pure soul unto his captain Christ,
Under whose colours he had fought so long.

331

Antony,
Leave thy lascivious wassails. When thou once
Wast beaten from Modena, where thou slew'st
Hirtius and Pansa, consuls, at thy heel

Did famine follow; whom thou fought'st against,
Though daintily brought up, with patience more
Than savages could suffer: thou didst drink
The stale of horses, and the gilded puddle
Which beasts would cough at: thy palate then did
 deign
The roughest berry in the rudest hedge;
Yea, like the stag, when snow the pasture sheets,
The barks of trees thou browsed'st; on the Alps
It is reported thou didst eat strange flesh,
Which some did die to look on: and all this—
It wounds thine honour that I speak it now—
Was borne so like a soldier, that thy cheek
So much as lankt not.

332   Cut me to pieces, Volsces; men and lads,
Stain all your edges on me.—Boy! false hound!
If you have writ your annals true, 'tis there,
That, like an eagle in a dove-cote, I
Flutter'd your Volscians in Corioli:
Alone I did it.—Boy!

333   O, now, for ever
Farewell the tranquil mind! farewell content!
Farewell the plumed troop, and the big wars,
That make ambition virtue! O, farewell!
Farewell the neighing steed, and the shrill trump,
The spirit-stirring drum, th'ear-piercing fife,
The royal banner, and all quality,
Pride, pomp, and circumstance of glorious war!
And, O you mortal engines, whose rude throats
Th'immortal Jove's dread clamours counterfeit,
Farewell! Othello's occupation's gone!

334   This royal throne of kings, this scepter'd isle,
This earth of majesty, this seat of Mars,
This other Eden, demi-Paradise;
This fortress built by Nature for herself
Against infection and the hand of war;
This happy breed of men, this little world;
This precious stone set in the silver sea,
Which serves it in the office of a wall,
Or as a moat defensive to a house,
Against the envy of less happier lands;
This blessed plot, this earth, this realm, this England,
This nurse, this teeming womb of royal kings,
Fear'd by their breed, and famous by their birth,
Renowned for their deeds as far from home,—
For Christian service and true chivalry,—
As is the sepulchre, in stubborn Jewry,
Of the world's ransom, blessed Mary's Son;—
This land of such dear souls, this dear dear land,
Dear for her reputation through the world,
Is now leased out—I die pronouncing it—
Like to a tenement or pelting farm:
England, bound in with the triumphant sea,
Whose rocky shore beats back the envious siege
Of watery Neptune, is now bound in with shame,
With inky blots, and rotten parchment bonds:
That England, that was wont to conquer others,
Hath made a shameful conquest of itself.

335   This England never did, nor never shall,
Lie at the proud foot of a conqueror,
But when it first did help to wound itself.
Now these her princes are come home again,
Come the three corners of the world in arms,
And we shall shock them; naught shall make us rue,
If England to itself do rest but true.

DUKE OF BOURBON

Normans, but bastard Normans, Norman bastards!
Mort de ma vie! if they march along
Unfought withal, but I will sell my dukedom,
To buy a slobbery and a dirty farm
In that nook-shotten isle of Albion.

THE CONSTABLE OF FRANCE

Dieu de batailles! where have they this mettle?
Is not their climate foggy, raw, and dull;
On whom, as in despite, the sun looks pale,
Killing their fruit with frowns? Can sodden water,
A drench for sur-rein'd jades, their barley-broth,
Decoct their cold blood to such valiant heat?
And shall our quick blood, spirited with wine,
Seem frosty? O, for honour of our land,
Let us not hang like roping icicles
Upon our houses' thatch, whiles a more frosty people
Sweat drops of gallant youth in our rich fields.

Mad world! mad kings! mad composition!
John, to stop Arthur's title in the whole,
Hath willingly departed with a part;
And France,—whose armour conscience buckled on,
Whom zeal and charity brought to the field
As God's own soldier,—rounded in the ear
With that same purpose-changer, that sly devil;
That broker, that still breaks the pate of faith;
That daily break-vow; he that wins of all,
Of kings, of beggars, old men, young men, maids,—
Who having no external thing to lose
But the word 'maid,' cheats the poor maid of that;
That smooth-faced gentleman, tickling Commodity—
Commodity, the bias of the world;
The world, who of itself is peised well,
Made to run even upon even ground,

Till this advantage, this vile-drawing bias,
This sway of motion, this Commodity,
Makes it take head from all indifferency,
From all direction, purpose, course, intent,
And this same bias, this Commodity,
This bawd, this broker, this all-changing word,
Clapt on the outward eye of fickle France,
Hath drawn him from his own determined aid,
From a resolved and honourable war,
To a most base and vile-concluded peace.

338   O inglorious league!
Shall we, upon the footing of our land,
Send fair-play orders, and make compromise,
Insinuation, parley, and base truce,
To arms invasive? shall a beardless boy,
A cocker'd silken wanton, brave our fields,
And flesh his spirit in a warlike soil,
Mocking the air with colours idly spread,
And find no check? Let us, my liege, to arms!

339   This apish and unmannerly approach,
This harness'd mask and unadvised revel,
This unhair'd sauciness and boyish troops,
The king doth smile at; and is well prepared
To whip this dwarfish war, these pigmy arms,
From out the circle of his territories.
Shall that victorious hand be feebled here,
That in your chambers gave you chastisement?
No: know the gallant monarch is in arms:
And, like an eagle o'er his aery, towers
To souse annoyance that comes near his nest.—
And you degenerate, you ingrate revolts,

You bloody Neroes, ripping up the womb
Of your dear mother England, blush for shame;
For your own ladies and pale-visaged maids,
Like Amazons, come tripping after drums,
Their thimbles into armed gauntlets change,
Their needles to lances, and their gentle hearts
To fierce and bloody inclination.

340   Arm, arm, you heavens, against these perjured kings
A widow cries; be husband to me, heavens!
Let not the hours of this ungodly day
Wear out the day in peace; but, ere sunset,
Set armed discord 'twixt these perjured kings!
Hear me, O, hear me!

341   O heavens,
If you do love old men, if your sweet sway
Allow obedience, if yourselves are old,
Make it your cause; send down, and take my part!

342   Go, bear him in thine arms.—
I am amazed, methinks; and lose my way
Among the thorns and dangers of this world.—
How easy dost thou take all England up!
From forth this morsel of dead royalty,
The life, the right, and truth of all this realm
Is fled to heaven; and England now is left
To tug and scamble, and to part by th' teeth
The unowed interest of proud-swelling state.
Now for the bare-pickt bone of majesty
Doth dogged war bristle his angry crest,
And snarleth in the gentle eyes of peace:

Now powers from home and discontents at home
Meet in one line; and vast confusion waits,
As doth a raven on a sick-fall'n beast,
The imminent decay of wrested pomp.
Now happy he whose cloak and cincture can
Hold out this tempest.

343 O, pardon me, thou bleeding piece of earth,
That I am meek and gentle with these butchers!
Thou art the ruins of the noblest man
That ever lived in the tide of times.
Woe to the hand that shed this costly blood!
Over thy wounds now do I prophesy,—
Which, like dumb mouths, do ope their ruby lips,
To beg the voice and utterance of my tongue,—
A curse shall light upon the limbs of men;
Domestic fury and fierce civil strife
Shall cumber all the parts of Italy;
Blood and destruction shall be so in use,
And dreadful objects so familiar,
That mothers shall but smile when they behold
Their infants quarter'd with the hands of war;
All pity choked with custom of fell deeds:
And Cæsar's spirit, ranging for revenge,
With Ate by his side come hot from hell,
Shall in these confines with a monarch's voice
Cry 'Havoc,' and let slip the dogs of war;
That this foul deed shall smell above the earth
With carrion men, groaning for burial.

344 Let it not disgrace me,
If I demand, before this royal view,
What rub or what impediment there is,
Why that the naked, poor, and mangled Peace,
Dear nurse of arts, plenties, and joyful births,

Should not, in this best garden of the world,
Our fertile France, put up her lovely visage?
Alas, she hath from France too long been chased!
And all her husbandry doth lie on heaps,
Corrupting in its own fertility.
Her vine, the merry cheerer of the heart,
Unpruned dies; her hedges even-pleacht,
Like prisoners wildly overgrown with hair,
Put forth disorder'd twigs; her fallow leas
The darnel, hemlock, and rank fumitory,
Do root upon, while that the coulter rusts,
That should deracinate such savagery;
The even mead, that erst brought sweetly forth
The freckled cowslip, burnet, and green clover,
Wanting the scythe, all uncorrected, rank,
Conceives by idleness, and nothing teems
But hateful docks, rough thistles, kecksies, burs,
Losing both beauty and utility.
And as our vineyards, fallows, meads, and hedges.
Defective in their natures, grow to wildness,
Even so our houses, and ourselves and children,
Have lost, or do not learn for want of time,
The sciences that should become our country;
But grow, like savages,—as soldiers will,
That nothing do but meditate on blood,—
To swearing, and stern looks, diffused attire,
And every thing that seems unnatural.

345   Should we be silent and not speak, our raiment
       And state of bodies would bewray what life
       We have led since thy exile. Think with thyself
       How more unfortunate than all living women
       Are we come hither: since that thy sight, which
           should
       Make our eyes flow with joy, hearts dance with
           comforts,

Constrains them weep, and shake with fear and
    sorrow;
Making the mother, wife, and child, to see
The son, the husband, and the father, tearing
His country's bowels out. And to poor we
Thine enmity's most capital: thou barr'st us
Our prayers to the gods, which is a comfort
That all but we enjoy; for how can we,
Alas, how can we for our country pray,
Whereto we are bound,—together with thy victory,
Whereto we are bound? alack, or we must lose
The country, our dear nurse, or else thy person,
Our comfort in the country. We must find
An evident calamity, though we had
Our wish, which side should win; for either thou
Must, as a foreign recreant, be led
With manacles through our streets, or else
Triumphantly tread on thy country's ruin,
And bear the palm for having bravely shed
Thy wife and children's blood. For myself, son,
I purpose not to wait on fortune till
These wars determine: if I cannot persuade thee
Rather to show a noble grace to both parts
Than seek the end of one, thou shalt no sooner
March to assault thy country than to tread—
Trust to't, thou shalt not—on thy mother's womb
That brought thee to this world.

346   Though I speak it to you, I think the king is but a
man, as I am: the violet smells to him as it doth to
me; the element shows to him as it does to me; all
his senses have but human conditions: his ceremonies
laid by, in his nakedness he appears but a man; and
though his affections are higher mounted than ours,
yet, when they stoop, they stoop with the like wing.

347   Not all the water in the rough rude sea
Can wash the balm from an anointed king;
The breath of worldly men cannot depose
The deputy elected by the Lord.

348   And shall the figure of God's majesty,
His captain, steward, deputy elect,
Anointed, crowned, planted many years,
Be judged by subject and inferior breath,
And he himself not present? O, forfend it, God,
That in a Christian climate, souls refined
Should show so heinous, black, obscene a deed!
I speak to subjects, and a subject speaks,
Stirr'd up by God, thus boldly for his king.

349   What infinite heart's-ease must kings neglect,
That private men enjoy!
And what have kings, that privates have not too,
Save ceremony,—save general ceremony?
And what art thou, thou idol ceremony?
What kind of god art thou, that suffer'st more
Of mortal griefs than do thy worshippers?
What are thy rents? what are thy comings-in?
O ceremony, show me but thy worth!
What is thy soul, O adoration?
Art thou aught else but place, degree, and form,
Creating awe and fear in other men?
Wherein thou art less happy being fear'd
Than they in fearing.
What drink'st thou oft, instead of homage sweet,
But poison'd flattery? O, be sick, great greatness,
And bid thy ceremony give thee cure!
Think'st thou the fiery fever will go out
With titles blown from adulation?

Will it give place to flexure and low bending?
Canst thou, when thou command'st the beggar's
    knee,
Command the health of it? No, thou proud dream,
That play'st so subtly with a king's repose:
I am a king that find thee; and I know
'Tis not the balm, the sceptre, and the ball,
The sword, the mace, the crown imperial,
The intertissued robe of gold and pearl,
The farced title running 'fore the king,
The throne he sits on, nor the tide of pomp
That beats upon the high shore of this world,—
No, not all these, thrice-gorgeous ceremony,
Not all these, laid in bed majestical,
Can sleep so soundly as the wretched slave,
Who, with a body fill'd and vacant mind,
Gets him to rest, cramm'd with distressful bread;
Never sees horrid night, the child of hell;
But, like a lackey, from the rise to set,
Sweats in the eye of Phœbus, and all night
Sleeps in Elysium; next day, after dawn,
Doth rise, and help Hyperion to his horse;
And follows so the ever-running year,
With profitable labour, to his grave:
And, but for ceremony, such a wretch,
Winding up days with toil and nights with sleep,
Had the fore-hand and vantage of a king.
The slave, a member of the country's peace,
Enjoys it; but in gross brain little wots
What watch the king keeps to maintain the peace,
Whose hours the peasant best advantages.

350   O God! methinks it were a happy life,
    To be no better than a homely swain;
    To sit upon a hill, as I do now,
    To carve out dials quaintly, point by point,

Thereby to see the minutes how they run,—
How many makes the hour full complete;
How many hours brings about the day;
How many days will finish up the year;
How many years a mortal man may live.
When this is known, then to divide the times:—
So many hours must I tend my flock;
So many hours must I take my rest;
So many hours must I contemplate;
So many hours must I sport myself;
So many days my ewes have been with young;
So many weeks ere the poor fools will ean;
So many months ere I shall shear the fleece:
So minutes, hours, days, months, and years,
Past over to the end they were created,
Would bring white hairs unto a quiet grave.
Ah, what a life were this! how sweet! how lovely!
Gives not the hawthorn-bush a sweeter shade
To shepherds looking on their silly sheep,
Than doth a rich-embroider'd canopy
To kings that fear their subjects' treachery?
O, yes, it doth; a thousand-fold it doth.
And to conclude,—the shepherd's homely curds,
His cold thin drink out of his leather bottle,
His wonted sleep under a fresh tree's shade,
All which secure and sweetly he enjoys,
Is far beyond a prince's delicates,
His viands sparkling in a golden cup,
His body couched in a curious bed,
When care, mistrust, and treason waits on him.

351   Sir, I am a true labourer: I earn that I eat, get that
I wear; owe no man hate, envy no man's happiness;
glad of other men's good, content with my harm;
and the greatest of my pride is, to see my ewes graze
and my lambs suck.

JOHN BATES

He [the King] may show what outward courage he will; but I believe, as cold a night as 'tis, he could wish himself in Thames up to the neck;—and so I would he were, and I by him, at all adventures, so we were quit here.

KING HENRY (*incognito*)

By my troth, I will speak my conscience of the king: I think he would not wish himself any where but where he is.

JOHN BATES

Then I would he were here alone; so should he be sure to be ransom'd, and a many poor men's lives saved.

KING HENRY

I dare say you love him not so ill, to wish him here alone, howsoever you speak this, to feel other men's minds: methinks I could not die any where so contented as in the king's company,—his cause being just, and his quarrel honourable.

MICHAEL WILLIAMS

That's more than we know.

JOHN BATES

Ay, or more than we should seek after; for we know enough, if we know we are the king's subjects: if his cause be wrong, our obedience to the king wipes the crime of it out of us.

MICHAEL WILLIAMS

But if the cause be not good, the king himself hath a heavy reckoning to make, when all those legs and arms and heads, chopt off in battle, shall join together at the latter day, and cry all, 'We died at such a place;' some swearing; some crying for a surgeon; some, upon their wives left poor behind them; some, upon the debts they owe; some, upon their children rawly left. I am afeard there are few die well that die in battle, for how can they charitably dispose of any thing, when blood is their argument? Now, if these men do not die well, it will be a black matter for the king that led them to it; who to disobey were against all proportion of subjection.

KING HENRY

So, if a son, that is by his father sent about merchandise, do sinfully miscarry upon the sea, the imputation of his wickedness, by your rule, should be imposed upon his father that sent him: or if a servant, under his master's command transporting a sum of money, be assail'd by robbers, and die in many irreconciled iniquities, you may call the business of the master the author of the servant's damnation:—but this is not so: the king is not bound to answer the particular endings of his soldiers, the father of his son, nor the master of his servant; for they purpose not their death, when they purpose their services. Besides, there is no king, be his cause never so spotless, if it come to the arbitrement of swords, can try it out with all unspotted soldiers: some peradventure have on them the guilt of premeditated and contrived murder; some, of beguiling virgins with the broken seals of perjury; some, making the wars their bulwark, that have before gored the gentle bosom of peace with pillage and robbery. Now, if these men have defeated the law and outrun native punishment, though they can outstrip men, they have no wings to fly from God: war is His beadle, war is His vengeance; so that here men are punisht for before-breach of the king's laws in now the king's quarrel: where they fear'd the death, they have borne life away; and where they would be safe, they perish: then if they die unprovided, no more is the king guilty of their damnation, than he was before guilty of those impieties for the which they are now visited. Every subject's duty is the king's; but every subject's soul is his own

Therefore should every soldier in the wars do as every sick man in his bed,—wash every mote out of his conscience: and dying so, death is to him advantage; or not dying, the time was blessedly lost wherein such preparation was gain'd: and in him that escapes, it were not sin to think that, making God so free an offer, He let him outlive that day to see His greatness, and to teach others how they should prepare.

MICHAEL WILLIAMS

'Tis certain, every man that dies ill, the ill upon his own head,—the king is not to answer it.

JOHN BATES

I do not desire he should answer for me; and yet I determine to fight lustily for him.

353

HENRY PERCY

See, see, King Richard doth himself appear,
As doth the blushing discontented sun
From out the fiery portal of the east,
When he perceives the envious clouds are bent
To dim his glory, and to stain the track
Of his bright passage to the occident.
Yet looks he like a king: behold, his eye,
As bright as is the eagle's, lightens forth
Controlling majesty:—alack, alack, for woe,
That any harm should stain so fair a show!

KING RICHARD

We are amazed; and thus long have we stood
To watch the fearful bending of thy knee,
Because we thought ourself thy lawful king:
And if we be, how dare thy joints forget
To pay their awful duty to our presence?
If we be not, show us the hand of God
That hath dismist us from our stewardship;

For well we know, no hand of blood and bone
Can gripe the sacred handle of our sceptre,
Unless he do profane, steal, or usurp.
And though you think that all, as you have done
Have torn their souls by turning them from us,
And we are barren and bereft of friends;
Yet know,—my master, God omnipotent,
Is mustering in his clouds, on our behalf,
Armies of pestilence; and they shall strike
Your children yet unborn and unbegot,
That lift your vassal hands against my head,
And'threat the glory of my precious crown.

———

What must the king do now? must he submit?
The king shall do it: must he be deposed?
The king shall be contented: must he lose
The name of king? o' God's name, let it go·
I'll give my jewels for a set of beads,
My gorgeous palace for a hermitage,
My gay apparel for an almsman's gown,
My figured goblets for a dish of wood,
My sceptre for a palmer's walking-staff,
My subjects for a pair of carved saints,
And my large kingdom for a little grave,
A little little grave, an obscure grave;—
Or I'll be buried in the king's highway,
Some way of common trade, where subjects' feet
May hourly trample on their sovereign's head;
For on my heart they tread now whilst I live.

354 Alack, why am I sent for to a king,
Before I have shook off the regal thoughts
Wherewith I reign'd? I hardly yet have learn'd
To insinuate, flatter, bow, and bend my knee:
Give sorrow leave awhile to tutor me

THE AGES OF MAN

To this submission. Yet I well remember
The favours of these men: were they not mine?
Did they not sometime cry, 'All hail!' to me?
So Judas did to Christ: but he, in twelve,
Found truth in all but one; I, in twelve thousand,
    none.
God save the king!—Will no man say amen?
Am I both priest and clerk? well then, amen.
God save the king! although I be not he;
And yet, amen, if heaven do think him me.

———

Give me the crown.—Here, cousin, seize the crown;
Here, cousin:
On this side my hand, and on that side yours.
Now is this golden crown like a deep well
That owes two buckets, filling one another;
The emptier ever dancing in the air,
The other down, unseen, and full of water:
That bucket down and full of tears am I,
Drinking my griefs, whilst you mount up on high.

———

Now mark me, how I will undo myself:—
I give this heavy weight from off my head,
And this unwieldy sceptre from my hand,
The pride of kingly sway from out my heart;
With mine own tears I wash away my balm,
With mine own hands I give away my crown,
With mine own tongue deny my sacred state,
With mine own breath release all duty's rites:
All pomp and majesty I do forswear;
My manors, rents, revenues I forgo;
My acts, decrees, and statutes I deny:
God pardon all oaths that are broke to me!
God keep all vows unbroke that swear to thee!
Make me, that nothing have, with nothing grieved,
And thou with all pleased, that hast all achieved!

———

Nay, all of you that stand and look upon,
Whilst that my wretchedness doth bait myself,—
Though some of you, with Pilate, wash your hands,
Showing an outward pity; yet you Pilates
Have here deliver'd me to my sour cross,
And water cannot wash away your sin.

O, that I were a mockery-king of snow,
Standing before the sun of Bolingbroke,
To melt myself away in water-drops!

Good king,—great king,—and yet not greatly
  good,—
An if my word be sterling yet in England,
Let it command a mirror hither straight,
That it may show me what a face I have,
Since it is bankrupt of his majesty.
Give me the glass, and therein will I read.—
No deeper wrinkles yet? hath sorrow struck
So many blows upon this face of mine,
And made no deeper wounds!—O flattering glass,
Like to my followers in prosperity,
Thou dost beguile me! Was this face the face
That every day under his household roof
Did keep ten thousand men? was this the face
That, like the sun, did make beholders wink?
Was this the face that faced so many follies,
And was at last out-faced by Bolingbroke?
A brittle glory shineth in this face:
As brittle as the glory is the face.

355   Poor broken glass, I often did behold
In thy sweet semblance my old age new born;
But now that fair fresh mirror, dim and old,
Shows me a bare-boned death by time outworn:

O, from thy cheeks my image thou hast torn,
And shiver'd all the beauty of my glass,
That I no more can see what once I was.

356   Beauty is but a vain and doubtful good;
A shining gloss that vadeth suddenly;
A flower that dies when first it gins to bud;
A brittle glass that's broken presently:
    A doubtful good, a gloss, a glass, a flower,
    Lost, vaded, broken, dead within an hour.

357   GROOM
I was a poor groom of thy stable, king,
When thou wert king; who, travelling towards York
With much ado at length have gotten leave
To look upon my sometimes royal master's face.
O, how it yearn'd my heart, when I beheld,
In London streets, that coronation-day,
When Bolingbroke rode on roan Barbary,—
That horse that thou so often hast bestrid,
That horse that I so carefully have drest!
           KING RICHARD
Rode he on Barbary? Tell me, gentle friend,
How went he under him?
                 GROOM
So proudly as if he disdain'd the ground.
           KING RICHARD
So proud that Bolingbroke was on his back!
That jade hath eat bread from my royal hand;
This hand hath made him proud with clapping him.
Would he not stumble? would he not fall down,—
Since pride must have a fall,—and break the neck
Of that proud man that did usurp his back?

Forgiveness, horse! why do I rail on thee,
Since thou, created to be awed by man,
Wast born to bear? I was not made a horse
And yet I bear a burden like an ass,
Spur-gall'd and tired by jauncing Bolingbroke.

358   Come hither, Harry, sit thou by my bed;
And hear, I think, the very latest counsel
That ever I shall breathe. God knows, my son,
By what by-paths and indirect crookt ways
I met this crown; and I myself know well
How troublesome it sat upon my head:
To thee it shall descend with better quiet,
Better opinion, better confirmation;
For all the soil of the achievement goes
With me into the earth. It seem'd in me
But as an honour snatcht with boisterous hand;
And I had many living to upbraid
My gain of it by their assistances;
Which daily grew to quarrel and to bloodshed,
Wounding supposed peace: all these bold fears
Thou see'st with peril I have answered;
For all my reign hath been but as a scene
Acting that argument: and now my death
Changes the mode; for what in me was purchased,
Falls upon thee in a more fairer sort;
So thou the garland wear'st successively.

359   When that the general is not like the hive,
To whom the foragers shall all repair,
What honey is expected? Degree being vizarded,
Th'unworthiest shows as fairly in the mask.
The heavens themselves, the planets, and this centre
Observe degree, priority, and place,

Insisture, course, proportion, season, form,
Office, and custom, in all line of order:
And therefore is the glorious planet Sol
In noble eminence enthroned and sphered
Amidst the other; whose med'cinable eye
Corrects the ill aspects of planets evil,
And posts, like the commandment of a king,
Sans check, to good and bad: but when the planets,
In evil mixture, to disorder wander,
What plagues, and what portents, what mutiny,
What raging of the sea, shaking of earth,
Commotion in the winds, frights, changes, horrors,
Divert and crack, rend and deracinate
The unity and married calm of states
Quite from their fixure! O, when degree is shaked,
Which is the ladder to all high designs,
The enterprise is sick! How could communities,
Degrees in schools, and brotherhoods in cities,
Peaceful commerce from dividable shores,
The primogenity and due of birth,
Prerogative of age, crowns, sceptres, laurels,
But by degree, stand in authentic place?
Take but degree away, untune that string,
And, hark, what discord follows!

360   For government, though high, and low, and lower,
Put into parts, doth keep in one concent,
Congreeing in a full and natural close,
Like music.

361   Therefore doth heaven divide
The state of man in divers functions,
Setting endeavour in continual motion;
To which is fixed, as an aim or butt,
Obedience: for so work the honey-bees,

THE HONEY-BEES

Creatures that, by a rule in nature, teach
The art of order to a peopled kingdom.
They have a king, and officers of sorts:
Where some, like magistrates, correct at home;
Others, like merchants, venture trade abroad;
Others, like soldiers, armed in their stings,
Make boot upon the summer's velvet buds;
Which pillage they with merry march bring home
To the tent-royal of their emperor:
Who, busied in his majesty, surveys
The singing masons building roofs of gold;
The civil citizens kneading-up the honey;
The poor mechanic porters crowding in
Their heavy burdens at his narrow gate;
The sad-eyed justice, with his surly hum,
Delivering o'er to executors pale
The lazy yawning drone. I this infer,—
That many things, having full reference
To one concent, may work contrariously:
As many arrows, loosed several ways,
Fly to one mark;
As many several ways meet in one town;
As many fresh streams run in one self sea;
As many lines close in the dial's centre;
So may a thousand actions, once afoot,
End in one purpose, and be all well borne
Without defeat.

362   Music do I hear?
Ha, ha! keep time:—how sour sweet music is,
When time is broke and no proportion kept!
So is it in the music of men's lives.
And here have I the daintiness of ear
To check time broke in a disorder'd string;
But, for the concord of my state and time,
Had not an ear to hear my true time broke.

363
            Therefore the poet
Did feign that Orpheus drew trees, stones, and floods;
Since naught so stockish, hard, and full of rage,
But music for the time doth change his nature.
The man that hath no music in himself,
Nor is not moved with concord of sweet sounds,
Is fit for treasons, stratagems, and spoils;
The motions of his spirit are dull as night,
And his affections dark as Erebus:
Let no such man be trusted.

364
            Orpheus with his lute made trees,
            And the mountain-tops that freeze,
                Bow themselves, when he did sing:
            To his music plants and flowers
            Ever sprung; as sun and showers
                There had made a lasting spring.
            Every thing that heard him play,
            Even the billows of the sea,
                Hung their heads, and then lay by.
            In sweet music is such art,
            Killing care and grief of heart
                Fall asleep, or hearing, die.

365   GARDENER
Go, bind thou up yon dangling apricocks,
Which, like unruly children, make their sire
Stoop with oppression of their prodigal weight:
Give some supportance to the bending twigs.—
Go thou, and, like an executioner,
Cut off the heads of too-fast-growing sprays,
That look too lofty in our commonwealth:
All must be even in our government.—

ENGLAND, A GARDEN

You thus employ'd, I will go root away
The noisome weeds, that without profit suck
The soil's fertility from wholesome flowers.
                    SERVANT
Why should we, in the compass of a pale,
Keep law and form and due proportion,
Showing, as in a model, our firm estate,
When our sea-walled garden, the whole land,
Is full of weeds; her fairest flowers choked up,
Her fruit-trees all unpruned, her hedges ruin'd,
Her knots disorder'd, and her wholesome herbs
Swarming with caterpillars?
                    GARDENER
                        Hold thy peace:—
He that hath suffer'd this disorder'd spring
Hath now himself met with the fall of leaf:
                        O, what pity is it
That he had not so trimm'd and drest his land
As we this garden! We at time of year
Do wound the bark, the skin of our fruit-trees,
Lest, being over-proud in sap and blood,
With too much riches it confound itself:
Had he done so to great and growing men,
They might have lived to bear, and he to taste
Their fruits of duty. All superfluous branches
We lop away, that bearing boughs may live:
Had he done so, himself had borne the crown,
Which waste of idle hours hath quite thrown down.

366   The providence that's in a watchful state
       Knows almost every grain of Pluto's gold;
       Finds bottom in th'uncomprehensive deeps;
       Keeps place with thought, and almost, like the gods,
       Does thoughts unveil in their dumb cradles

There is a mystery—with whom relation
Durst never meddle—in the soul of state;
Which hath an operation more divine
Than breath or pen can give expressure to.

367   Had I so lavish of my presence been,
So common-hackney'd in the eyes of men,
So stale and cheap to vulgar company,—
Opinion, that did help me to the crown,
Had still kept loyal to possession,
And left me in reputeless banishment,
A fellow of no mark nor likelihood.
By being seldom seen, I could not stir
But, like a comet, I was wonder'd at;
That men would tell their children, 'This is he;'
Others would say, 'Where, which is Bolingbroke?'
And then I stole all courtesy from heaven,
And drest myself in such humility
That I did pluck allegiance from men's hearts,
Loud shouts and salutations from their mouths,
Even in the presence of the crowned king.
Thus did I keep my person fresh and new;
My presence, like a robe pontifical,
Ne'er seen but wonder'd at: and so my state,
Seldom but sumptuous, show'd like a feast,
And won by rareness such solemnity.
The skipping king, he ambled up and down
With shallow jesters and rash bavin wits,
Soon kindled and soon burnt; carded his state;
Mingled his royalty with capering fools;
Had his great name profaned with their scorns;
And gave his countenance, against his name,
To laugh at gibing boys, and stand the push
Of every beardless vain comparative;
Grew a companion to the common streets,

Enfeoft himself to popularity;
That, being daily swallow'd by men's eyes,
They surfeited with honey, and began
To loathe the taste of sweetness, whereof a little
More than a little is by much too much.
So, when he had occasion to be seen,
He was but as the cuckoo is in June,
Heard, not regarded,—seen, but with such eyes
As, sick and blunted with community,
Afford no extraordinary gaze,
Such as is bent on sun-like majesty
When it shines seldom in admiring eyes;
But rather drowzed, and hung their eyelids down,
Slept in his face, and render'd such aspect
As cloudy men use to their adversaries,
Being with his presence glutted, gorged, and full.

368   My father is gone wild into his grave,
For in his tomb lie my affections;
And with his spirit sadly I survive,
To mock the expectation of the world,
To frustrate prophecies, and to raze out
Rotten opinion, who hath writ me down
After my seeming. The tide of blood in me
Hath proudly flow'd in vanity till now:
Now doth it turn, and ebb back to the sea,
Where it shall mingle with the state of floods,
And flow henceforth in formal majesty.

369   JACK CADE
Be brave, then; for your captain is brave, and vows
reformation. There shall be in England seven halfpenny loaves sold for a penny: the three-hoop'd pot
shall have ten hoops; and I will make it felony to

drink small beer: all the realm shall be in common; and in Cheapside shall my palfrey go to grass: and when I am king,—as king I will be,—

ALL

God save your majesty!

JACK CADE

I thank you, good people:—there shall be no money; all shall eat and drink on my score; and I will apparel them all in one livery, that they may agree like brothers, and worship me their lord.

DICK

The first thing we do, let's kill all the lawyers.

JACK CADE

Nay, that I mean to do. Is not this a lamentable thing, that of the skin of an innocent lamb should be made parchment? that parchment, being scribbled o'er, should undo a man? Some say the bee stings: but I say, 'tis the bee's wax; for I did but seal once to a thing, and I was never mine own man since.

370

GONZALO

Had I plantation of this isle, my lord,—

ANTONIO

He'd sow't with nettle-seed.

SEBASTIAN

                Or docks, or mallows

GONZALO

And were the king on't, what would I do?

SEBASTIAN

Scape being drunk for want of wine.

GONZALO

I'the commonwealth I would by contraries
Execute all things; for no kind of traffic
Would I admit; no name of magistrate;
Letters should not be known; riches, poverty,

And use of service, none; contract, succession,
Bourn, bound of land, tilth, vineyard, none;
No use of metal, corn, or wine, or oil;
No occupation; all men idle, all;
And women too,—but innocent and pure;
No sovereignty,—

SEBASTIAN
Yet he would be king on't.

ANTONIO
The latter end of his commonwealth forgets the
beginning.

GONZALO
All things in common nature should produce
Without sweat or endeavour: treason, felony,
Sword, pike, knife, gun, or need of any engine,
Would I not have, but nature should bring forth,
Of it own kind, all foison, all abundance,
To feed my innocent people.

SEBASTIAN
No marrying 'mong his subjects?

ANTONIO
None, man; all idle; whores and knaves.

GONZALO
I would with such perfection govern, sir,
T'excel the golden age.

SEBASTIAN
'Save his majesty!

ANTONIO
Long live Gonzalo!

371   MENENIUS AGRIPPA
There was a time when all the body's members
Rebell'd against the belly; thus accused it:—
That only like a gulf it did remain

I'the midst o'the body, idle and unactive,
Still cupboarding the viand, never bearing
Like labour with the rest; where th'other instruments
Did see and hear, devise, instruct, walk, feel,
And, mutually participate, did minister
Unto the appetite and affection common
Of the whole body. The belly answer'd,—

FIRST CITIZEN

Well, sir, what answer made the belly?

MENENIUS AGRIPPA

Sir, I shall tell you.—With a kind of smile,
Which ne'er came from the lungs, but even thus—
For, look you, I may make the belly smile
As well as speak—it tauntingly replied
To the discontented members, the mutinous parts
That envied his receipt; even so most fitly
As you malign our senators for that
They are not such as you.

FIRST CITIZEN

Your belly's answer? What!
The kingly-crowned head, the vigilant eye,
The counsellor heart, the arm our soldier,
Our steed the leg, the tongue our trumpeter,
With other muniments and petty helps
In this our fabric, if that they—

MENENIUS AGRIPPA

What then?—
'Fore me, this fellow speaks!—what then?—what
then?

FIRST CITIZEN

Should by the cormorant belly be restrain'd,
Who is the sink o'the body,—

MENENIUS AGRIPPA

Well, what then?

FIRST CITIZEN

The former agents, if they did complain,
What could the belly answer?

THE BELLY'S ANSWER

MENENIUS AGRIPPA
                              I will tell you;
If you'll bestow a small—of what you have little—
Patience awhile, you'st hear the belly's answer.
          FIRST CITIZEN
Y'are long about it.
          MENENIUS AGRIPPA
                         Note me this, good friend;
Your most grave belly was deliberate,
Not rash like his accusers, and thus answer'd:
'True is it, my incorporate friends,' quoth he,
'That I receive the general food at first,
Which you do live upon; and fit it is,
Because I am the store-house and the shop
Of the whole body: but, if you do remember,
I send it through the rivers of your blood,
Even to the court, the heart,—to the seat o'the
    brain;
And, through the cranks and offices of man,
The strongest nerves and small inferior veins
From me receive that natural competency
Whereby they live: and though that all at once,
You, my good friends,'—this says the belly, mark
    me,—
          FIRST CITIZEN
Ay, sir; well, well.
          MENENIUS AGRIPPA
                    'Though all at once can not
See what I do deliver out to each,
Yet I can make my audit up, that all
From me do back receive the flour of all,
And leave me but the bran.'—What say you to't?
          FIRST CITIZEN
It was an answer: how apply you this?
          MENENIUS AGRIPPA
The senators of Rome are this good belly,
And you the mutinous members: for examine

Their counsels and their cares; digest things rightly
Touching the weal o'the common; you shall find,
No public benefit which you receive
But it proceeds or comes from them to you,
And no way from yourselves.

372

FISHERMAN
Master, I marvel how the fishes live in the sea.
SECOND FISHERMAN
Why, as men do a-land,—the great ones eat up the
little ones: I can compare our rich misers to nothing
so fitly as to a whale; a' plays and tumbles, driving
the poor fry before him, and at last devours them all
at a mouthful: such whales have I heard on o'the
land, who never leave gaping till they've swallow'd
the whole parish, church, steeple, bells, and all.

373

I cannot tell what you and other men
Think of this life; but, for my single self,
I had as lief not be as live to be
In awe of such a thing as I myself.
I was born free as Cæsar; so were you:
We both have fed as well; and we can both
Endure the winter's cold as well as he:
For once, upon a raw and gusty day,
The troubled Tiber chafing with her shores,
Cæsar said to me, 'Darest thou, Cassius, now
Leap in with me into this angry flood,
And swim to yonder point?' Upon the word,
Accoutred as I was, I plunged in,
And bade him follow: so, indeed, he did.
The torrent roar'd; and we did buffet it
With lusty sinews, throwing it aside

And stemming it with hearts of controversy:
But ere we could arrive the point proposed,
Cæsar cried, 'Help me, Cassius, or I sink!'
I, as Aeneas, our great ancestor,
Did from the flames of Troy upon his shoulder
The old Anchises bear, so from the waves of Tiber
Did I the tired Cæsar: and this man
Is now become a god; and Cassius is
A wretched creature, and must bend his body,
If Cæsar carelessly but nod on him.
He had a fever when he was in Spain,
And, when the fit was on him, I did mark
How he did shake; 'tis true, this god did shake:
His coward lips did from their colour fly;
And that same eye, whose bend doth awe the world,
Did lose his lustre: I did hear him groan:
Ay, and that tongue of his, that bade the Romans
Mark him, and write his speeches in their books,
Alas, it cried, 'Give me some drink, Titinius,'
As a sick girl. Ye gods, it doth amaze me,
A man of such a feeble temper should
So get the start of the majestic world,
And bear the palm alone.

374   Why, man, he doth bestride the narrow world
Like a Colossus; and we petty men
Walk under his huge legs, and peep about
To find ourselves dishonourable graves.

375   I could be well moved, if I were as you;
If I could pray to move, prayers would move me:
But I am constant as the northern star,
Of whose true-fixt and resting quality

There is no fellow in the firmament.
The skies are painted with unnumber'd sparks,
They are all fire, and every one doth shine;
But there's but one in all doth hold his place:
So in the world,—'tis furnisht well with men,
And men are flesh and blood, and apprehensive;
Yet in the number I do know but one
That unassailable holds on his rank,
Unshaked of motion: and that I am he.

376   It hath been taught us from the primal state,
        That he which is was wisht until he were;
        And the ebb'd man, ne'er loved till ne'er worth love,
        Comes dear'd by being lackt. This common body,
        Like to a vagabond flag upon the stream,
        Goes to and back, lackeying the varying tide,
        To rot itself with motion.

377   An habitation giddy and unsure
        Hath he that buildeth on the vulgar heart.
        O thou fond many! with what loud applause
        Didst thou beat heaven with blessing Bolingbroke,
        Before he was what thou wouldst have him be!
        And being now trimm'd in thine own desires,
        Thou, beastly feeder, art so full of him,
        That thou provokest thyself to cast him up.
        So, so, thou common dog, didst thou disgorge
        Thy glutton bosom of the royal Richard;
        And now thou wouldst eat thy dead vomit up,
        And howl'st to find it. What trust is in these times?
        They that, when Richard lived, would have him die,
        Are now become enamour'd on his grave:
        Thou, that threw'st dust upon his goodly head

When through proud London he came sighing on
After th'admired heels of Bolingbroke,
Cry'st now, 'O earth, yield us that king again,
And take thou this!' O thoughts of men accurst!
Past, and to come, seems best; things present, worst.

378   Ah, simple men, you know not what you swear!
Look, as I blow this feather from my face,
And as the air blows it to me again,
Obeying with my wind when I do blow,
And yielding to another when it blows,
Commanded always by the greater gust;
Such is the lightness of you common men.

379   What many men desire!—that many may be meant
By the fool multitude, that choose by show,
Not learning more than the fond eye doth teach;
Which pries not to th' interior, but, like the martlet,
Builds in the weather on the outward wall.
Even in the force and road of casualty.
I will not choose what many men desire,
Because I will not jump with common spirits,
And rank me with the barbarous multitudes.

380   CAIUS MARCIUS CORIOLANUS
Must I go show them my unbarb'd sconce? must I
With my base tongue give to my noble heart
A lie that it must bear? Well, I must do't:
Away, my disposition, and possess me
Some harlot's spirit! my throat of war be turn'd,
Which quired with my drum, into a pipe

Small as an eunuch, or the virgin voice
That babies lulls asleep! the smiles of knaves
Tent in my cheeks; and schoolboys' tears take up
The glasses of my sight! a beggar's tongue
Make motion through my lips; and my arm'd knees,
Who bow'd but in my stirrup, bend like his
That hath received an alms!—I will not do't;
Lest I surcease to honour mine own truth,
And by my body's action teach my mind
A most inherent baseness.

VOLUMNIA

                At thy choice, then:
To beg of thee, it is my more dishonour
Than thou of them. Come all to ruin: let
Thy mother rather feel thy pride than fear
Thy dangerous stoutness; for I mock at death
With as big heart as thou. Do as thou list.
Thy valiantness was mine, thou suck'dst it from me;
But owe thy pride thyself.

CAIUS MARCIUS CORIOLANUS

                Pray, be content:
Mother, I am going to the market-place;
Chide me no more. I'll mountebank their loves,
Cog their hearts from them, and come home beloved
Of all the trades in Rome.

381   Open your ears; for which of you will stop
The vent of hearing when loud Rumour speaks?
I, from the orient to the drooping west,
Making the wind my post-horse, still unfold
The acts commenced on this ball of earth:
Upon my tongues continual slanders ride,
The which in every language I pronounce,
Stuffing the ears of men with false reports.
I speak of peace, while covert enmity,

SLANDER

Under the smile of safety, wounds the world:
And who but Rumour, who but only I,
Make fearful musters and prepared defence,
Whilst the big year, swoln with some other grief
Is thought with child by the stern tyrant war,
And no such matter? Rumour is a pipe
Blown by surmises, jealousies, conjectures;
And of so easy and so plain a stop,
That the blunt monster with uncounted heads,
The still-discordant wavering multitude,
Can play upon it. But what need I thus
My well-known body to anatomise
Among my household? Why is Rumour here?
I run before King Harry's victory

382
                                    No, 'tis slander;
Whose edge is sharper than the sword; whose tongue
Outvenoms all the worms of Nile; whose breath
Rides on the posting winds, and doth belie
All corners of the world: kings, queens, and states,
Maids, matrons, nay, the secrets of the grave
This viperous slander enters.

383   The shrug, the hum, or ha,—these petty brands
        That calumny doth use.

384   Tired with all these, for restful death I cry,—
        As, to behold Desert a beggar born,
        And needy Nothing trimm'd in jollity,
        And purest Faith unhappily forsworn,
        And gilded Honour shamefully misplaced,

And maiden Virtue rudely strumpeted,
And right Perfection wrongfully disgraced,
And Strength by limping Sway disabled,
And Art made tongue-tied by Authority,
And Folly, doctor-like, controlling Skill,
And simple Truth miscall'd Simplicity,
And captive Good attending captain Ill:
    Tired with all these, from these would I be gone,
    Save that, to die, I leave my love alone.

385   O, that estates, degrees, and offices,
Were not derived corruptly! and that clear honour
Were purchased by the merit of the wearer!
How many then should cover that stand bare!
How many be commanded that command!
How much low peasantry would then be glean'd
From the true seed of honour! and how much honour
Pickt from the chaff and ruin of the times,
To be new-varnisht!

386   O Opportunity, thy guilt is great!
'Tis thou that executest the traitor's treason;
Thou sett'st the wolf where he the lamb may get;
Whoever plots the sin, thou point'st the season;
'Tis thou that spurn'st at right, at law, at reason;
    And in thy shady cell, where none may spy him.
    Sits Sin, to seize the souls that wander by him.

When wilt thou be the humble suppliant's friend,
And bring him where his suit may be obtained?
When wilt thou sort an hour great strifes to end?
Or free that soul which wretchedness hath chained?
Give physic to the sick, ease to the pained?
    The poor, lame, blind, halt, creep, cry out for thee;
    But they ne'er meet with Opportunity.

The patient dies while the physician sleeps;
The orphan pines while the oppressor feeds;
Justice is feasting while the widow weeps;
Advice is sporting while infection breeds:
Thou grant'st no time for charitable deeds:
    Wrath, envy, treason, rape, and murder's rages,
    Thy heinous hours wait on them as their pages.

387   Pleasure and revenge
Have ears more deaf than adders to the voice
Of any true decision.

388   Could great men thunder
As Jove himself does, Jove would ne'er be quiet,
For every pelting, petty officer
Would use his heaven for thunder. Nothing but
    thunder!
Merciful Heaven,
Thou rather with thy sharp and sulphurous bolt
Splitt'st the unwedgeable and gnarled oak
Than the soft myrtle: but man, proud man,
Drest in a little brief authority,—
Most ignorant of what he's most assured,
His glassy essence,—like an angry ape,
Plays such fantastic tricks before high heaven
As make the angels weep; who, with our spleens,
Would all themselves laugh mortal.

389   Earth, yield me roots!
Who seeks for better of thee, sauce his palate
With thy most operant poison!—What is here?

Gold? yellow, glittering, precious gold? No, gods,
I am no idle votarist: roots, your clear heavens!
Thus much of this will make black white; foul, fair;
Wrong, right; base, noble; old, young; coward, valiant.
Ha, you gods! why this? what this, you gods? Why, this
Will lug your priests and servants from your sides;
Pluck stout men's pillows from below their heads:
This yellow slave
Will knit and break religions; bless th'accurst;
Make the hoar leprosy adored; place thieves,
And give them title, knee, and approbation,
With senators on the bench: this is it
That makes the wappen'd widow wed again;
She, whom the spital-house and ulcerous sores
Would cast the gorge at, this embalms and spices
To th'April day again.

390   O thou sweet king-killer, and dear divorce
'Twixt natural son and sire! thou bright defiler
Of Hymen's purest bed! thou valiant Mars!
Thou ever young, fresh, loved, and delicate wooer,
Whose blush doth thaw the consecrated snow
That lies on Dian's lap! thou visible god,
That solder'st close impossibilities,
And makest them kiss! that speak'st with every
    tongue,
To every purpose! O thou touch of hearts!
Think, thy slave man rebels; and by thy virtue
Set them into confounding odds, that beasts
May have the world in empire!

391   Through tatter'd clothes small vices do appear;
Robes and furr'd gowns hide all. Plate sin with gold,
And the strong lance of justice hurtless breaks;
Arm it in rags, a pigmy's straw does pierce it.
None does offend, none,—I say, none.

392
       Heavens, deal so still!
Let the superfluous and lust-dieted man,
That slaves your ordinance, that will not see
Because he doth not feel, feel your power quickly;
So distribution should undo excess,
And each man have enough.

393
Poor naked wretches, wheresoe'er you are,
That bide the pelting of this pitiless storm,
How shall your houseless heads and unfed sides,
Your loopt and window'd raggedness, defend you
From seasons such as these? O, I have ta'en
Too little care of this! Take physic, pomp;
Expose thyself to feel what wretches feel,
That thou mayst shake the superflux to them,
And show the heavens more just.

394
Why, thou wert better in thy grave than to answer
with thy uncover'd body this extremity of the
skies.—Is man no more than this? Consider him well.
Thou owest the worm no silk, the beast no hide, the
sheep no wool, the cat no perfume.—Ha! here's
three on's are sophisticated!—Thou art the thing
itself: unaccommodated man is no more but such a
poor, bare, forkt animal as thou art.—Off, off, you
lendings!—come, unbutton here.

395
       HAMLET
Good, my lord, will you see the players well bestow'd? Do you hear, let them be well used; for they
are the abstract and brief chronicles of the time: after
your death you were better have a bad epitaph than
their ill report while you live.

POLONIUS

My lord, I will use them according to their desert.

HAMLET

God's bodykins, man, better: use every man after his desert, and who should scape whipping? Use them after your own honour and dignity: the less they deserve, the more merit is in your bounty.

396   Let the great gods,
That keep this dreadful pudder o'er our heads,
Find out their enemies now. Tremble, thou wretch,
That hast within thee undivulged crimes,
Unwhipt of justice: hide thee, thou bloody hand;
Thou perjured, and thou simular of virtue
That art incestuous: caitiff, to pieces shake,
That under covert and convenient seeming
Has practised on man's life: close pent-up guilts,
Rive your concealing continents, and cry
These dreadful summoners grace.

397 Marry, then, sweet wag, when thou art king, let not us that are squires of the night's body be call'd thieves of the day's beauty: let us be Diana's foresters, gentlemen of the shade, minions of the moon; and let men say we be men of good government, being govern'd, as the sea is, by our noble and chaste mistress the moon, under whose countenance we steal.

398   Rascal thieves,
Here's gold. Go, suck the subtle blood o' the grape,
Till the high fever seethe your blood to froth,
And so scape hanging: trust not the physician;
His antidotes are poison, and he slays

More than you rob: take wealth and lives together;
Do villainy, do, since you protest to do't,
Like workmen. I'll example you with thievery:
The sun's a thief, and with his great attraction
Robs the vast sea: the moon's an arrant thief,
And her pale fire she snatches from the sun:
The sea's a thief, whose liquid surge resolves
The moon into salt tears: the earth's a thief,
That feeds and breeds by a composture stoln
From general excrement: each thing's a thief:
The laws, your curb and whip, in their rough power
Have uncheckt theft. Love not yourselves: away,
Rob one another.

399   Discomfortable cousin! know'st thou not
That when the searching eye of heaven is hid
Behind the globe, that lights the lower world,
Then thieves and robbers range abroad unseen,
In murders and in outrage, boldly here;
But when, from under this terrestrial ball,
He fires the proud tops of the eastern pines,
And darts his light through every guilty hole,
Then murders, treasons, and detested sins,
The cloak of night being pluckt from off their backs,
Stand bare and naked, trembling at themselves?

400   While I may scape,
I will preserve myself: and am bethought
To take the basest and most poorest shape
That ever penury, in contempt of man,
Brought near to beast: my face I'll grime with filth;
Blanket my loins; elf all my hair in knots;
And with presented nakedness out-face

THE AGES OF MAN

The winds and persecutions of the sky.
The country gives me proof and precedent
Of Bedlam beggars, who, with roaring voices,
Strike in their numb'd and mortified bare arms
Pins, wooden pricks, nails, sprigs of rosemary;
And with this horrible object, from low farms,
Poor pelting villages, sheep-cotes, and mills,
Sometime with lunatic bans, sometime with prayers,
Enforce their charity.

401   O, reason not the need: our basest beggars
Are in the poorest thing superfluous:
Allow not nature more than nature needs,
Man's life is cheap as beast's: thou art a lady;
If only to go warm were gorgeous,
Why, nature needs not what thou gorgeous wear'st,
Which scarcely keeps thee warm.

402   And his poor self,
A dedicated beggar to the air,
With his disease of all-shunn'd poverty,
Walks, like contempt, alone.

403   My derivation was from ancestors
Who stood equivalent with mighty kings:
But time hath rooted out my parentage,
And to the world and awkward casualties
Bound me in servitude.

404   Had it pleased heaven
To try me with affliction; had they rain'd
All kinds of sores and shames on my bare head;
Steept me in poverty to the very lips:

Given to captivity me and and my utmost hopes;
I should have found in some place of my soul
A drop of patience: but, alas, to make me
A fixed figure for the time of scorn
To point his slow unmoving finger at!—
Yet could I bear that too; well, very well:
But there, where I have garner'd up my heart,
Where either I must live, or bear no life,—
The fountain from the which my current runs,
Or else dries up; to be discarded thence!
Or keep it as a cistern for foul toads
To knot and gender in!—turn thy complexion there.
Patience, thou young and rose-lipt cherubin,—
Ay, there, look grim as hell!

405 The little dogs and all,
   Tray, Blanch, and Sweetheart, see, they bark at me!

406 And pity, like a naked new-born babe,
   Striding the blast, or heaven's cherubin, horsed
   Upon the sightless couriers of the air.
   Shall blow the horrid deed in every eye,
   That tears shall drown the wind.

407   What is he whose grief
   Bears such an emphasis; whose phrase of sorrow
   Conjures the wandering stars, and makes them stand
   Like wonder-wounded hearers?

408 I will instruct my sorrows to be proud;
   For grief is proud, and makes his owner stoop;
   To me, and to the state of my great grief,

Let kings assemble; for my grief's so great,
That no supporter but the huge firm earth
Can hold it up: here I and sorrows sit;
Here is my throne, bid kings come bow to it.

KING PHILIP

Bind up those tresses.—O, what love I note
In the fair multitude of those her hairs!
Where but by chance a silver drop hath fall'n,
Even to that drop ten thousand wiry friends
Do glue themselves in sociable grief;
Like true, inseparable, faithful loves,
Sticking together in calamity.

CONSTANCE

To England, if you will.

KING PHILIP

                    Bind up your hairs

CONSTANCE

Yes, that I will; and wherefore will I do it?
I tore them from their bonds, and cried aloud,
'O, that these hands could so redeem my son,
As they have given these hairs their liberty!'
But now I envy at their liberty,
And will again commit them to their bonds,
Because my poor child is a prisoner.—
And, father cardinal, I have heard you say
That we shall see and know our friends in heaven:
If that be true, I shall see my boy again;
For since the birth of Cain, the first male child,
To him that did but yesterday suspire,
There was not such a gracious creature born.
But now will canker-sorrow eat my bud,
And chase the native beauty from his cheek,
And he will look as hollow as a ghost,
As dim and meagre as an ague's fit;

HECUBA

And so he'll die; and, rising so again,
When I shall meet him in the court of heaven
I shall not know him: therefore never, never
Must I behold my pretty Arthur more.

410   To this well-painted piece is Lucrece come,
To find a face where all distress is stell'd.
Many she sees where cares have carved some,
But none where all distress and dolour dwell'd,
Till she despairing Hecuba beheld,
    Staring on Priam's wounds with her old eyes,
    Which bleeding under Pyrrhus' proud foot lies.

In her the painter had anatomized
Time's ruin, beauty's wrack, and grim care's reign:
Her cheeks with chops and wrinkles were disguised;
Of what she was no semblance did remain:
Her blue blood changed to black in every vein,
    Wanting the spring that those shrunk pipes had
      fed,
    Show'd life imprison'd in a body dead.

411   But who, O, who had seen the mobled queen
Run barefoot up and down, threat'ning the flames
With bisson rheum; a clout upon that head
Where late the diadem stood; and for a robe,
About her lank and all o'er-teemed loins,
A blanket, in th'alarm of fear caught up;—
Who this had seen, with tongue in venom steept,
'Gainst Fortune's state would treason have pro-
      nounced:
But if the gods themselves did see her then,
When she saw Pyrrhus make malicious sport

In mincing with his sword her husband's limbs,
The instant burst of clamour that she made—
Unless things mortal move them not at all—
Would have made milch the burning eyes of heaven,
And passion in the gods.

412   Is it not monstrous, that this player here,
But in a fiction, in a dream of passion,
Could force his soul so to his own conceit,
That, from her working, all his visage wann'd;
Tears in his eyes, distraction in's aspect,
A broken voice, and his whole function suiting
With forms to his conceit? and all for nothing!
For Hecuba!
What's Hecuba to him, or he to Hecuba,
That he should weep for her?

413   For sorrow, like a heavy-hanging bell,
Once set on ringing, with his own weight goes;
Then little strength rings out the doleful knell.

414   A fearful eye thou hast: where is that blood
That I have seen inhabit in those cheeks?
So foul a sky clears not without a storm:
Pour down thy weather: how goes all in France?

415   Yea, this man's brow, like to a title-leaf,
Foretells the nature of a tragic volume:
So looks the strond whereon the imperious flood
Hath left a witness'd usurpation.

416
Even such a man, so faint, so spiritless,
So dull, so dead in look, so woe-begone,
Drew Priam's curtain in the dead of night,
And would have told him half his Troy was burnt;
But Priam found the fire ere he his tongue.

417
MACBETH
The devil damn thee black, thou cream-faced loon!
Where gott'st thou that goose look?
SERVANT
There is ten thousand—
MACBETH
Geese, villain?
SERVANT
Soldiers, sir.
MACBETH
Go prick thy face, and over-red thy fear,
Thou lily-liver'd boy. What soldiers, patch?
Death of thy soul! those linen cheeks of thine
Are counsellors to fear. What soldiers, whey-face?

418
But, O, how bitter a thing it is
to look into happiness through another man's eyes!

419
Patience and sorrow strove
Who should express her goodliest. You have seen
Sunshine and rain at once: her smiles and tears
Were like a better way: those happy smilets
That play'd on her ripe lip seem'd not to know
What guests were in her eyes; which parted thence
As pearls from diamonds dropt.—In brief,
Sorrow would be a rarity most beloved,
If all could so become it.

420 I think affliction may subdue the cheek,
     But not take in the mind

421 When sorrows come, they come not single spies,
     But in battalions!

422 Irreparable is the loss; and patience
     Says it is past her cure.

423 Thou must be patient; we came crying hither:
     Thou know'st, the first time that we smell the air,
     We wawl and cry.—I will preach to thee: mark.
     When we are born, we cry that we are come
     To this great stage of fools.

424   I would I were at home.

425 Sir, I desire you do me right and justice;
     And to bestow your pity on me: for
     I am a most poor woman, and a stranger,
     Born out of your dominions; having here
     No judge indifferent, nor no more assurance
     Of equal friendship and proceeding. Alas, sir,
     In what have I offended you? what cause
     Hath my behaviour given to your displeasure,
     That thus you should proceed to put me off,
     And take your good grace from me? Heaven witness,

I have been to you a true and humble wife,
At all times to your will conformable;
Ever in fear to kindle your dislike,
Yea, subject to your countenance,—glad or sorry,
As I saw it inclined. When was the hour
I ever contradicted your desire,
Or made it not mine too? Or which of your friends
Have I not strove to love, although I knew
He were mine enemy? what friend of mine
That had to him derived your anger, did I
Continue in my liking? nay, gave notice
He was from thence discharged? Sir, call to mind
That I have been your wife, in this obedience,
Upward of twenty years, and have been blest
With many children by you: if, in the course
And process of this time, you can report,
And prove it too, against mine honour aught,
My bond to wedlock, or my love and duty,
Against my sacred person, in God's name,
Turn me away; and let the foul'st contempt
Shut door upon me, and so give me up
To the sharp'st kind of justice.

26 The quality of mercy is not strain'd,—
It droppeth as the gentle rain from heaven
Upon the place beneath: it is twice blest,—
It blesseth him that gives, and him that takes:
'Tis mightiest in the mightiest: it becomes
The throned monarch better than his crown;
His sceptre shows the force of temporal power,
The attribute to awe and majesty,
Wherein doth sit the dread and fear of kings;
But mercy is above this sceptred sway,—
It is enthroned in the hearts of kings,
It is an attribute to God himself;

And earthly power doth then show likest God's
When mercy seasons justice. Therefore, Jew,
Though justice be thy plea, consider this,—
That, in the course of justice, none of us
Should see salvation: we do pray for mercy;
And that same prayer doth teach us all to render
The deeds of mercy. I have spoke thus much
To mitigate the justice of thy plea

427
                              Alas, alas!
Why, all the souls that were were forfeit once;
And He that might the vantage best have took
Found out the remedy. How would you be,
If He, which is the top of judgement, should
But judge you as you are? O, think on that;
And mercy then will breathe within your lips,
Like man new-made. . .
No ceremony that to great ones 'longs,
Not the king's crown nor the deputed sword,
The marshal's truncheon nor the judge's robe,
Become them with one half so good a grace
As mercy does.
If he had been as you, and you as he,
You would have slipp'd like him; but he, like you,
Would not have been so stern.

428
                         Whereto serves mercy
But to confront the visage of offence?
And what's in prayer but this twofold force,
To be forestalled ere we come to fall,
Or pardon'd being down?

429
ESCALUS
Let but your honour know,—
Whom I believe to be most strait in virtue,—
That, in the working of your own affections,
Had time cohered with place, or place with wishing,
Or that the resolute acting of your blood
Could have attain'd th'effect of your own purpose,
Whether you had not sometime in your life
Err'd in this point which now you censure him,
And pull'd the law upon you.
ANGELO
'Tis one thing to be tempted, Escalus,
Another thing to fall. I not deny,
The jury, passing on the prisoner's life,
May in the sworn twelve have a thief or two
Guiltier than him they try. What's open made to
    justice,
That justice seizes: what know the laws
That thieves do pass on thieves? 'Tis very pregnant,
The jewel that we find, we stoop and take't.
Because we see it; but what we do not see
We tread upon, and never think of it.
You may not so extenuate his offence
For I have had such faults; but rather tell me,
When I, that censure him, do so offend,
Let mine own judgement pattern out my death,
And nothing come in partial.

430
KING LEAR
See how yond justice rails upon yond simple thief. Hark, in thine ear: change places; and, handy-dandy, which is the justice, which is the thief?—Thou hast seen a farmer's dog bark at a beggar?

EARL OF GLOSTER

Ay, sir.

KING LEAR

And the creature run from the cur? There thou
mightst behold the great image of authority: a dog's
obey'd in office.

431
                                        Go to your bosom;
Knock there, and ask your heart what it doth know
That's like my brother's fault: if it confess
A natural guiltiness such as is his,
Let it not sound a thought upon your tongue
Against my brother's life.

432
ARIEL
        Your charm so strongly works 'em,
That if you now beheld them, your affections
Would become tender.

PROSPERO
                Dost thou think so, spirit?

ARIEL

Mine would, sir, were I human.

PROSPERO
                        And mine shall.
Hast thou, which art but air, a touch, a feeling
Of their afflictions, and shall not myself,
One of their kind, that relish all as sharply,
Passion as they, be kindlier moved than thou art?
Though with their high wrongs I am struck to the
        quick,
Yet, with my nobler reason, 'gainst my fury

Do I take part: the rarer action is
In virtue than in vengeance: they being penitent,
The sole drift of my purpose doth extend
Not a frown further. Go release them, Ariel.

433   Kneel not to me:
The power that I have on you is to spare you;
The malice towards you to forgive you: live,
And deal with others better.

434   O, wonder!
How many goodly creatures are there here!
How beauteous mankind is! O brave new world,
That has such people in't!

435   Blow, blow, thou winter wind,
    Thou art not so unkind
     As man's ingratitude;
    Thy tooth is not so keen,
    Because thou art not seen,
     Although thy breath be rude.
Heigh-ho! sing, heigh-ho! unto the green holly:
Most friendship is feigning, most loving mere folly:
    Then, heigh-ho, the holly!
     This life is most jolly.
    Freeze, freeze, thou bitter sky,
    That dost not bite so nigh
     As benefits forgot:
    Though thou the waters warp,
    Thy sting is not so sharp
     As friend remember'd not.

436   Ingratitude, thou marble-hearted fiend,
        More hideous when thou show'st thee in a child
        Than the sea-monster!

437   I hate ingratitude more in a man
        Than lying, vainness, babbling, drunkenness,
        Or any taint of vice whose strong corruption
        Inhabits our frail blood.

438   Blow, winds, and crack your cheeks! rage! blow!
        You cataracts and hurricanoes, spout
        Till you have drencht our steeples, drown'd the
            cocks!
        You sulphurous and thought-executing fires,
        Vaunt-couriers to oak-cleaving thunderbolts,
        Singe my white head! And thou, all-shaking thunder,
        Strike flat the thick rotundity o'the world!
        Crack nature's moulds, all germens spill at once,
        That make ingrateful man!

439   That nature, being sick of man's unkindness,
        Should yet be hungry!—Common mother, thou,
        Whose womb unmeasurable, and infinite breast,
        Teems, and feeds all; whose self-same mettle,
        Whereof thy proud child, arrogant man, is puft,
        Engenders the black toad and adder blue,
        The gilded newt and eyeless venom'd worm,
        With all th'abhorred births below crisp heaven
        Whereon Hyperion's quickening fire both shine;
        Yield him, who all thy human sons doth hate,
        From forth thy plenteous bosom, one poor root!

Ensear thy fertile and conceptious womb,
Let it no more bring out ingrateful man!
Go great with tigers, dragons, wolves, and bears;
Teem with new monsters, whom thy upward face
Hath to the marbled mansion all above
Never presented!—O, a root,—dear thanks!—
Dry up thy marrows, vines, and plough-torn leas;
Whereof ingrateful man, with liquorish draughts
And morsels unctuous, greases his pure mind,
That from it all consideration slips!

440

As it fell upon a day
In the merry month of May,
Sitting in a pleasant shade
Which a grove of myrtles made,
Beasts did leap and birds did sing,
Trees did grow and plants did spring;
Every thing did banish moan,
Save the nightingale alone:
She, poor bird, as all forlorn,
Lean'd her breast up-till a thorn,
And there sung the dolefull'st ditty,
That to hear it was great pity:
'Fie, fie, fie,' now would she cry;
'Tereu, Tereu!' by and by;
That to hear her so complain,
Scarce I could from tears refrain;
For her griefs so lively shown
Made me think upon mine own.
Ah, thought I, thou mourn'st in vain!
None takes pity on thy pain:
Senseless trees they cannot hear thee;
Ruthless beasts they will not cheer thee:
King Pandion he is dead;

THE AGES OF MAN

All thy friends are lapt in lead;
All thy fellow birds do sing,
Careless of thy sorrowing.
Even so, poor bird, like thee,
None alive will pity me.
Whilst as fickle Fortune smiled,
Thou and I were both beguiled.

Every one that flatters thee
Is no friend in misery.
Words are easy, like the wind;
Faithful friends are hard to find·
Every man will be thy friend
Whilst thou hast wherewith to spend;
But if store of crowns be scant,
No man will supply thy want.
If that one be prodigal,
Bountiful they will him call,
And with such-like flattering,
'Pity but he were a king;'
If he be addict to vice,
Quickly him they will entice;
If to women he be bent,
They have at commandement:
But if Fortune once do frown,
Then farewell his great renown;
They that fawn'd on him before
Use his company no more.
He that is thy friend indeed,
He will help thee in thy need:
If thou sorrow, he will weep;
If thou wake, he cannot sleep;
Thus of every grief in heart
He with thee doth bear a part.
These are certain signs to know
Faithful friend from flattering foe.

441 If you suspect my husbandry or falsehood,
Call me before the exactest auditors,
And set me on the proof. So the gods bless me,
When all our offices have been opprest
With riotous feeders; when out vaults have wept
With drunken spilth of wine; when every room
Hath blazed with lights and bray'd with minstrelsy
I have retired me to a wasteful cock,
And set mine eyes at flow.

442 Had I a steward
So true, so just, and now so comfortable?
It almost turns my dangerous nature mild.
Let me behold thy face. Surely, this man
Was born of woman.—
Forgive my general and exceptless rashness,
You perpetual-sober gods! I do proclaim
One honest man,—mistake me not,—but one;
No more, I pray,—and he's a steward.—
How fain would I have hated all mankind!
And thou redeem'st thyself.

443   ADAM
I have five hundred crowns,
The thrifty hire I saved under your father,
Which I did store to be my foster-nurse
When service should in my old limbs lie lame
And unregarded age in corners thrown:
Take that; and He that doth the ravens feed,
Yea, providently caters for the sparrow,
Be comfort to my age! Here is the gold;
All this I give you. Let me be your servant.
     ORLANDO
O good old man, how well in thee appears
The constant service of the antique world,

When service sweat for duty, not for meed!
Thou art not for the fashion of these times,
Where none will sweat but for promotion,
And having that, do choke their service up
Even with the having: it is not so with thee.

444   What poor duty cannot do,
Noble respect takes it in might, not merit.
Where I have come, great clerks have purposed
To greet me with premeditated welcomes;
Where I have seen them shiver and look pale,
Make periods in the midst of sentences,
Throttle their practised accent in their fears,
And, in conclusion, dumbly have broke off,
Not paying me a welcome. Trust me, sweet,
Out of this silence yet I pickt a welcome;
And in the modesty of fearful duty
I read as much as from the rattling tongue
Of saucy and audacious eloquence.
Love, therefore, and tongue-tied simplicity,
In least speak most, to my capacity.

445   We are fellows still,
Serving alike in sorrow: leakt is our bark;
And we, poor mates, stand on the dying deck,
Hearing the surges threat: we must all part
Into this sea of air.

446 O world, thy slippery turns! Friends now fast sworn,
Whose double bosoms seems to wear one heart,
Whose hours, whose bed, whose meal, and exercise,
Are still together, who twin, as 'twere, in love

Unseparable, shall within this hour,
On a dissension of a doit, break out
To bitterest enmity: so, fellest foes,
Whose passions and whose plots have broke their
    sleep
To take the one the other, by some chance,
Some trick not worth an egg, shall grow dear friends
And interjoin their issues

447

FALSTAFF

If sack and sugar be a fault, God help the wicked! if to
be old and merry be a sin, then many an old host that
I know is damn'd: if to be fat be to be hated, then
Pharaoh's lean kine are to be loved. No, my good
lord; banish Peto, banish Bardolph, banish Pointz:
but, for sweet Jack Falstaff, kind Jack Falstaff, true
Jack Falstaff, valiant Jack Falstaff, and therefore
more valiant, being. as he is, old Jack Falstaff, banish
not him thy Harry's company, banish not him thy
Harry's company:—banish plump Jack, and banish
all the world.

PRINCE HENRY

I do, I will.

448   Full many a glorious morning have I seen
Flatter the mountain-tops with sovereign eye,
Kissing with golden face the meadows green,
Gilding pale streams with heavenly alchemy;
Anon permit the basest clouds to ride
With ugly rack on his celestial face,
And from the forlorn world his visage hide,
Stealing unseen to west with this disgrace:

Even so my sun one early morn did shine
With all-triumphant splendour on my brow;
But, out, alack! he was but one hour mine,
The region cloud hath maskt him from me now.
    Yet him for this my love no whit disdaineth;
    Suns of the world may stain when heaven's sun
    staineth.

449   Two loves I have of comfort and despair,
Which like two spirits do suggest me still:
The better angel is a man right fair,
The worser spirit a woman colour'd ill.
To win me soon to hell, my female evil
Tempteth my better angel from my side,
And would corrupt my saint to be a devil,
Wooing his purity with her foul pride.
And whether that my angel be turn'd fiend
Suspect I may, yet not directly tell;
But being both from me, both to each friend,
I guess one angel in another's hell:
    Yet this shall I ne'er know, but live in doubt,
    Till my bad angel fire my good one out.

450   There's no art
To find the mind's construction in the face:
He was a gentleman on whom I built
An absolute trust.

451   Has friendship such a faint and milky heart,
It turns in less than two nights?

452
                           Thou hast described
A hot friend cooling: ever note, Lucilius,
When love begins to sicken and decay,
It useth an enforced ceremony.
There are no tricks in plain and simple faith:
But hollow men, like horses hot at hand,
Make gallant show and promise of their mettle;
But when they should endure the bloody spur,
They fall their crests, and, like deceitful jades,
Sink in the trial.

453
Friendship is constant in all other things
Save in the office and affairs of love:
Therefore all hearts in love use their own tongues;
Let every eye negotiate for itself,
And trust no agent; for beauty is a witch,
Against whose charms faith melteth into blood.
This is an accident of hourly proof,
Which I mistrusted not.

454
Is all the counsel that we two have shared,
The sisters' vows, the hours that we have spent,
When we have chid the hasty-footed time
For parting us,—O, and is all forgot?
All school-days' friendship, childhood innocence?
We, Hermia, like two artificial gods,
Have with our neelds created both one flower,
Both on one sampler, sitting on one cushion,
Both warbling of one song, both in one key;
As if our hands, our sides, voices, and minds,
Had been incorporate. So we grew together,
Like to a double cherry, seeming parted,
But yet an union in partition;
Two lovely berries moulded on one stem.

455 I was too young that time to value her;
But now I know her: if she be a traitor,
Why, so am I; we still have slept together,
Rose at an instant, learn'd, play'd, eat together;
And wheresoe'er we went, like Juno's swans,
Still we went coupled and inseparable.

456   EMILIA
                                   How his longing
Follows his friend! since his depart, his sports,
Though craving seriousness and skill, pass'd slightly
His careless execution, where nor gain
Made him regard, or loss consider; but
Playing one business in his hand, another
Directing in his head, his mind nurse equal
To these so differing twins. Have you observ'd him
Since our great lord departed?
                          HIPPOLITA
                               With much labour;
And I did love him for't. They two have cabin'd
In many as dangerous as poor a corner,
Peril and want contending; they have skiff'd
Torrents, whose roaring tyranny and power
I' the least of these was dreadful; and they have
Fought out together, where death's self was lodg'd;
Yet fate had brought them off. Their knot of love
Tied, weav'd, entangled, with so true, so long,
And with a finger of so deep a cunning,
May be out-worn, never undone. I think
Theseus cannot be umpire to himself,
Cleaving his conscience into twain, and doing
Each side like justice, which he loves best.
                          EMILIA
                               Doubtless
There is a best, and reason has no manners
To say it is not you. I was acquainted

"MY TRUE LOVE HATH MY HEART"

Once with a time, when I enjoy'd a playfellow;
You were at wars when she the grave enrich'd,
Who made too proud the bed, took leave o' the moon—
Which then looked pale at parting—when our count
Was each eleven

HIPPOLITA
'Twas Flavina.

EMILIA
Yes.

You talk of Pirithous' and Theseus' love:
Theirs has more ground, is more maturely season'd,
More buckled with strong judgment, and their needs
The one of th' other may be said to water
Their intertangled roots of love; but I,
And she I sigh and spoke of, were things innocent;
Lov'd for we did, and like the elements
That know not what nor why, yet do effect
Rare issues by their operance, our souls
Did as to one another: what she lik'd
Was then of me approv'd; what not, condemn'd,
No more arraignment; the flower that I would pluck
And put between my breasts, O'then but beginning
To swell about the blossom, she would long
Till she had such another, and commit it
To the like innocent cradle, where, phœnix-like,
They died in perfume; on my head no toy
But was her pattern; her affections—pretty,
Though happily her careless wear—I followed
For my most serious decking; had mine ear
Stol'n some new air, or at adventure humm'd one
From musical coinage, why, it was a note
Whereon her spirits would sojourn,—rather dwell
    on—
And sing it in her slumbers: this rehearsal,
Which every innocent wots well, has this end,
That the true love 'tween maid and maid may be
More than in sex dividual.

457   Suffolk first died: and York, all haggled over,
Comes to him, where in gore he lay insteept,
And takes him by the beard; kisses the gashes
That bloodily did yawn upon his face;
And cries aloud, 'Tarry, dear cousin Suffolk!
My soul shall thine keep company to heaven;
Tarry, sweet soul, for mine, then fly abreast;
As in this glorious and well-foughten field
We kept together in our chivalry!'

458   Since my dear soul was mistress of her choice,
And could of men distinguish, her election
Hath seal'd thee for herself: for thou hast been
As one, in suffering all, that suffers nothing;
A man that fortune's buffets and rewards
Hast ta'en with equal thanks: and blest are those
Whose blood and judgement are so well commingled,
That they are not a pipe for fortune's finger
To sound what stop she please. Give me that man
That is not passion's slave, and I will wear him
In my heart's core, ay, in my heart of heart,
As I do thee.

459

HAMLET
Will you play upon this pipe?
GUILDENSTERN
My lord, I cannot.
HAMLET
I pray you.
GUILDENSTERN
Believe me, I cannot.
HAMLET
I do beseech you.

GUILDENSTERN

I know no touch of it, my lord.

HAMLET

'Tis as easy as lying: govern these ventages with your finger and thumb, give it breath with your mouth, and it will discourse most eloquent music. Look you, these are the stops.

GUILDENSTERN

But these cannot I command to any utterance of harmony; I have not the skill.

HAMLET

Why, look you now, how unworthy a thing you make of me! You would play upon me; you would seem to know my stops; you would pluck out the heart of my mystery; you would sound me from my lowest note to the top of my compass: and there is much music, excellent voice, in this little organ; yet cannot you make it speak. 'Sblood, do you think I am easier to be play'd on than a pipe? Call me what instrument you will, though you can fret me, you cannot play upon me.

462

APEMANTUS

I was directed hither: men report
Thou dost affect my manners, and dost use them.

TIMON

'Tis, then, because thou dost not keep a dog,
Whom I would imitate: consumption catch thee!

APEMANTUS

This is in thee a nature but infected;
A poor unmanly melancholy sprung
From change of fortune. Why this spade? this place?
This slave-like habit; and these looks of care?
Thy flatterers yet wear silk, drink wine, lie soft;
Hug their diseased perfumes, and have forgot

That ever Timon was. Shame not these woods,
By putting on the cunning of a carper.
Be thou a flatterer now, and seek to thrive
By that which has undone thee: hinge thy knee,
And let his very breath, whom thou'lt observe,
Blow off thy cap; praise his most vicious strain,
And call it excellent: thou wast told thus;
Thou gavest thine ears like tapsters that bid welcome
To knaves and all approachers: 'tis most just
That thou turn rascal; hadst thou wealth again,
Rascals should have't. Do not assume my likeness.

TIMON

Were I like thee, I'ld throw away myself.

APEMANTUS

Thou hast cast away thyself, being like thyself;
A madman so long, now a fool. What, think'st
That the bleak air, thy boisterous chamberlain,
Will put thy shirt on warm? will these moss'd trees,
That have outlived the eagle, page thy heels,
And skip when thou point'st out? will the cold brook,
Candied with ice, caudle thy morning taste,
To cure thy o'er-night's surfeit? Call the creatures
Whose naked natures live in all the spite
Of wreakful heaven; whose bare unhoused trunks,
To the conflicting elements exposed,
Answer mere nature, bid them flatter thee.

TIMON

Thou art a slave, whom Fortune's tender arm
With favour never claspt; but bred a dog.
Hadst thou, like us from our first swath, proceeded
The sweet degrees that this brief world affords
To such as may the passive drugs of it
Freely command, thou wouldst have plunged thyself
In general riot; melted down thy youth
In different beds of lust; and never learn'd
The icy precepts of respect, but follow'd
The sugar'd game before thee. But myself,

Who had the world as my confectionary;
The mouths, the tongues, the eyes, and hearts of men
At duty, more than I could frame employment;
That numberless upon me stuck, as leaves
Do on the oak, have with one winter's brush
Fell from their boughs, and left me open, bare
For every storm that blows;—I, to bear this,
That never knew but better, is some burden:
Thy nature did commence in sufferance, time
Hath made thee hard in't. Why shouldst thou hate
    men?
They never flatter'd thee: what has thou given?
If thou wilt curse,—thy father, that poor rag,
Must be thy subject; who, in spite, put stuff
To some she-beggar, and compounded thee
Poor rogue hereditary. Hence, be gone!—
If thou hadst not been born the worst of men,
Thou hadst been a knave and flatterer.

461   In so profound abysm I throw all care
      Of others' voices, that my adder's sense
      To critic and to flatterer stopped are.

462   Who dares, who dares,
In purity of manhood stand upright,
And say, 'This man's a flatterer'? if one be,
So are they all; for every grise of fortune
Is smooth'd by that below: the learned pate
Ducks to the golden fool: all is oblique;
There's nothing level in our cursed natures,
But direct villainy. Therefore, be abhorr'd
All feasts, societies, and throngs of men!

463   Did you but know the city's usuries,
And felt them knowingly: the art o'the court,
As hard to leave as keep; whose top to climb
Is certain falling, or so slippery that
The fear's as bad as falling: the toil o'the war,
A pain that only seems to seek out danger
I'the name of fame and honour; which dies i'the
    search;
And hath as oft a slanderous epitaph
As record of fair act; nay, many times
Doth ill deserve by doing well; what's worse,
Must court'sy at the censure:—O boys, this story
The world may read in me: my body's markt
With Roman swords; and my report was once
First with the best of note: Cymbeline loved me;
And when a soldier was the theme, my name
Was not far off: then was I as a tree
Whose boughs did bend with fruit: but in one night,
A storm or robbery, call it what you will,
Shook down my mellow hangings, nay, my leaves,
And left me bare to weather.

464   A servingman, proud in heart and mind; that curl'd
my hair; wore gloves in my cap; served the lust of my
mistress' heart, and did the act of darkness with her;
swore as many oaths as I spake words, and broke
them in the sweet face of heaven: one that slept in
the contriving of lust, and waked to do it: wine loved
I deeply, dice dearly; and in woman out-paramour'd
the Turk: false of heart, light of ear, bloody of hand;
hog in sloth, fox in stealth, wolf in greediness, dog in
madness, lion in prey. Let not the creaking of shoes
nor the rustling of silks betray thy poor heart to
woman: keep thy foot out of brothels, thy hand out
of plackets, thy pen from lenders' books, and defy
the foul fiend.

465

HAMLET

Besides, to be demanded of a sponge!—what
replication should be made by the son of a king?

ROSENCRANTZ

Take you me for a sponge, my lord?

HAMLET

Ay, sir; that soaks up the king's countenance, his
rewards, his authorities. But such officers do the
king best service in the end: he keeps them, like an
ape, in the corner of his jaw; first mouth'd, to be last
swallow'd: when he needs what you have glean'd, it
is but squeezing you, and, sponge, you shall be dry
again.

466

This fellow pecks up wit as pigeons pease,
And utters it again when God doth please:
He is wit's pedlar, and retails his wares
At wakes and wassails, meetings, markets, fairs;
And we that sell by gross, the Lord doth know,
Have not the grace to grace it with such show.
This gallant pins the wenches on his sleeve;
Had he been Adam, he had tempted Eve;
A' can carve too, and lisp: why, this is he
That kist his hand away in courtesy;
This is the ape of form, monsieur the nice,
That, when he plays at tables, chides the dice
In honourable terms: nay, he can sing
A mean most meanly; and in ushering
Mend him who can: the ladies call him sweet;
The stairs, as he treads on them, kiss his feet:
This is the flower that smiles on every one,
To show his teeth as white as whales bone;
And consciences, that will not die in debt,
Pay him the due of honey-tongued Boyet.

467   Why, what a candy deal of courtesy
This fawning greyhound then did proffer me!

468   He does smile his face into more lines than is in the
new map, with the augmentation of the Indies: you
have not seen such a thing as 'tis; I can hardly forbear hurling things at him.

469   Signior Antonio, many a time and oft,
In the Rialto, you have rated me
About my moneys and my usances:
Still have I borne it with a patient shrug;
For sufferance is the badge of all our tribe:
You call me misbeliever, cut-throat dog,
And spit upon my Jewish gaberdine,
And all for use of that which is mine own.
Well, then, it now appears you need my help:
Go to, then; you come to me, and you say,
'Shylock, we would have moneys:'—you say so;
You, that did void your rheum upon my beard,
And foot me as you spurn a stranger cur
Over your threshold: moneys is your suit.
What should I say to you? Should I not say,
'Hath a dog money? is it possible
A cur can lend three thousand ducats?' or
Shall I bend low, and in a bondman's key,
With bated breath and whispering humbleness,
Say this,—
'Fair sir, you spit on me on Wednesday last;
You spurn'd me such a day; another time
You call'd me dog; and for these courtesies
I'll lend you thus much moneys'?

470 But I remember, when the fight was done,
When I was dry with rage and extreme toil,
Breathless and faint, leaning upon my sword,
Came there a certain lord, neat, and trimly drest,
Fresh as a bridegroom; and his chin new reapt
Show'd like a stubble-land at harvest-home;
He was perfumed like a milliner;
And 'twixt his finger and his thumb he held
A pouncet-box, which ever and anon
He gave his nose, and took't away again;—
Who therewith angry, when it next came there,
Took it in snuff:—and still he smiled and talkt;
And as the soldiers bore dead bodies by,
He call'd them untaught knaves, unmannerly,
To bring a slovenly unhandsome corse
Betwixt the wind and his nobility.
With many holiday and lady terms
He question'd me; amongst the rest, demanded
My prisoners in your majesty's behalf.
I then, all smarting with my wounds being cold,
To be so pester'd with a popinjay,
Out of my grief and my impatience,
Answer'd neglectingly, I know not what,—
He should, or he should not; for he made me mad
To see him shine so brisk, and smell so sweet,
And talk so like a waiting-gentlewoman
Of guns and drums and wounds,—God save
        mark!—
And telling me the sovereign'st thing on earth
Was parmaceti for an inward bruise;
And that it was great pity, so it was,
This villainous salt-petre should be digg'd
Out of the bowels of the harmless earth,
Which many a good tall fellow had destroy'd
So cowardly; and but for these vile guns,
He would himself have been a soldier.

471   Thou art like one of these fellows that, when he
enters the confines of a tavern, claps me his sword
upon the table, and says, 'God send me no need of
thee!' and, by the operation of the second cup, draws
it on the drawer, when, indeed, there is no need.
Thou! why, thou wilt quarrel with a man that hath a
hair more or a hair less in his beard than thou hast:
thou wilt quarrel with a man for cracking nuts, having
no other reason but because thou hast hazel eyes;—
what eye, but such an eye, would spy out such a
quarrel? Thy head is as full of quarrels as an egg is
full of meat; and yet thy head hath been beaten as
addle as an egg for quarrelling: thou hast quarrell'd
with a man for coughing in the street, because he
hath waken'd thy dog that hath lain asleep in the
sun: didst thou not fall out with a tailor for wearing
his new doublet before Easter? with another, for
tying his new shoes with old riband? and yet thou
wilt tutor me from quarrelling!

472   That such a slave as this should wear a sword,
Who wears no honesty. Such smiling rogues as
        these,
Like rats, oft bite the holy cords a-twain
Which are too intrinse t'unloose; smooth every
        passion
That in the natures of their lords rebel,
Bring oil to fire, snow to their colder moods;
Renege, affirm, and turn their halcyon beaks
With every gale and vary of their masters,
Knowing naught, like dogs, but following.—

473   They'll take suggestion as a cat laps milk;

KNAVES

474   A knave; a rascal; an eater of broken meats; a base, proud, shallow, beggarly, three-suited, hundred-pound, filthy, worsted-stocking knave; a lily-liver'd, action - taking, whoreson, glass - gazing, super - serviceable, finical rogue; one-trunk-inheriting slave; one that wouldst be a bawd in way of good service, and art nothing but the composition of a knave, beggar, coward, pandar, and the son and heir of a mongrel bitch: one whom I will beat into clamorous whining, if thou deniest the least syllable of thy addition.

475   Thou whoreson zed! thou unnecessary letter!

476   Thou idle immaterial skein of sleave-silk, thou green sarcenet flap for a sore eye, thou tassel of a prodigal's purse, thou! Ah, how the poor world is pestered with such water-flies—diminutives of nature.

477   This is some fellow,
Who, having been praised for bluntness, doth affect
A saucy roughness, and constrains the garb
Quite from his nature: he cannot flatter, he,—
An honest mind and plain,—he must speak truth!
An they will take it, so; if not, he's plain.
These kind of knaves I know, which in this plainness
Harbour more craft and more corrupter ends
Than twenty silly-ducking observants
That stretch their duties nicely.

478   I follow him to serve my turn upon him:
We cannot all be masters, nor all masters
Cannot be truly follow'd. You shall mark
Many a duteous and knee-crooking knave,
That, doting on his own obsequious bondage,
Wears out his time, much like his master's ass,
For naught but provender; and, when he's old,
    cashier'd:
Whip me such honest knaves. Others there are,
Who, trimm'd in forms and visages of duty,
Keep yet their hearts attending on themselves;
And, throwing but shows of service on their lords,
Do well thrive by them, and, when they have lined
    their coats,
Do themselves homage: these fellows have some soul;
And such a one do I profess myself.

479   But 'tis a common proof,
That lowliness is young ambition's ladder,
Whereto the climber-upward turns his face;
But when he once attains the upmost round,
He then unto the ladder turns his back,
Looks in the clouds, scorning the base degrees
By which he did ascend.

480   Cromwell, I charge thee, fling away ambition:
By that sin fell the angels; how can man, then,
The image of his Maker, hope to win by it?
Love thyself last; cherish those hearts that hate thee;
Corruption wins not more than honesty.
Still in thy right hand carry gentle peace,
To silence envious tongues. Be just, and fear not:
Let all the ends thou aim'st at be thy country's,

Thy God's, and truth's: then if thou fall'st, O Crom-
well,
Thou fall'st a blessed martyr! . . .
          O Cromwell, Cromwell!
Had I but served my God with half the zeal
I served my king, He would not in mine age
Have left me naked to mine enemies.

481   Angels are bright still, though the brightest fell.

482   KATHARINE
                 He was a man
Of an unbounded stomach, ever ranking
Himself with princes; one that by suggestion
Tithed all the kingdom: simony was fair-play;
His own opinion was his law: i'the presence
He would say untruths; and be ever double
Both in his words and meaning: he was never,
But where he meant to ruin, pitiful:
His promises were, as he then was, mighty;
But his performance, as he is now, nothing:
Of his own body he was ill, and gave
The clergy ill example.
                    GRIFFITH
                 Noble madam,
Men's evil manners live in brass; their virtues
We write in water. May it please your highness
To hear me speak his good now?
                    KATHARINE
                    Yes, good Griffith;
I were malicious else.
                    GRIFFITH
                    This cardinal,
Though from an humble stock, undoubtedly
Was fashion'd to much honour from his cradle.

He was a scholar, and a ripe and good one;
Exceeding wise, fair-spoken, and persuading:
Lofty and sour to them that lov'd him not;
But to those men that sought him sweet as summer.
And though he were unsatisfied in getting,—
Which was a sin,—yet in bestowing, madam,
He was most princely: ever witness for him
Those twins of learning that he raised in you,
Ipswich and Oxford! one of which fell with him,
Unwilling to outlive the good that did it;
The other, though unfinisht, yet so famous,
So excellent in art, and still so rising,
That Christendom shall ever speak his virtue.
His overthrow heapt happiness upon him;
For then, and not till then, he felt himself,
And found the blessedness of being little:
And, to add greater honours to his age
Than man could give him, he died fearing God.

483   He reads much;
He is a great observer, and he looks
Quite through the deeds of men: he loves no plays,
As thou dost, Antony; he hears no music:
Seldom he smiles; and smiles in such a sort
As if he mockt himself, and scorn'd his spirit
That could be moved to smile at any thing.
Such men as he be never at heart's ease
Whiles they behold a greater than themselves;
And therefore are they very dangerous.

484   He hath disgraced me, and hinder'd
me half a million; laught at my losses, mockt at my
gains, scorn'd my nation, thwarted my bargains,
cooled my friends, heated mine enemies: and what's
his reason? I am a Jew. Hath not a Jew eyes?

hath not a Jew hands, organs, dimensions, senses, affections, passions? fed with the same food, hurt with the same weapons, subject to the same diseases, heal'd by the same means, warm'd and cool'd by the same winter and summer, as a Christian is? If you prick us, do we not bleed? if you tickle us, do we not laugh? if you poison us, do we not die? and if you wrong us, shall we not revenge? if we are like you in the rest, we will resemble you in that. If a Jew wrong a Christian, what is his humility? revenge: if a Christian wrong a Jew, what should his sufferance be by Christian example? why, revenge. The villainy you teach me, I will execute; and it shall go hard but I will better the instruction.

485   You taught me language; and my profit on't
       Is, I know how to curse.

486   Get thee to a nunnery: why wouldst thou be a breeder of sinners? I am myself indifferent honest: but yet I could accuse me of such things, that it were better my mother had not borne me: I am very proud, revengeful, ambitious; with more offences at my beck than I have thoughts to put them in, imagination to give them shape, or time to act them in. What should such fellows as I do crawling between earth and heaven?

487   Then let them anatomize Regan; see what breeds about her heart. Is there any cause in nature that makes these hard hearts?

488 Why should the worm intrude the maiden bud?
Or hateful cuckoos hatch in sparrows' nests?
Or toads infect fair founts with venom mud?
Or tyrant folly lurk in gentle breasts?
Or kings be breakers of their own behests?
  But no perfection is so absolute,
  That some impurity doth not pollute.

489 Thou, nature, art my goddess; to thy law
My services are bound. Wherefore should I
Stand in the plague of custom, and permit
The curiosity of nations to deprive me,
For that I am some twelve or fourteen moonshines
Lag of a brother? Why bastard? wherefore base?
When my dimensions are as well compact,
My mind as generous, and my shape as true,
As honest madam's issue? Why brand they us
With base? with baseness? bastardy? base, base?
Who, in the lusty stealth of nature, take
More composition and fierce quality
Than doth, within a dull, stale, tired bed,
Go to th'creating a whole tribe of fops,
Got 'tween asleep and wake?

490 Now is the winter of our discontent
Made glorious summer by this sun of York;
And all the clouds that lour'd upon our house
In the deep bosom of the ocean buried.
Now are our brows bound with victorious wreaths;
Our bruised arms hung up for monuments;
Our stern alarums changed to merry meetings,
Our dreadful marches to delightful measures.
Grim-visaged war hath smooth'd his wrinkled front;

And now—instead of mounting barbed steeds
To fright the souls of fearful adversaries—
He capers nimbly in a lady's chamber
To the lascivious pleasing of a lute.
But I, that am not shaped for sportive tricks,
Nor made to court an amorous looking-glass;
I, that am rudely stampt, and want love's majesty
To strut before a wanton ambling nymph;
I, that am curtail'd of this fair proportion,
Cheated of feature by dissembling nature,
Deform'd, unfinisht, sent before my time
Into this breathing world, scarce half made up,
And that so lamely and unfashionable
That dogs bark at me as I halt by them;—
Why, I, in this weak piping time of peace,
Have no delight to pass away the time,
Unless to spy my shadow in the sun,
And descant on mine own deformity:
And therefore, since I cannot prove a lover,
To entertain these fair well-spoken days,
I am determined to prove a villain,
And hate the idle pleasures of these days.

491   Shine out, fair sun, till I have bought a glass,
That I may see my shadow as I pass.

492   I do remember an apothecary,—
And hereabouts he dwells,—which late I noted
In tatter'd weeds, with overwhelming brows,
Culling of simples; meagre were his looks,
Sharp misery had worn him to the bones:
And in his needy shop a tortoise hung,
An alligator stuft, and other skins

Of ill-shaped fishes; and about his shelves
A beggarly account of empty boxes,
Green earthen pots, bladders, and musty seeds,
Remnants of packthread, and old cakes of roses,
Were thinly scatter'd, to make up a show.
Noting this penury, to myself I said,
'An if a man did need a poison now,
Whose sale is present death in Mantua,
Here lives a caitiff wretch would sell it him.'

493   I bought an unction of a mountebank,
So mortal, that but dip a knife in it,
Where it draws blood no cataplasm so rare,
Collected from all simples that have virtue
Under the moon, can save the thing from death
That is but scratcht withal: I'll touch my point
With this contagion, that, if I gall him slightly,
It may be death.

494   O, mickle is the powerful grace that lies
In herbs, plants, stones, and their true qualities:
For naught so vile that on the earth doth live,
But to the earth some special good doth give;
Nor aught so good, but, strain'd from that fair use,
Revolts from true birth, stumbling on abuse:
Virtue itself turns vice, being misapplied;
And vice sometime's by action dignified.
Within the infant rind of this small flower
Poison hath residence, and medicine power:
For this, being smelt, with that part cheers each part;
Being tasted, slays all senses with the heart.
Two such opposed kings encamp them still
In man as well as herbs,—grace and rude will;
And where the worser is predominant,
Full soon the canker death eats up that plant.

495   There is a kind of character in thy life,
       That to th'observer doth thy history
       Fully unfold. Thyself and thy belongings
       Are not thine own so proper, as to waste
       Thyself upon thy virtues, they on thee.
       Heaven doth with us as we with torches do,
       Not light them for themselves; for if our virtues
       Did not go forth of us, 'twere all alike
       As if we had them not. Spirits are not finely touch'd
       But to fine issues; nor Nature never lends
       The smallest scruple of her excellence
       But, like a thrifty goddess, she determines
       Herself the glory of a creditor,
       Both thanks and use.

496   They that have power to hurt and will do none,
       That do not do the thing they most do show,
       Who, moving others, are themselves as stone,
       Unmoved, cold, and to temptation slow;
       They rightly do inherit heaven's graces,
       And husband nature's riches from expense;
       They are the lords and owners of their faces,
       Others but stewards of their excellence.
       The summer's flower is to the summer sweet,
       Though to itself it only live and die;
       But if that flower with base infection meet,
       The basest weed outbraves his dignity:
           For sweetest things turn sourest by their deeds;
           Lilies that fester smell far worse than weeds.

497   It is the bright day that brings forth the adder

ACHILLES
What are you reading?

ULYSSES
                    A strange fellow here
Writes me, 'That man—how dearly ever parted,
How much in having, or without or in—
Cannot make boast to have that which he hath,
Nor feels not what he owes, but by reflection;
As when his virtues shining upon others
Heat them, and they retort that heat again
To the first giver.'

ACHILLES
                    This is not strange, Ulysses.
The beauty that is borne here in the face
The bearer knows not, but commends itself
To others' eyes: nor doth the eye itself,
That most pure spirit of sense, behold itself,
Not going from itself; but eye to eye opposed
Salutes each other with each other's form:
For speculation turns not to itself,
Till it hath travell'd, and is mirror'd there
Where it may see itself. This is not strange at all.

ULYSSES
I do not strain at the position,—
It is familiar,—but at the author's drift;
Who, in his circumstance, expressly proves
That no man is the lord of any thing,
Though in and of him there be much consisting,
Till he communicate his parts to others;
Nor doth he of himself know them for aught
Till he behold them formed in th'applause
Where they're extended; who, like an arch, reverb'rates
The voice again; or, like a gate of steel
Fronting the sun, receives and renders back
His figure and his heat.

499   'Tis certain, greatness, once faln out with fortune,
Must fall out with men too: what the declined is,
He shall as soon read in the eyes of others
As feel in his own fall; for men, like butterflies,
Show not their mealy wings but to the summer;
And not a man, for being simply man,
Hath any honour, but honour for those honours
That are without him, as place, riches, favour,
Prizes of accident as oft as merit:
Which when they fall, as being slippery standers,
The love that lean'd on them as slippery too,
Do one pluck down another, and together
Die in the fall.

500   New honours come upon him,
Like our strange garments, cleave not to their mould
But with the aid of use.

501   ACHILLES
I see my reputation is at stake;
My fame is shrewdly gored.
                PATROCLUS
                O, then, beware;
Those wounds heal ill that men do give themselves:
Omission to do what is necessary
Seals a commission to a blank of danger:
And danger, like an ague, subtly taints
Even then when we sit idly in the sun.

502   Reputation, reputation, reputation! O, I have lost
my reputation! I have lost the immortal part of
myself, and what remains is bestial.

503   Good name in man and woman, dear my lord,
Is the immediate jewel of their souls:
Who steals my purse steals trash; 'tis something,
    nothing;
'Twas mine, 'tis his, and has been slave to thousands;
But he that filches from me my good name
Robs me of that which not enriches him,
And makes me poor indeed.

504   How far that little candle throws his beams!
So shines a good deed in a naughty world.

505   The web of our life is of a mingled yarn, good and
ill together: our virtues would be proud, if our faults
whipt them not: and our crimes would despair, if
they were not cherisht by our virtues.

506   Yet do I fear thy nature;
It is too full o'th'milk of human kindness
To catch the nearest way: thou wouldst be great;
Art not without ambition; but without
The illness should attend it: what thou wouldst
    highly,
That wouldst thou holily; wouldst not play false,
And yet wouldst wrongly win.

507   Blunt not his love,
Nor lose the good advantage of his grace
By seeming cold or careless of his will;
For he is gracious, if he be observed:

He hath a tear for pity, and a hand
Open as day for melting charity:
Yet notwithstanding, being incensed, he's flint;
As humorous as winter, and as sudden
As flaws congealed in the spring of day.
His temper, therefore, must be well observed:
Chide him for faults, and do it reverently,
When you perceive his blood inclined to mirth;
But, being moody, give him line and scope,
Till that his passions, like a whale on ground,
Confound themselves with working.

508 The colour of the king doth come and go
Between his purpose and his conscience.
Like heralds 'twixt two dreadful battles set:
His passion is so ripe, it needs must break.

509 May one be pardon'd, and retain th'offence?
In the corrupted currents of this world
Offence's gilded hand may shove by justice;
And oft 'tis seen the wicked prize itself
Buys out the law: but 'tis not so above;
There is no shuffling,—there the action lies
In his true nature; and we ourselves compell'd,
Even to the teeth and forehead of our faults,
To give in evidence. What then? what rests?
Try what repentance can: what can it not?
Yet what can it when one can not repent?
O wretched state! O bosom black as death!
O limed soul, that, struggling to be free,
Art more engaged! Help, angels! Make assay:
Bow, stubborn knees; and, heart with strings of steel
Be soft as sinews of the new-born babe!
All may be well.

510   What's this, what's this? Is this her fault or mine?
The tempter or the tempted, who sins most, ha?
Not she; nor doth she tempt: but it is I
That, lying by the violet in the sun,
Do as the carrion does, not as the flower,
Corrupt with virtuous season. Can it be
That modesty may more betray our sense
Than woman's lightness? Having waste ground
    enough,
Shall we desire to raze the sanctuary,
And pitch our evils there? O, fie, fie, fie!
O cunning enemy, that, to catch a saint,
With saints dost bait thy hook! Most dangerous
Is that temptation that doth goad us on
To sin in loving virtue: never could the strumpet,
With all her double vigour, art and nature,
Once stir my temper; but this virtuous maid
Subdues me quite:—ever till now,
When men were fond, I smiled, and wonder'd how

511   Virtue! a fig! 'tis in ourselves that we are thus or
thus. Our bodies are gardens; to the which our wills
are gardeners: so that if we will plant nettles, or sow
lettuce; set hyssop, and weed-up thyme; supply it
with one gender of herbs, or distract it with many;
either to have it sterile with idleness, or manured
with industry; why, the power and corrigible authority of this lies in our wills. If the balance of our
lives had not one scale of reason to poise another of
sensuality, the blood and baseness of our natures
would conduct us to most preposterous conclusions:
but we have reason to cool our raging motions, our
carnal stings, our unbitted lusts; whereof I take this
that you call love to be a sect or scion.

512 This is the excellent foppery of the world, that, when we are sick in fortune,—often the surfeit of our own behaviour,—we make guilty of our disasters the sun, the moon, and the stars: as if we were villains by necessity; fools by heavenly compulsion; knaves, thieves, and treachers, by spherical predominance; drunkards, liars, and adulterers, by an enforced obedience of planetary influence; and all that we are evil in, by a divine thrusting on: an admirable evasion of whore-master man, to lay his goatish disposition to the charge of a star! My father compounded with my mother under the dragon's tail; and my nativity was under *ursa major;* so that it follows, I am rough and lecherous.—Fut, I should have been that I am, had the maidenliest star in the firmament twinkled on my bastardizing

513 The sweets we wish for turn to loathed sours
Even in the moment that we call them ours.

514 Our wills and fates do so contrary run
That our devices still are overthrown;
Our thoughts are ours, their ends none of our own.

515 Something may be done that we will not
And sometimes we are devils to ourselves,
When we will tempt the frailty of our powers
Presuming on their changeful potency.

516 There lives within the very flame of love
A kind of wick or snuff that will abate it;
And nothing is at a like goodness still;
For goodness, growing to a plurisy,

Dies in his own too-much: that we would do,
We should do when we would; for this 'would'
   changes,
And hath abatements and delays as many
As there are tongues, are hands, are accidents;
And then this 'should' is like a spendthrift sigh,
That hurts by easing.

517   But when we in our viciousness grow hard,—
O misery on't!—the wise gods seel our eyes;
In our own filth drop our clear judgements; make us
Adore our errors; laugh at's, while we strut
To our confusion.

518   The gods are just, and of our pleasant vices
Make instruments to plague us.

519   As flies to wanton boys, are we to the gods,
They kill us for their sport.

520   It is the stars,
The stars above us, govern our conditions;
Else one self mate and mate could not beget
Such different issues.

521   Our remedies oft in ourselves do lie,
Which we ascribe to heaven: the fated sky
Gives us free scope; only doth backward pull
Our slow designs when we ourselves are dull.

522   The fault, dear Brutus, is not in our stars,
But in ourselves, that we are underlings.

523   Hang up philosophy!
Unless philosophy can make a Juliet,
Displant a town, reverse a prince's doom,
It helps not, it prevails not: talk no more.

524   O, who can hold a fire in his hand
By thinking on the frosty Caucasus?
Or cloy the hungry edge of appetite
By bare imagination of a feast?
Or wallow naked in December snow
By thinking on fantastic summer's heat?
O, no! the apprehension of the good
Gives but the greater feeling to the worse:
Fell sorrow's tooth doth never rankle more
Than when he bites, but lanceth not the sore.

525   For there was never yet philosopher
That could endure the toothache patiently,
However they have writ the style of gods,
And made a push at chance and sufferance.

Book III ★ Age

DEATH

SICKNESS

SLEEP

MAN AGAINST HIMSELF

OLD AGE

TIME

FINIS

The miserable have no other medicine
But only hope:
I have hope to live, and am prepared to die.

DUKE

Be absolute for death; either death or life
Shall thereby be the sweeter. Reason thus with
  life:—
If I do lose thee, I do lose a thing
That none but fools would keep: a breath thou art,
Servile to all the skyey influences
That do this habitation, where thou keep'st,
Hourly afflict: merely, thou art death's fool;
For him thou labour'st by thy flight to shun,
And yet runn'st toward him still. Thou art not noble;
For all th'accommodations that thou bear'st
Are nursed by baseness. Thou'rt by no means
  valiant;
For thou dost fear the soft and tender fork
Of a poor worm. Thy best of rest is sleep,
And that thou oft provokest; yet grossly fear'st
Thy death, which is no more. Thou art not thyself;
For thou exists on many a thousand grains
That issue out of dust. Happy thou art not;
For what thou hast not, still thou strivest to get,
And what thou hast, forgett'st. Thou art not certain;
For thy complexion shifts to strange affects,
After the moon. If thou art rich, thou'rt poor;
For, like an ass whose back with ingot bows,
Thou bear'st thy heavy riches but a journey,
And death unloads thee. Friend hast thou none;
For thine own bowels, which do call thee sire,
The mere effusions of thy proper loins,
Do curse the gout, serpigo, and the rheum,
For ending thee no sooner. Thou hast nor youth nor
  age,
But, as it were, an after-dinner's sleep,

Dreaming on both; for all thy blessed youth
Becomes as aged, and doth beg the alms
Of palsied eld; and when thou art old and rich,
Thou hast neither heat, affection, limb, nor beauty,
To make thy riches pleasant. What's yet in this
That bears the name of life? Yet in this life
Lie hid moe thousand deaths: yet death we fear,
That makes these odds all even.

527

ISABELLA

                    Darest thou die?
The sense of death is most in apprehension;
And the poor beetle that we tread upon,
In corporal sufferance finds a pang as great
As when a giant dies.

CLAUDIO

                    Why give you me this shame?
Think you I can a resolution fetch
From flowery tenderness? If I must die,
I will encounter darkness as a bride,
And hug it in mine arms.

ISABELLA

There spake my brother; there my father's grave
Did utter forth a voice!

528

Ay, but to die, and go we know not where;
To lie in cold obstruction, and to rot;
This sensible warm motion to become
A kneaded clod; and the delighted spirit
To bathe in fiery floods, or to reside
In thrilling region of thick-ribbed ice;
To be imprison'd in the viewless winds,
And blown with restless violence round about

The pendent world; or to be worse than worst
Of those that lawless and incertain thought
Imagine howling!—'tis too horrible!
The weariest and most loathed worldly life
That age, ache, penury, and imprisonment
Can lay on nature, is a paradise
To what we fear of death.

529   Cowards die many times before their deaths;
The valiant never taste of death but once.
Of all the wonders that I yet have heard,
It seems to me most strange that men should fear;
Seeing that death, a necessary end,
Will come when it will come.

530   We defy augury: there's a special providence in the
fall of a sparrow. If it be now, 'tis not to come; if it
be not to come, it will be now; if it be not now, yet
it will come: the readiness is all: since no man has
aught of what he leaves, what is't to leave betimes?
Let be.

531   What, in ill thoughts again? Men must endure
Their going hence, even as their coming hither:
Ripeness is all.

532   And a man's life's no more than to say 'one.'

533   A man that apprehends death no more dreadfully
but as a drunken sleep; careless, reckless, and fearless
of what's past, present, or to come; insensible of
mortality, and desperately mortal.

534   I have lived long enough: my way of life
Is faln into the sear, the yellow leaf;
And that which should accompany old age,
As honour, love, obedience, troops of friends,
I must not look to have; but, in their stead,
Curses not loud but deep, mouth-honour, breath,
Which the poor heart would fain deny, and dare not.

535   To-morrow, and to-morrow, and to-morrow,
Creeps in this petty pace from day to day,
To the last syllable of recorded time;
And all our yesterdays have lighted fools
The way to dusty death. Out, out, brief candle!
Life's but a walking shadow; a poor player,
That struts and frets his hour upon the stage,
And then is heard no more: it is a tale
Told by an idiot, full of sound and fury,
Signifying nothing.

536   There's nothing in this world can make me joy:
Life is as tedious as a twice-told tale
Vexing the dull ear of a drowsy man;
And bitter shame hath spoil'd the sweet world's taste,
That it yields naught but shame and bitterness.

537   I have of late—but wherefore I know not—lost all
my mirth, forgone all custom of exercises; and,
indeed, it goes so heavily with my disposition that
this goodly frame, the earth, seems to me a sterile
promontory; this most excellent canopy, the air,
look you, this brave o'erhanging firmament, this

majestical roof fretted with golden fire,--why, it
appears no other thing to me than a foul and pestilent
congregation of vapours. What a piece of work is
man! how noble in reason! how infinite in faculty!
in form and moving how express and admirable! in
action how like an angel! in apprehension how like
a god! the beauty of the world! the paragon of
animals! And yet, to me, what is this quintessence
of dust?

538   When, in disgrace with fortune and men's eyes,
I all alone beweep my outcast state,
And trouble deaf heaven with my bootless cries,
And look upon myself, and curse my fate,
Wishing me like to one more rich in hope,
Featured like him, like him with friends possest,
Desiring this man's art, and that man's scope,
With what I most enjoy contented least;
Yet in these thoughts myself almost despising,
Haply I think on thee,—and then my state,
Like to the lark at break of day arising
From sullen earth, sings hymns at heaven's gate;
    For thy sweet love remember'd such wealth brings,
    That then I scorn to change my state with kings.

539   When to the sessions of sweet silent thought
I summon up remembrance of things past,
I sigh the lack of many a thing I sought,
And with old woes new wail my dear time's waste:
Then can I drown an eye, unused to flow,
For precious friends hid in death's dateless night,
And weep afresh love's long-since-cancell'd woe,
And moan the expense of many a vanisht sight:

Then can I grieve at grievances foregone,
And heavily from woe to woe tell o'er
The sad account of fore-bemoaned moan,
Which I new pay as if not paid before.
    But if the while I think on thee, dear friend,
    All losses are restored, and sorrows end.

540   I have neither the scholar's melancholy, which is emulation; nor the musician's, which is fantastical; nor the courtier's, which is proud; nor the soldier's, which is ambitious; nor the lawyer's, which is politic; nor the lady's, which is nice; nor the lover's, which is all these;—but it is a melancholy of mine own, compounded of many simples, extracted from many objects, and, indeed, the sundry contemplation of my travels, which, by often rumination, wraps me in a most humorous sadness.

541   But thou wouldst not think how ill all's here about my heart: but it is no matter. It is but foolery; but it is such a kind of gain-giving as would perhaps trouble a woman.

542   O, that this too too solid flesh would melt,
Thaw, and resolve itself into a dew!
Or that the Everlasting had not fixt
His canon 'gainst self-slaughter! O God! God!
How weary, stale, flat, and unprofitable
Seem to me all the uses of this world?
Fie on't! O, fie! 'tis an unweeded garden,
That grows to seed; things rank and gross in nature
Possess it merely.

543   Then hate me when thou wilt; if ever, now;
Now, while the world is bent my deeds to cross,
Join with the spite of fortune, make me bow,
And do not drop in for an after-loss:
Ah, do not, when my heart hath scaped this sorrow,
Come in the rearward of a conquer'd woe;
Give not a windy night a rainy morrow,
To linger out a purposed overthrow.
If thou wilt leave me, do not leave me last,
When other petty griefs have done their spite,
But in the onset come: so shall I taste
At first the very worst of fortune's might;
     And other strains of woe, which now seem woe,
     Compared with loss of thee will not seem so.

544   The deep of night is crept upon our talk,
And nature must obey necessity;
Which we will niggard with a little rest.

545   I talk of dreams;
Which are the children of an idle brain,
Begot of nothing but vain fantasy;
Which is as thin of substance as the air;
And more inconstant than the wind, who wooes
Even now the frozen bosom of the north,
And, being anger'd, puffs away from thence,
Turning his face to the dew-dropping south.

546   DUKE OF CLARENCE
O, I have pass'd a miserable night,
So full of fearful dreams, of ugly sights,
That, as I am a Christian faithful man,

THE AGES OF MAN

I would not spend another such a night
Though 'twere to buy a world of happy days—
So full of dismal terror was the time!

SIR ROBERT BRAKENBURY

What was your dream, my lord? I pray you, tell me.

DUKE OF CLARENCE

Methought that I had broken from the Tower,
And was embarkt to cross to Burgundy;
And, in my company, my brother Gloster;
Who from my cabin tempted me to walk
Upon the hatches: thence we lookt toward England,
And cited up a thousand heavy times,
During the wars of York and Lancaster,
That had befaln us. As we paced along
Upon the giddy footing of the hatches,
Methought that Gloster stumbled; and, in falling,
Struck me, that thought to stay him, overboard
Into the tumbling billows of the main.
Lord, Lord! methought, what pain it was to drown!
What dreadful noise of waters in mine ears!
What ugly sights of death within mine eyes!
Methought I saw a thousand fearful wracks;
Ten thousand men that fishes gnaw'd upon;
Wedges of gold, great anchors, heaps of pearl,
Inestimable stones, unvalued jewels,
All scatt'red in the bottom of the sea:
Some lay in dead men's skulls; and, in those holes
Where eyes did once inhabit, there were crept,
As 'twere in scorn of eyes, reflecting gems,
That woo'd the slimy bottom of the deep,
And mockt the dead bones that lay scatt'red by.

SIR ROBERT BRAKENBURY

Had you such leisure in the time of death
To gaze upon the secrets of the deep?

DUKE OF CLARENCE

Methought I had; and often did I strive
To yield the ghost: but still the envious flood

Kept in my soul, and would not let it forth
To seek the empty, vast, and wandering air;
But smother'd it within my panting bulk,
Which almost burst to belch it in the sea.

SIR ROBERT BRAKENBURY

Awaked you not with this sore agony?

DUKE OF CLARENCE

No, no, my dream was lengthen'd after life;
O, then began the tempest to my soul!
I past, methought, the melancholy flood,
With that grim ferryman which poets write of,
Unto the kingdom of perpetual night.
The first that there did greet my stranger soul,
Was my great father-in-law, renowned Warwick;
Who cried aloud, 'What scourge for perjury
Can this dark monarchy afford false Clarence?'
And so he vanisht: then came wandering by
A shadow like an angel, with bright hair
Dabbled in blood; and he shriekt out loud,
'Clarence is come; false, fleeting, perjured Clarence,
That stabb'd me in the field by Tewksbury:
Seize on him, Furies, take him to your torments!'
With that, methought, a legion of foul fiends
Environ'd me, and howled in mine ears
Such hideous cries, that, with the very noise,
I trembling waked, and, for a season after,
Could not believe but that I was in hell,—
Such terrible impression made my dream.

547   Not poppy, nor mandragora,
Nor all the drowsy syrups of the world,
Shall ever medicine thee to that sweet sleep
Which thou owedst yesterday.

548

DOCTOR

Our foster-nurse of nature is repose,
The which he lacks; that to provoke in him
Are many simples operative, whose power
Will close the eye of anguish.

CORDELIA

All bless'd secrets,
All you unpublish'd virtues of the earth,
Spring with my tears! be aidant and remediate
In the good man's distress!

549

The innocent sleep,
Sleep that knits up the ravell'd sleave of care,
The death of each day's life, sore labour's bath,
Balm of hurt minds, great nature's second course,
Chief nourisher in life's feast.

550

Infected minds
To their deaf pillows will discharge their secrets.

551   O God, I could be bounded in a nut-shell, and count
myself a king of infinite space, were it not that I have
bad dreams.

552   How many thousand of my poorest subjects
Are at this hour asleep!—O sleep, O gentle sleep,
Nature's soft nurse, how have I frighted thee,
That thou no more wilt weigh my eyelids down,
And steep my senses in forgetfulness?
Why rather, sleep, liest thou in smoky cribs,

Upon uneasy pallets stretching thee,
And husht with buzzing night-flies to thy slumber,
Than in the perfumed chambers of the great,
Under the canopies of costly state,
And lull'd with sound of sweetest melody?
O thou dull god, why liest thou with the vile
In loathsome beds, and leavest the kingly couch
A watch-case or a common 'larum-bell?
Wilt thou upon the high and giddy mast
Seal up the ship-boy's eyes, and rock his brains
In cradle of the rude imperious surge,
And in the visitation of the winds,
Who take the ruffian billows by the top,
Curling their monstrous heads, and hanging them
With deafening clamour in the slippery shrouds,
That, with the hurly, death itself awakes?—
Canst thou, O partial sleep, give thy repose
To the wet sea-boy in an hour so rude;
And in the calmest and most stillest night,
With all appliances and means to boot,
Deny it to a king? Then, happy low, lie down!
Uneasy lies the head that wears a crown.

553   O, the fierce wretchedness that glory brings us!

554   Infirmity doth still neglect all office
Whereto our health is bound; we are not ourselves
When nature, being opprest, commands the mind
To suffer with the body.

555   Why doth the crown lie there upon his pillow,
Being so troublesome a bedfellow?
O polisht perturbation! golden care!
That keep'st the ports of slumber open wide

To many a watchful night!—sleep with it now!
Yet not so sound and half so deeply sweet
As he whose brow with homely biggen bound
Snores out the watch of night. O majesty!
When thou dost pinch thy bearer, thou dost sit
Like a rich armour worn in heat of day,
That scalds with safety. By his gates of breath
There lies a downy feather which stirs not:
Did he suspire, that light and weightless down
Perforce must move.—My gracious lord! my father!—
This sleep is sound indeed; this is a sleep,
That from this golden rigol hath divorced
So many English kings.

556   Give me an ounce of civet, good apothecary,
       to sweeten my imagination.

557   Canst thou not minister to a mind diseased;
       Pluck from the memory a rooted sorrow;
       Raze out the written troubles of the brain;
       And with some sweet oblivious antidote
       Cleanse the stuft bosom of that perilous stuff
       Which weighs upon the heart?

558   You lack the season of all natures, sleep.

559   Between the acting of a dreadful thing
       And the first motion, all the interim is
       Like a phantasma or a hideous dream:
       The Genius and the mortal instruments
       Are then in council; and the state of man,
       Like to a little kingdom, suffers then
       The nature of an insurrection.

560   Why do you keep alone,
Of sorriest fancies your companions making;
Using those thoughts which should indeed have died
With them they think on? Things without all remedy
Should be without regard: what's done is done.

561 Let me have men about me that are fat;
Sleek-headed men, and such as sleep o' nights.

562 To be, or not to be,—that is the question,—
Whether 'tis nobler in the mind to suffer
The slings and arrows of outrageous fortune,
Or to take arms against a sea of troubles,
And by opposing end them?—To die,—to sleep,—
No more; and by a sleep to say we end
The heart-ache, and the thousand natural shocks
That flesh is heir to, 'tis a consummation
Devoutly to be wisht. To die,—to sleep;—
To sleep! perchance to dream: ay, there's the rub;
For in that sleep of death what dreams may come,
When we have shuffled off this mortal coil,
Must give us pause: there's the respect
That makes calamity of so long life;
For who would bear the whips and scorns of time,
The oppressor's wrong, the proud man's contumely,
The pangs of despised love, the law's delay,
The insolence of office, and the spurns
That patient merit of the unworthy takes,
When he himself might his quietus make
With a bare bodkin? who would fardels bear,
To grunt and sweat under a weary life,
But that the dread of something after death,—
The undiscover'd country, from whose bourn
No traveller returns,—puzzles the will,

And makes us rather bear those ills we have
Than fly to others that we know not of?
Thus conscience does make cowards of us all;
And thus the native hue of resolution
Is sicklied o'er with the pale cast of thought;
And enterprises of great pith and moment,
With this regard, their currents turn awry,
And lose the name of action.

563   But let the frame of things disjoint, both the worlds
          suffer,
       Ere we will eat our meal in fear, and sleep
       In the affliction of these terrible dreams
       That shake us nightly: better be with the dead,
       Whom we, to gain our peace, have sent to peace,
       Than on the torture of the mind to lie
       In restless ecstasy. Duncan is in his grave;
       After life's fitful fever he sleeps well;
       Treason has done his worst: nor steel, nor poison,
       Malice domestic, foreign levy, nothing,
       Can touch him further.

564   O' let me not be mad, not mad, sweet heaven!
       Keep me in temper: I would not be mad!

565   Alas, 'tis true I have gone here and there,
       And made myself a motley to the view,
       Gored mine own thoughts, sold cheap what is most
          dear,
       Made old offences of affections new;
       Most true it is that I have lookt on truth

Askance and strangely: but, by all above,
These blenches gave my heart another youth,
And worse essays proved thee my best of love.
Now all is done, have what shall have no end:
Mine appetite I never more will grind
On newer proof, to try an older friend,
A god in love, to whom I am confined.
  Then give me welcome, next my heaven the best,
  Even to thy pure and most loving breast.

566　O, what a noble mind is here o'erthrown!
The courtier's, soldier's, scholar's eye, tongue, sword;
Th'expectancy and rose of the fair state,
The glass of fashion and the mould of form,
Th'observ'd of all observers,—quite, quite down!
And I, of ladies most deject and wretched,
That suckt the honey of his music vows,
Now see that noble and most sovereign reason,
Like sweet bells jangled, out of tune and harsh;
That unmatcht form and feature of blown youth
Blasted with ecstasy: O, woe is me
T'have seen what I have seen, see what I see!

567　　　　　　　Good night, sweet prince;
And flights of angels sing thee to thy rest!

568　Vex not his ghost: O' let him pass! he hates him
That would upon the rack of this tough world
Stretch him out longer.

569   Come, you spirits
That tend on mortal thoughts, unsex me here;
And fill me, from the crown to the toe, top-full
Of direst cruelty! make thick my blood,
Stop up th'access and passage to remorse,
That no compunctious visitings of nature
Shake my fell purpose, nor keep peace between
Th'effect and it! Come to my woman's breasts,
And take my milk for gall, you murd'ring ministers,
Wherever in your sightless substances
You wait on nature's mischief! Come, thick night,
And pall thee in the dunnest smoke of hell,
That my keen knife see not the wound it makes,
Nor heaven peep through the blanket of the dark,
To cry 'Hold, hold!'

570   Arise, black vengeance, from the hollow hell!
Yield up, O love, thy crown and hearted throne
To tyrannous hate! Swell, bosom, with thy fraught,
For 'tis of aspics' tongues!

571   Like to the Pontic sea,
Whose icy current and compulsive course
Ne'er feels retiring ebb, but keeps due on
To the Propontic and the Hellespont;
Even so my bloody thoughts, with violent pace,
Shall ne'er look back, ne'er ebb to humble love,
Till that a capable and wide revenge
Swallow them up.

572   Anger's my meat; I sup upon myself,
And so shall starve with feeding.—Come, let's go:
Leave this faint puling, and lament as I do,
In anger, Juno-like. Come, come, come.

573   I have given suck, and know
How tender 'tis to love the babe that milks me:
I would, while it was smiling in my face,
Have pluckt my nipple from his boneless gums,
And dasht the brains out, had I so sworn as you
Have done to this.

574   Hear, nature, hear; dear goddess, hear!
Suspend thy purpose, if thou didst intend
To make this creature fruitful!
Into her womb convey sterility!
Dry up in her the organs of increase;
And from her derogate body never spring
A babe to honour her! If she must teem,
Create her child of spleen; that it may live,
And be a thwart disnatured torment to her!
Let it stamp wrinkles in her brow of youth;
With cadent tears fret channels in her cheeks;
Turn all her mother's pains and benefits
To laughter and contempt,—that she may feel
How sharper than a serpent's tooth it is
To have a thankless child!—Away, away!

575   All the stored vengeances of heaven fall
On her ingrateful top! Strike her young bones,
You taking airs, with lameness!
You nimble lightnings, dart your blinding flames
Into her scornful eyes! Infect her beauty,
You fen-suckt fogs, drawn by the powerful sun,
To fall and blast her pride!

576   Piety, and fear,
Religion to the gods, peace, justice, truth,
Domestic awe, night-rest, and neighbourhood,

Instruction, manners, mysteries, and trades,
Degrees, observances, customs, and laws,
Decline to your confounding contraries,
And let confusion live!—Plagues incident to men,
Your potent and infectious fevers heap
On Athens, ripe for stroke! thou cold sciatica,
Cripple our senators, that their limbs may halt
As lamely as their manners! lust and liberty,
Creep in the minds and marrows of our youth,
That 'gainst the stream of virtue they may strive,
And drown themselves in riot! itches, blains,
Sow all the Athenian bosoms; and their crop
Be general leprosy! breath infect breath;
That their society, as their friendship, may
Be merely poison! Nothing I'll bear from thee
But nakedness, thou detestable town!

577 Be as a planetary plague, when Jove
Will o'er some high-viced city hang his poison
In the sick air: let not thy sword skip one:
Pity not honour'd age for his white beard,—
He is an usurer: strike me the counterfeit matron,—
It is her habit only that is honest,
Herself's a bawd: let not the virgin's cheek
Make soft thy trenchant sword; for those milk-paps,
That through the window-bars bore at men's eyes,
Are not within the leaf of pity writ,
But set down horrible traitors: spare not the babe,
Whose dimpled smiles from fools exhaust their
 mercy;
Think it a bastard, whom the oracle
Hath doubtfully pronounced thy throat shall cut,
And mince it sans remorse: swear against objects;
Put armour on thine ears and on thine eyes,
Whose proof, nor yells of mothers, maids, nor babes,

Nor sight, of priests in holy vestments bleeding
Shall pierce a jot. There's gold to pay thy soldiers:
Make large confusion; and, thy fury spent,
Confounded be thyself! Speak not, be gone.

578   Come, seeling night,
Scarf up the tender eye of pitiful day;
And with thy bloody and invisible hand
Cancel and tear to pieces that great bond
Which keeps me pale!—Light thickens; and the crow
Makes wing to th'rooky wood:
Good things of day begin to droop and drowse;
Whiles night's black agents to their preys do rouse.

579   Let's kill him boldly, but not wrathfully;
Let's carve him as a dish fit for the gods,
Not hew him as a carcass fit for hounds.

580   If it were done—when 'tis done—then 'twere well
It were done quickly: if th'assassination
Could trammel up the consequence, and catch,
With his surcease, success; that but this blow
Might be the be-all and the end-all here,
But here, upon this bank and shoal of time,
We'ld jump the life to come. But in these cases
We still have judgement here; that we but teach
Bloody instructions, which, being taught, return
To plague th'inventor: this even-handed justice
Commends th'ingredients of our poison'd chalice
To our own lips.

581   Had I but died an hour before this chance,
I had lived a blessed time; for, from this instant,
There's nothing serious in mortality:
All is but toys: renown and grace is dead;
The wine of life is drawn, and the mere lees
Is left this vault to brag of.

582   Now o'er the one half-world
Nature seems dead, and wicked dreams abuse
The curtain'd sleep; now witchcraft celebrates
Pale Hecate's offerings; and wither'd murder,
Alarum'd by his sentinel, the wolf,
Whose howl's his watch, thus with his stealthy pace,
With Tarquin's ravishing strides, towards his design
Moves like a ghost.

583   Ere the bat hath flown
His cloister'd flight; ere, to black Hecate's summons
The shard-borne beetle with his drowsy hums
Hath rung night's yawning peal, there shall be done
A deed of dreadful note.

584   Shake off this downy sleep, death's counterfeit,
And look on death itself! up, up, and see
The great doom's image!

585   Will all great Neptune's ocean wash this blood
Clean from my hand? No; this my hand will rather
The multitudinous seas incarnadine,
Making the green one red.

586   Blood hath been shed ere now, i'th'olden time,
Ere human statute purged the gentle weal;
Ay, and since too, murders have been perform'd
Too terrible for the ear: the time has been,
That, when the brains were out, the man would die,
And there an end; but now they rise again,
With twenty mortal murders on their crowns,
And push us from our stools.

587   It will have blood; they say blood will have blood:
Stones have been known to move, and trees to speak;
Augurs, and understood relations have
By maggot-pies and choughs and rooks brought forth
The secret'st man of blood.

588   Here's the smell of the blood still: all the perfumes
of Arabia will not sweeten this little hand. Oh, oh,
oh!

589   I am in blood
Stept in so far, that, should I wade no more,
Returning were as tedious as go o'er.

590   Upon his bloody finger he doth wear
A precious ring, that lightens all the hole,
Which, like a taper in some monument,
Doth shine upon the dead man's earthy cheeks,
And shows the ragged entrails of the pit:
So pale did shine the moon on Pyramus
When he by night lay bathed in maiden blood.

591   When beggars die, there are no comets seen;
The heavens themselves blaze forth the death of
   princes.

592   The night has been unruly: where we lay,
Our chimneys were blown down; and, as they say,
Lamentings heard i'th'air; strange screams of death;
And prophesying, with accents terrible,
Of dire combustion and confused events
New hatcht to th'woeful time: the obscure bird
Clamour'd the livelong night: some say, the earth
Was feverous and did shake.

593   **ROSS**
Thou seest, the heavens, as troubled with man's act
Threatens his bloody stage: by th'clock 'tis day,
And yet dark night strangles the travelling lamp:
Is't night's predominance, or the day's shame,
That darkness does the face of earth entomb,
When living light should kiss it?
                OLD MAN
                     'Tis unnatural,
Even like the deed that's done. On Tuesday last,
A falcon, towering in her pride of place,
Was by a mousing owl hawkt at and kill'd.
                ROSS
And Duncan's horses,—a thing most strange and
   certain,—
Beauteous and swift, the minions of their race,
Turn'd wild in nature, broke their stalls, flung out,
Contending 'gainst obedience, as they would make
War with mankind.

594   In the most high and palmy state of Rome,
A little ere the mightiest Julius fell,
The graves stood tenantless, and the sheeted dead
Did squeak and gibber in the Roman streets.

595   These late eclipses in the sun and moon portend no
good to us: though the wisdom of nature can reason
it thus and thus, yet nature finds itself scourged by
the sequent effects: love cools, friendship falls off,
brothers divide: in cities, mutinies, in countries,
discord; in palaces, treason; and the bond crackt
'twixt son and father. We have seen the best of our
time: machinations, hollowness, treachery, and all
ruinous disorders, follow us disquietly to our graves.

596

FIRST WITCH
Thrice the brinded cat hath mew'd.
SECOND WITCH
Thrice and once the hedge-pig whined.
THIRD WITCH
Harpier cries:—'tis time, 'tis time.
FIRST WITCH
Round about the caldron go;
In the poison'd entrails throw.—
Toad, that under cold stone
Days and nights has thirty-one
Swelter'd venom sleeping got,
Boil thou first i'the charmed pot.
ALL
Double, double toil and trouble;
Fire, burn; and, caldron, bubble.
SECOND WITCH
Fillet of a fenny snake,
In the caldron boil and bake;
Eye of newt, and toe of frog,

THE AGES OF MAN

Wool of bat, and tongue of dog,
Adder's fork, and blind-worm's sting,
Lizard's leg, and howlet's wing,—
For a charm of powerful trouble,
Like a hell-broth boil and bubble.

ALL

Double, double toil and trouble;
Fire, burn; and, caldron, bubble.

THIRD WITCH

Scale of dragon; tooth of wolf;
Witches' mummy; maw and gulf
Of the ravin'd salt-sea shark;
Root of hemlock digg'd i'the dark;
Liver of blaspheming Jew;
Gall of goat; and slips of yew
Sliver'd in the moon's eclipse;
Nose of Turk, and Tartar's lips;
Finger of birth-strangled babe
Ditch-deliver'd by a drab,—
Make the gruel thick and slab:
Add thereto a tiger's chaudron,
For th'ingredients of our caldron.

ALL

Double, double toil and trouble;
Fire, burn; and, caldron, bubble.

SECOND WITCH

Cool it with a baboon's blood,
Then the charm is firm and good.
By the pricking of my thumbs,
Something wicked this way comes:—
           Open, locks,
           Whoever knocks!

MACBETH

How now, you secret, black, and midnight hags!
What is't you do?

ALL
           A deed without a name

MACBETH

I conjure you, by that which you profess,—
Howe'er you come to know it,—answer me:
Though you untie the winds, and let them fight
Against the churches; though the yesty waves
Confound and swallow navigation up;
Though bladed corn be lodged, and trees blown
    down;
Though castles topple on their warders' heads;
Though palaces and pyramids do slope
Their heads to their foundations; though the treasure
Of nature's germens tumble all together,
Even till destruction sicken,—answer me
To what I ask you.

597   They love not poison that do poison need,
Nor do I thee: though I did wish him dead,
I hate the murderer, love him murdered.
The guilt of conscience take thou for thy labour,
But neither my good word nor princely favour:
With Cain go wander through the shades of night,
And never show thy head by day nor light.

598   KING JOHN
It is the curse of kings to be attended
By slaves that take their humours for a warrant
To break within the bloody house of life;
And, on the winking of authority,
To understand a law; to know the meaning
Of dangerous majesty, when perchance it frowns
More upon humour than advised respect.
          HUBERT DE BURGH
Here is your hand and seal for what I did.

KING JOHN

O, when the last account 'twixt heaven and earth
Is to be made, then shall this hand and seal
Witness against us to damnation!
How oft the sight of means to do ill deeds
Make deeds ill done! Hadst not thou been by,
A fellow by the hand of nature markt,
Quoted, and sign'd, to do a deed of shame,
This murder had not come into my mind.

599 For God's sake, let us sit upon the ground,
And tell sad stories of the death of kings:—
How some have been deposed; some slain in war;
Some haunted by the ghosts they have deposed;
Some poison'd by their wives; some sleeping kill'd;
All murder'd:—for within the hollow crown
That rounds the mortal temples of a king
Keeps Death his court; and there the antick sits,
Scoffing his state, and grinning at his pomp;
Allowing him a breath, a little scene,
To monarchize, be fear'd, and kill with looks;
Infusing him with self and vain conceit,—
As if this flesh, which walls about our life,
Were brass impregnable; and humour'd thus,
Comes at the last, and with a little pin
Bores through his castle-wall, and—farewell king!

600

KING JOHN

Ay, marry, now my soul hath elbow-room;
It would not out at windows nor at doors.
There is so hot a summer in my bosom,
That all my bowels crumble up to dust:
I am a scribbled form, drawn with a pen
Upon a parchment; and against this fire
Do I shrink up.

PROUD DEATH

PRINCE HENRY
How fares your majesty?
KING JOHN
Poison'd,—ill fare;—dead, forsook, cast off:
And none of you will bid the winter come,
To thrust his icy fingers in my maw;
Nor let my kingdom's rivers take their course
Through my burn'd bosom; nor entreat the north
To make his bleak winds kiss my parched lips,
And comfort me with cold:—I do not ask you much,
I beg cold comfort; and you are so strait,
And so ingrateful, you deny me that

601   O death, made proud with pure and princely beauty!
The earth had not a hole to hide this deed.

602   O proud Death,
What feast is toward in thine eternal cell,
That thou so many princes at a shot
So bloodily hast struck?

603   Let's talk of graves, of worms, and epitaphs;
Make dust our paper, and with rainy eyes
Write sorrow on the bosom of the earth.
Let's choose executors, and talk of wills:
And yet not so,—for what can we bequeath,
Save our deposed bodies to the ground?

604   More are men's ends markt than their lives before:
The setting sun, and music at the close,
As the last taste of sweets, is sweetest last,
Writ in remembrance more than things long past.

605
                But I have spoke
With one that saw him die: who did report,
That very frankly he confest his treasons;
Implored your highness' pardon; and set forth
A deep repentance: nothing in his life
Became him like the leaving it; he died
As one that had been studied in his death
To throw away the dearest thing he owed,
As 'twere a careless trifle.

606
This was the noblest Roman of them all:
All the conspirators, save only he,
Did that they did in envy of great Cæsar;
He only, in a general honest thought,
And common good to all, made one of them.
His life was gentle; and the elements
So mixt in him, that Nature might stand up
And say to all the world, 'This was a man!'

607
                BRUTUS
                Stoop, Romans, stoop,
And let us bathe our hands in Cæsar's blood
Up to the elbows, and besmear our swords:
Then walk we forth; even to the market-place,
And, waving our red weapons o'er our heads,
Let's all cry, 'Peace, freedom, and liberty!'
                CASSIUS
Stoop then, and wash.—How many ages hence
Shall this our lofty scene be acted over
In states unborn and accents yet unknown!
                BRUTUS
How many times shall Cæsar bleed in sport,
That now on Pompey's basis lies along
No worthier than the dust!

CASSIUS
      So oft as that shall be,
So often shall the knot of us be call'd
The men that gave their country liberty.

608   O mighty Cæsar! dost thou lie so low?
Are all thy conquests, glories, triumphs, spoils,
Shrunk to this little measure?

609   If you have tears, prepare to shed them now.
You all do know this mantle: I remember
The first time ever Cæsar put it on;
'Twas on a summer's evening, in his tent,
That day he overcame the Nervii:—
Look, in this place ran Cassius' dagger through:
See what a rent the envious Casca made:
Through this the well-beloved Brutus stabb'd;
And, as he pluckt his cursed steel away,
Mark how the blood of Cæsar follow'd it,
As rushing out of doors, to be resolved
If Brutus so unkindly knockt, or no;
For Brutus, as you know, was Cæsar's angel:
Judge, O you gods, how dearly Cæsar loved him!
This was the most unkindest cut of all;
For when the noble Cæsar saw him stab,
Ingratitude, more strong than traitors' arms,
Quite vanquisht him: then burst his mighty heart;
And, in his mantle muffling up his face,
Even at the base of Pompey's statua,
Which all the while ran blood, great Cæsar fell.
O, what a fall was there, my countrymen!

610   Ill-weaved ambition, how much art thou shrunk!

CLEOPATRA

Give me my robe, put on my crown; I have
Immortal longings in me: now no more
The juice of Egypt's grape shall moist this lip:—
Yare, yare, good Iras; quick.—Methinks I hear
Antony call; I see him rouse himself
To praise my noble act; I hear him mock
The luck of Cæsar, which the gods give men
To excuse their after wrath:—husband, I come:
Now to that name my courage prove my title!
I am fire and air; my other elements
I give to baser life.—So,—have you done?
Come then, and take the last warmth of my lips.
Farewell, kind Charmian;—Iras, long farewell.
Have I the aspic in my lips? Dost fall?
If thou and nature can so gently part,
The stroke of death is as a lover's pinch,
Which hurts, and is desired. Dost thou lie still?
If thus thou vanishest, thou tell'st the world
It is not worth leave-taking.

CHARMIAN

Dissolve, thick cloud, and rain; that I may say
The gods themselves do weep!

CLEOPATRA

                    This proves me base:
If she first meet the curled Antony,
He'll make demand of her, and spend that kiss
Which is my heaven to have.—Come, thou mortal
        wretch,
With thy sharp teeth this knot intrinsicate
Of life at once untie: poor venomous fool,
Be angry, and dispatch. O, couldst thou speak,
That I might hear thee call great Cæsar ass
Unpolicied!

CHARMIAN

O eastern star!

CLEOPATRA
        Peace, peace!
Dost thou not see my baby at my breast,
That sucks the nurse asleep?

CHARMIAN
        O break! O, break!

CLEOPATRA
As sweet as balm, as soft as air, as gentle,—
O Antony!—Nay, I will take thee too:—
What should I stay—

CHARMIAN
In this vile world?—So, fare thee well.—
Now boast thee, death, in thy possession lies
A lass unparallel'd.—Downy windows, close;
And golden Phœbus never be beheld
Of eyes again so royal!—Your crown's awry;
I'll mend it, and then play.

FIRST GUARD
Where is the queen?

CHARMIAN
      Speak softly, wake her not.

FIRST GUARD
Cæsar hath sent—

CHARMIAN
      Too slow a messenger.
O come apace, dispatch: I partly feel thee.

FIRST GUARD
What work is here! Charmian, is this well done?

CHARMIAN
It is well done, and fitting for a princess
Descended of so many royal kings.

      She looks like sleep,
As she would catch another Antony
In her strong toil of grace.

613   Alas, poor Yorick!—I knew him, Horatio: a
fellow of infinite jest, of most excellent fancy: he hath
borne me on his back a thousand times; and now,
how abhorred in my imagination it is! my gorge rises
at it. Here hung those lips that I have kist I know
not how oft. Where be your gibes now? your
gambols? your songs? your flashes of merriment, that
were wont to set the table on a roar? Not one now,
to mock your own grinning? quite chop-faln? Now
get you to my lady's chamber, and tell her, let her
paint an inch thick, to this favour she must come
make her laugh at that.

614   Soft you; a word or two before you go.
I have done the state some service, and they know't;
No more of that.—I pray you, in your letters,
When you shall these unlucky deeds relate,
Speak of me as I am; nothing extenuate,
Nor set down aught in malice; then must you speak
Of one that loved not wisely, but too well;
Of one not easily jealous, but, being wrought,
Perplext in the extreme; of one whose hand,
Like the base Indian, threw a pearl away
Richer than all his tribe; of one whose subdued eyes,
Albeit unused to the melting mood,
Drop tears as fast as the Arabian trees
Their medicinable gum. Set you down this;
And say besides, that in Aleppo once,
Where a malignant and a turban'd Turk
Beat a Venetian and traduced the state,
I took by th'throat the circumcised dog,
And smote him—thus.

615   I do not set my life at a pin's fee;
And for my soul, what can it do to that,
Being a thing immortal as itself?

616   How oft when men are at the point of death
Have they been merry? which their keepers call
A lightning before death: O, how may I
Call this a lightning? O my love! my wife!
Death, that hath suckt the honey of thy breath,
Hath had no power yet upon thy beauty:
Thou art not conquer'd; beauty's ensign yet
Is crimson in thy lips and in thy cheeks,
And death's pale flag is not advanced there.
Tybalt, liest thou there in thy bloody sheet?
O, what more favour can I do to thee,
Than with that hand that cut thy youth in twain
To sunder his that was thine enemy?
Forgive me, cousin!—Ah, dear Juliet,
Why art thou yet so fair? shall I believe
That unsubstantial Death is amorous;
And that the lean abhorred monster keeps
Thee here in dark to be his paramour?
For fear of that, I still will stay with thee;
And never from this palace of dim night
Depart again: here, here will I remain
With worms that are thy chamber-maids; O, here
Will I set up my everlasting rest;
And shake the yoke of inauspicious stars
From this world-wearied flesh.—Eyes, look your last!
Arms, take your last embrace! and, lips, O you
The doors of breath, seal with a righteous kiss
A dateless bargain to engrossing death!—
Come, bitter conduct, come, unsavoury guide!
Thou desperate pilot, now at once run on
The dashing rocks thy sea-sick weary bark!
Here's to my love!—O true apothecary!
Thy drugs are quick.—Thus with a kiss I die.

617   O, our lives' sweetness!
That we the pain of death would hourly die
Rather than die at once!

618 Look, who comes here! a grave unto a soul;
Holding th'eternal spirit, against her will,
In the vile prison of afflicted breath.

619
ABHORSON

Sirrah, bring Barnardine hither.

POMPEY

Master Barnardine! you must rise and be hang'd,
Master Barnardine!

ABHORSON

What, ho, Barnardine!

BARNARDINE

A pox o' your throats! Who makes that noise there?
Who are you?

POMPEY

Your friends, sir; the hangman. You must be so
good, sir, to rise and be put to death.

BARNARDINE

Away, you rogue, away! I am sleepy.

ABHORSON

Tell him he must awake, and that quickly too.

POMPEY

Pray, Master Barnardine, awake till you are executed, and sleep afterwards.

ABHORSON

Go in to him, and fetch him out.

POMPEY

He is coming, sir, he is coming; I hear his straw rustle.

ABHORSON

Is the axe upon the block, sirrah?

POMPEY

Very ready, sir.

LAERTES

O heat, dry up my brains! tears seven-times salt,
Burn out the sense and virtue of mine eye!—
By heaven, thy madness shall be paid by weight,
Till our scale turn the beam. O rose of May!
Dear maid, kind sister, sweet Ophelia!—
O heavens! is't possible a young maid's wits
Should be as mortal as an old man's life?
Nature is fine in love; and, where 'tis fine,
It sends some precious instance of itself
After the thing it loves.

OPHELIA

They bore him barefaced on the bier;
Hey non nonny, nonny, hey nonny;
And in his grave rain'd many a tear,—
Fare you well, my dove!

LAERTES

Hadst thou thy wits, and didst persuade revenge,
It could not move thus.

OPHELIA

There's rosemary, that's for remembrance; pray
you, love, remember: and there is pansies, that's for
thoughts.

LAERTES

A document in madness,—thoughts and remembrance fitted.

OPHELIA

There's fennel for you, and columbines:—there's
rue for you; and here's some for me:—we may call
it herb-grace o' Sundays:—O, you must wear your
rue with a difference.—There's a daisy:—I would
give you some violets, but they wither'd all when my
father died:—they say he made a good end,—
For bonny sweet Robin is all my joy,—

LAERTES

Thought and affliction, passion, hell itself,
She turns to favour and to prettiness.

BARNARDINE

How now, Abhorson! what's the news with you?

ABHORSON

Truly, sir, I would desire you to clap into your prayers; for, look you, the warrant's come.

BARNARDINE

You rogue, I have been drinking all night; I am not fitted for't.

POMPEY

O, the better, sir; for he that drinks all night, and is hang'd betimes in the morning, may sleep the sounder all the next day.

ABHORSON

Look you, sir; here comes your ghostly father: do we jest now, think you?

DUKE

Sir, induced by my charity, and hearing how hastily you are to depart, I am come to advise you, comfort you, and pray with you.

BARNARDINE

Friar, not I: I have been drinking hard all night, and I will have more time to prepare me, or they shall beat out my brains with billets: I will not consent to die this day, that's certain

DUKE

O, sir, you must: and therefore I beseech you
Look forward on the journey you shall go.

BARNARDINE

I swear I will not die to-day for any man's persuasion.

DUKE

But hear you,—

BARNARDINE

Not a word: if you have anything to say to me, come to my ward; from thence will not I to-day.

OPHELIA

And will a' not come again?
And will a' not come again?
　No, no, he is dead:
　Go to thy death-bed:
He never will come again.

His beard was as white as snow,
All flaxen was his poll:
　He is gone, he is gone,
　And we cast away moan:
God ha' mercy on his soul!
And of all Christian souls, I pray God.—God be wi'
you.

LAERTES

Do you see this, O God?

621　There is a willow grows aslant a brook,
That shows his hoar leaves in the glassy stream;
There with fantastic garlands did she come
Of crow-flowers, nettles, daisies, and long purples
That liberal shepherds give a grosser name,
But our cold maids do dead men's fingers call them:
There, on the pendent boughs her coronet weeds
Clambering to hang, an envious sliver broke;
When down her weedy trophies and herself
Fell in the weeping brook. Her clothes spread wide,
And, mermaid-like, awhile they bore her up;
Which time she chanted snatches of old tunes,
As one incapable of her own distress,
Or like a creature native and indued
Unto that element: but long it could not be
Till that her garments, heavy with their drink,
Pull'd the poor wretch from her melodious lay
To muddy death.

622   Lay her i'th'earth;—
And from her fair and unpolluted flesh
May violets spring!—I tell thee, churlish priest,
A ministering angel shall my sister be,
When thou liest howling.

623   With fairest flowers,
Whilst summer lasts, and I live here, Fidele,
I'll sweeten thy sad grave: thou shalt not lack
The flower that's like thy face, pale primrose; nor
The azured harebell, like thy veins; no, nor
The leaf of eglantine, whom not to slander,
Out-sweeten'd not thy breath: the ruddock would,
With charitable bill,—O bill, sore-shaming
Those rich-left heirs that let their fathers lie
Without a monument!—bring thee all this;
Yea, and furr'd moss besides, when flowers are none,
To winter-ground thy corse.

624   Death lies on her like an untimely frost
Upon the sweetest flower of all the field.

625   If thou didst ever hold me in thy heart,
Absent thee from felicity awhile,
And in this harsh world draw thy breath in pain,
To tell my story.

626   Come not to me again: but say to Athens,
Timon hath made his everlasting mansion
Upon the beached verge of the salt flood;
Who once a day with his embossed froth
The turbulent surge shall cover.

627   Death, death:—O amiable lovely death!
Thou odoriferous stench! sound rottenness!
Arise forth from the couch of lasting night,
Thou hate and terror to prosperity,
And I will kiss thy detestable bones;
And put my eyeballs in thy vaulty brows;
And ring these fingers with thy household worms;
And stop this gap of breath with fulsome dust;
And be a carrion monster like thyself:
Come, grin on me; and I will think thou smilest,
And buss thee as thy wife! Misery's love,
O, come to me!

628   Howl, howl, howl, howl!—O, you are men of stone:
Had I your tongues and eyes, I'ld use them so
That heaven's vault should crack.—She's gone for
    ever!—
I know when one is dead, and when one lives;
She's dead as earth.—Lend me a looking-glass;
If that her breath will mist or stain the stone,
Why, then she lives.
This feather stirs; she lives! if it be so,
It is a chance which does redeem all sorrows
That ever I have felt.

629   O, the charity of a penny cord! it sums up
thousands in a trice: you have no true debitor and
creditor but it; of what's past, is, and to come, the
discharge:—your neck, sir, is pen, book, and counters;
so the acquittance follows.

630   Like as the waves make towards the pebbled shore,
So do our minutes hasten to their end;
Each changing place with that which goes before,

In sequent toil all forwards do contend.
Nativity, once in the main of light,
Crawls to maturity, wherewith being crown'd,
Crooked eclipses 'gainst his glory fight,
And Time that gave doth now his gift confound.
Time doth transfix the flourish set on youth,
And delves the parallels in beauty's brow;
Feeds on the rarities of nature's truth,
And nothing stands but for his scythe to mow:
 And yet, to times in hope my verse shall stand,
 Praising thy worth, despite his cruel hand.

631 That time of year thou mayst in me behold
When yellow leaves, or none, or few, do hang
Upon those boughs which shake against the cold,
Bare ruin'd choirs, where late the sweet birds sang.
In me thou see'st the twilight of such day
As after sunset fadeth in the west;
Which by and by black night doth take away,
Death's second self, that seals up all in rest.
In me thou see'st the glowing of such fire,
That on the ashes of his youth doth lie,
As the death-bed whereon it must expire,
Consumed with that which it was nourisht by.
 This thou perceivest, which makes thy love more
  strong,
 To love that well which thou must leave ere long.

632 Let's take the instant by the forward top;
For we are old, and on our quick'st decrees
Th'inaudible and noiseless foot of Time
Steals ere we can effect them.

633

LORD CHIEF JUSTICE

Do you set down your name in the scroll of youth, that
are written down old with all the characters of age?
Have you not a moist eye? a dry hand? a yellow
cheek? a white beard? a decreasing leg? an increasing
belly? is not your voice broken? your wind short?
your chin double? your wit single? and every part
about you blasted with antiquity? and will you yet
call yourself young? Fie, fie, fie, Sir John!

FALSTAFF

My lord, I was born about three of the clock in the
afternoon, with a white head and something a round
belly. For my voice,—I have lost it with hallooing,
and singing of anthems. To approve my youth
further, I will not: the truth is, I am only old in
judgement and understanding; and he that will
caper with me for a thousand marks, let him lend me
the money, and have at him.

634

Slanders, sir: for the satirical rogue says here, that
old men have gray beards; that their faces are
wrinkled; their eyes purging thick amber and plum-
tree gum; and that they have a plentiful lack of wit,
together with most weak hams: all which, sir,
though I most powerfully and potently believe, yet I
hold it not honesty to have it thus set down; for
yourself, sir, shall grow old as I am, if, like a crab,
you could go backward.

635

These old fellows
Have their ingratitude in them hereditary:
Their blood is caked, 'tis cold, it seldom flows;
'Tis lack of kindly warmth they are not kind;
And nature, as it grows again toward earth,
Is fashion'd for the journey, dull and heavy.

636
> Let me play the fool:
> With mirth and laughter let old wrinkles come;
> And let my liver rather heat with wine
> Than my heart cool with mortifying groans.
> Why should a man, whose blood is warm within,
> Sit like his grandsire cut in alabaster?
> Sleep when he wakes? and creep into the jaundice
> By being peevish? I tell thee what, Antonio,—
> I love thee, and it is my love that speaks,—
> There are a sort of men, whose visages
> Do cream and mantle like a standing pond;
> And do a wilful stillness entertain,
> With purpose to be drest in an opinion
> Of wisdom, gravity, profound conceit;
> As who should say, 'I am Sir Oracle,
> And when I ope my lips, let no dog bark!'

637
> I know thee not, old man: fall to thy prayers;
> How ill white hairs become a fool and jester!
> I have long dream'd of such a kind of man,
> So surfeit-swell'd, so old, and so profane;
> But, being awaked, I do despise my dream.

638
> KING OF FRANCE
> I would I had that corporal soundness now
> As when thy father and myself in friendship
> First tried our soldiership! He did look far
> Into the service of the time, and was
> Discipled of the bravest: he lasted long;
> But on us both did haggish age steal on,
> And wore us out of act. It much repairs me
> To talk of your good father. In his youth
> He had the wit, which I can well observe
> To-day in our young lords; but they may jest,

Till their own scorn return to them unnoted,
Ere they can hide their levity in honour
So like a courtier: contempt nor bitterness
Were in his pride, or sharpness; if they were,
His equal had awaked them; and his honour,
Clock to itself, knew the true minute when
Exception bid him speak, and at this time
His tongue obey'd his hand: who were below him
He used as creatures of another place;
And bow'd his eminent top to their low ranks,
Making them proud of his humility,
In their poor praise he humbled. Such a man
Might be a copy to these younger times;
Which, follow'd well, would demonstrate them now
But goers backward.

HELENA

His good remembrance, sir,
Lies richer in your thoughts than on his tomb;
So in approof lives not his epitaph
As in your royal speech.

KING OF FRANCE

Would I were with him! He would always say,—
Methinks I hear him now; his plausive words
He scatter'd not in ears, but grafted them,
To grow there, and to bear,—'Let me not live,'—
Thus his good melancholy oft began,
On the catastrophe and heel of pastime,
When it was out,—'Let me not live,' quoth he,
'After my flame lacks oil, to be the snuff
Of younger spirits, whose apprehensive senses
All but new things disdain; whose judgements are
Mere fathers of their garments; whose constancies
Expire before their fashions:'—this he wisht:
I, after him, do after him wish too,
Since I nor wax nor honey can bring home,
I quickly were dissolved from my hive,
To give some labourer room.

639   You see me here, you gods, a poor old man,
As full of grief as age; wretched in both!
If it be you that stir these daughters' hearts
Against their father, fool me not so much
To bear it tamely; touch me with noble anger,
And let not women's weapons, water-drops,
Stain my man's cheeks!—No, you unnatural hags,
I will have such revenges on you both,
That all the world shall—I will do such things,—
What they are, yet I know not; but they shall be
The terrors of the earth. You think I'll weep;
No, I'll not weep:—
I have full cause of weeping; but this heart
Shall break into a hundred thousand flaws,
Or e'er I'll weep.—O fool, I shall go mad!

640   I have seen the day
That I have worn a visor; and could tell
A whispering tale in a fair lady's ear,
Such as would please; 'tis gone, 'tis gone, 'tis gone.

641   I have seen the day
That with this little arm and this good sword,
I have made my way through more impediments
Than twenty times your stop:—but, O vain boast!
Who can control his fate? 'tis not so now.

642   Tell him of Nestor, one that was a man
When Hector's grandsire suckt: he is old now;
But if there be not in our Grecian host
One noble man that hath one spark of fire,

To answer for his love, tell him from me,—
I'll hide my silver beard in a gold beaver,
And in my vantbrace put this wither'd brawn;
And, meeting him, will tell him that my lady
Was fairer than his grandam, and as chaste
As may be in the world; his youth in flood,
I'll prove this truth with my three drops of blood.

643   I have seen the day, with my good biting falchion
I would have made them skip: I am old now,
And these same crosses spoil me.

644

SHALLOW

I was once of Clement's-inn, where I think they
will talk of mad Shallow yet.

SILENCE

You were call'd 'lusty Shallow' then, cousin.

SHALLOW

By the mass, I was call'd any thing; and I would have
done any thing indeed too, and roundly too. There
was I, and little John Doit of Staffordshire, and black
George Barnes, and Francis Pickbone, and Will
Squele a Cotsall man,—you had not four such
swinge-bucklers in all the inns o' court again: and, I
may say to you, we knew where the bona-robas were,
and had the best of them all at commandment.
Then was Jack Falstaff, now Sir John, a boy, and
page to Thomas Mowbray, duke of Norfolk.

SILENCE

This Sir John, cousin, that comes hither anon about
soldiers?

SHALLOW

The same Sir John, the very same. I see him break
Skogan's head at the court-gate, when a' was a crack

not thus high: and the very same day did I fight with one Sampson Stockfish, a fruiterer, behind Gray's-inn. Jesu, Jesu, the mad days that I have spent! and to see how many of my old acquaintance are dead!

SILENCE

We shall all follow, cousin.

SHALLOW

Certain, 'tis certain; very sure, very sure: death, as the Psalmist saith, is certain to all; all shall die — How a good yoke of bullocks at Stamford fair?

SILENCE

Truly, cousin, I was not there.

SHALLOW

Death is certain.—Is old Double of your town living yet?

SILENCE

Dead, sir.

SHALLOW

Jesu, Jesu, dead!—a' drew a good bow;—and dead!—a' shot a fine shoot:—John o' Gaunt loved him well, and betted much money on his head. Dead!—a' would have clapt i' th' clout at twelve score; and carried you a forehand shaft a fourteen and fourteen and a half, that it would have done a man's heart good to see.—How a score of ewes now?

SILENCE

Thereafter as they be: a score of good ewes may be worth ten pounds.

SHALLOW

And is old Double dead?

645 A good old man, sir; he will be talking: as they say, When the age is in, the wit is out: God help us! it is a world to see!—Well said, i'faith, neighbour Verges:—well, God's a good man; an two men ride of a horse, one must ride behind.—An honest soul, i'faith, sir; by my troth, he is, as ever broke bread: but God is to be worshipt: all men are not alike,—alas, good neighbour!

646

SHALLOW

O, Sir John, do you remember since we lay all night in the windmill in Saint George's field?

FALSTAFF

No more of that, good Master Shallow, no more of that.

SHALLOW

Ha, 'twas a merry night. And is Jane Nightwork alive?

FALSTAFF

She lives, Master Shallow.

SHALLOW

She never could away with me.

FALSTAFF

Never, never; she would always say she could not abide Master Shallow.

SHALLOW

By the mass, I could anger her to the heart. She was then a bona-roba. Doth she hold her own well?

FALSTAFF

Old, old, Master Shallow.

SHALLOW

Nay, she must be old; she cannot choose but be old; certain she's old; and had Robin Nightwork by old Nightwork before I came to Clement's-inn.

SILENCE

That's fifty-five year ago.

SHALLOW

Ha, cousin Silence, that thou hadst seen that that this knight and I have seen!—Ha, Sir John, said I vell?

FALSTAFF

We have heard the chimes at midnight, Master
Shallow.

SHALLOW

That we have, that we have, that we have; in faith,
Sir John, we have: our watch-word was, 'Hem, boys!'
—Come, let's to dinner; come, let's to dinner:—
Jesus, the days that we have seen!—come, come.

647   O God! that one might read the book of fate,
And see the revolution of the times
Make mountains level, and the continent,
Weary of solid firmness, melt itself
Into the sea! and, other times, to see
The beachy girdle of the ocean
Too wide for Neptune's hips; how chances mock,
And changes fill the cup of alteration
With divers liquors! O, if this were seen,
The happiest youth,—viewing his progress through,
What perils past, what crosses to ensue,—
Would shut the book, and sit him down and die.

648   What's past and what's to come is strew'd with husks
And formless ruin of oblivion.

649   PISTOL
Bardolph, a soldier, firm and sound of heart,
And of buxom valour, hath, by cruel fate,
And giddy Fortune's furious fickle wheel,—
That goddess blind,
That stands upon the rolling restless stone,—

BLIND FORTUNE

FLUELLEN

By your patience, Auncient Pistol. Fortune is painted plind, with a muffler afore her eyes, to signify to you that Fortune is plind; and she is painted also with a wheel, to signify to you, which is the moral of it, that she is turning, and inconstant, and mutability, and variation: and her foot, look you, is fixt upon a spherical stone, which rolls, and rolls, and rolls:—in good truth, the poet makes a most excellent description of it: Fortune is an excellent moral.

650   Out, out, thou strumpet, Fortune! All you gods,
In general synod, take away her power;
Break all the spokes and fellies from her wheel,
And bowl the round nave down the hill of heaven,
As low as to the fiends!

651   When I do count the clock that tells the time,
And see the brave day sunk in hideous night;
When I behold the violet past prime,
And sable curls all silver'd o'er with white;
When lofty trees I see barren of leaves,
Which erst from heat did canopy the herd,
And summer's green, all girded up in sheaves,
Borne on the bier with white and bristly beard;
Then of thy beauty do I question make,
That thou among the wastes of time must go,
Since sweets and beauties do themselves forsake,
And die as fast as they see others grow;
    And nothing 'gainst Time's scythe can make defence
    Save breed, to brave him when he takes thee hence.

652 When I have seen by Time's fell hand defaced
The rich proud cost of outworn buried age;
When sometime lofty towers I see down-razed,
And brass eternal slave to mortal rage;
When I have seen the hungry ocean gain
Advantage on the kingdom of the shore,
And the firm soil win of the watery main,
Increasing store with loss, and loss with store;
When I have seen such interchange of state,
Or state itself confounded to decay;
Ruin hath taught me thus to ruminate,—
That Time will come and take my love away.
 This thought is as a death, which cannot choose
 But weep to have that which it fears to lose.

653 When I consider every thing that grows
Holds in perfection but a little moment,
That this huge stage presenteth naught but shows
Whereon the stars in secret influence comment;
When I perceive that men as plants increase,
Cheered and checkt even by the self-same sky,
Vaunt in their youthful sap, at height decrease,
And wear their brave state out of memory;
Then the conceit of this inconstant stay
Sets you most rich in youth before my sight,
Where wasteful Time debateth with Decay,
To change your day of youth to sullied night;
 And, all in war with Time, for love of you,
 As he takes from you, I engraft you new.

654 There is a tide in the affairs of men,
Which, taken at the flood, leads on to fortune;
Omitted, all the voyage of their life
Is bound in shallows and in miseries.

On such a full sea are we now afloat;
And we must take the current when it serves,
Or lose our ventures.

655   There is a history in all men's lives,
Figuring the nature of the times deceased;
The which observed, a man may prophesy,
With a near aim, of the main chance of things
As yet not come to life, which in their seeds
And weak beginnings lie intreasured.
Such things become the hatch and brood of time.

656   A fool, a fool! I met a fool i'th'forest,
A motley fool; a miserable world!
As I do live by food, I met a fool;
Who laid him down and baskt him in the sun,
And rail'd on Lady Fortune in good terms,
In good set terms, and yet a motley fool.
'Good morrow, fool,' quoth I. 'No, sir,' quoth he,
'Call me not fool till heaven hath sent me fortune:'
And then he drew a dial from his poke,
And, looking on it with lack-lustre eye,
Says very wisely, 'It is ten o'clock:
Thus we may see,' quoth he, 'how the world wags:
'Tis but an hour ago since it was nine,
And after one hour more 'twill be eleven;
And so, from hour to hour, we ripe and ripe,
And then, from hour to hour, we rot and rot;
And thereby hangs a tale.' When I did hear
The motley fool thus moral on the time,
My lungs began to crow like chanticleer,
That fools should be so deep-contemplative;
And I did laugh sans intermission
An hour by his dial. O noble fool!
A worthy fool! Motley's the only wear.

657
              O that I were a fool!
I am ambitious for a motley coat.
                I must have liberty
Withal, as large a charter as the wind,
To blow on whom I please; for so fools have:
And they that are most galled with my folly,
They most must laugh.
Invest me in my motley; give me leave
To speak my mind, and I will through and through
Cleanse the foul body of th'infected world,
If they will patiently receive my medicine.

658
             'Tis a knavish piece of work: but what
o'that? your majesty, and we that have free souls, it
touches us not: let the gall'd jade wince, our withers
are unwrung.

659
Time hath, my lord, a wallet at his back,
Wherein he puts alms for oblivion,
A great-sized monster of ingratitudes:
Those scraps are good deeds past; which are devour'd
As fast as they are made, forgot as soon
As done: perseverance, dear my lord,
Keeps honour bright: to have done, is to hang
Quite out of fashion, like a rusty mail
In monumental mockery. Take the instant way;
For honour travels in a strait so narrow,
Where one but goes abreast: keep, then, the path;
For emulation hath a thousand sons,
That one by one pursue: if you give way,
Or hedge aside from the direct forthright,
Like to an enter'd tide, they all rush by,
And leave you hindmost;

Or, like a gallant horse faln in first rank,
Lie there for pavement to the abject rear,
O'er-run and trampled on: then what they do in
    present,
Though less than yours in past, must o'ertop yours;
For time is like a fashionable host,
That slightly shakes his parting guest by th'hand,
And with his arms outstretcht, as he would fly,
Grasps-in the comer: welcome ever smiles,
And farewell goes out sighing. O, let not virtue seek
Remuneration for the thing it was;
For beauty, wit,
High birth, vigour of bone, desert in service,
Love, friendship, charity, are subjects all
To envious and calumniating time.
One touch of nature makes the whole world kin,—
That all, with one consent, praise new-born gawds,
Though they are made and moulded of things past,
And give to dust, that is a little gilt,
More laud than gilt o'er-dusted.
The present eye praises the present object.

660   Devouring Time, blunt thou the lion's paws,
And make the earth devour her own sweet brood;
Pluck the keen teeth from the fierce tiger's jaws,
And burn the long-lived phœnix in her blood;
Make glad and sorry seasons as thou fleets,
And do whate'er thou wilt, swift-footed Time,
To the wide world and all her fading sweets;
But I forbid thee one most heinous crime:
O, carve not with thy hours my love's fair brow,
Nor draw no lines there with thine antique pen;
Him in thy course untainted do allow
For beauty's pattern to succeeding men.
    Yet, do thy worst, old Time: despite thy wrong,
    My love shall in my verse ever live young.

661   In the dark backward and abysm of time

662

ROSALIND

Time travels in divers paces with divers persons: I'll tell you who Time ambles withal, who Time trots withal, who Time gallops withal, and who he stands still withal.

ORLANDO

I prithee, who doth he trot witha.

ROSALIND

Marry, he trots hard with a young maid between the contract of her marriage and the day it is solemnized: if the interim be but a se'nnight, Time's pace is so hard that it seems the length of seven year.

ORLANDO

Who ambles Time withal?

ROSALIND

With a priest that lacks Latin, and a rich man that hath not the gout; for the one sleeps easily, because he cannot study; and the other lives merrily, because he feels no pain: the one lacking the burthen of lean and wasteful learning; the other knowing no burthen of heavy tedious penury: these Time ambles withal.

ORLANDO

Who doth he gallop withal?

ROSALIND

With a thief to the gallows; for though he go as softly as foot can fall, he thinks himself too soon there.

ORLANDO

Who stays it still withal?

ROSALIND

With lawyers in the vacation; for they sleep between term and term, and then they perceive not how Time moves.

663   Time's glory is to calm contending kings,
To unmask falsehood, and bring truth to light,
To stamp the seal of time in aged things,
To wake the morn, and sentinel the night,
To wrong the wronger till he render right,
    To ruinate proud buildings with thy hours,
    And smear with dust their glittering golden
      towers;

To fill with worm-holes stately monuments,
To feed oblivion with decay of things,
To blot old books and alter their contents,
To pluck the quills from ancient raven's wings,
To dry the old oak's sap, and cherish springs,
    To spoil antiquities of hammer'd steel,
    And turn the giddy round of Fortune's wheel;

To show the beldam daughters of her daughter,
To make the child a man, the man a child,
To slay the tiger that doth live by slaughter,
To tame the unicorn and lion wild,
To mock the subtle in themselves beguiled,
    To cheer the ploughman with increaseful crops,
    And waste huge stones with little water-drops.

664   Since brass, nor stone, nor earth, nor boundless sea,
But sad mortality o'ersways their power,
How with this rage shall beauty hold a plea,
Whose action is no stronger than a flower?
O, how shall summer's honey breath hold out
Against the wrackful siege of battering days,
When rocks impregnable are not so stout,
Nor gates of steel so strong, but Time decays?
O fearful meditation! where, alack,
Shall Time's best jewel from Time's chest lie hid?

Or what strong hand can hold his swift foot back?
Or who his spoil of beauty can forbid?
   O, none, unless this miracle have might,
   That in black ink my love may still shine bright.

665   Not marble, nor the gilded monuments
Of princes, shall outlive this powerful rime;
But you shall shine more bright in these contents
Than unswept stone, besmear'd with sluttish time.
When wasteful war shall statues overturn,
And broils root out the work of masonry,
Nor Mars his sword nor war's quick fire shall burn
The living record of your memory.
'Gainst death and all-oblivious enmity
Shall you pace forth; your praise shall still find room
Even in the eyes of all posterity
That wears this world out to the ending doom.
   So, till the judgement that yourself arise,
   You live in this, and dwell in lovers' eyes.

666   Nor stony tower, nor walls of beaten brass
Nor airless dungeon, nor strong links of iron,
Can be retentive to the strength of spirit;
But life, being weary of these worldly bars,
Never lacks power to dismiss itself.
So every bondman in his own hand bears
The power to cancel his captivity.

667   Nay then, farewell.
I have toucht the highest point of all my greatness
And, from that full meridian of my glory,
I haste now to my setting: I shall fall
Like a bright exhalation in the evening,
And no man see me more.

668   Down, down I come; like glistering Phaëthon,
        Wanting the manage of unruly jades.

669   Farewell, a long farewell, to all my greatness!
        This is the state of man: to-day he puts forth
        The tender leaves of hope; to-morrow blossoms,
        And bears his blushing honours thick upon him;
        The third day comes a frost, a killing frost,
        And—when he thinks, good easy man, full surely
        His greatness is a-ripening—nips his root,
        And then he falls, as I do. I have ventured,
        Like little wanton boys that swim on bladders,
        This many summers in a sea of glory;
        But far beyond my depth: my high-blown pride
        At length broke under me; and now has left me,
        Weary and old with service, to the mercy
        Of a rude stream, that must for ever hide me.
        Vain pomp and glory of this world, I hate ye:
        I feel my heart new open'd. O, how wretched
        Is that poor man that hangs on princes' favours!
        There is, betwixt that smile we would aspire to,
        That sweet aspect of princes, and their ruin,
        More pangs and fears than wars or women have;
        And when he falls, he falls like Lucifer,
        Never to hope again.

670   The soul and body rive not more in parting
        Than greatness going off.

671   I see thy glory, like a shooting star,
        Fall to the base earth from the firmament!

672   Poor painted queen, vain flourish of my fortune!
Why strew'st thou sugar on that bottled spider,
Whose deadly web ensnareth thee about?

673   I call'd thee then vain flourish of my fortune;
I call'd thee then poor shadow, painted queen;
The presentation of but what I was;
The flattering index of a direful pageant;
One heaved a-high, to be hurl'd down below;
A mother only mockt with two sweet babes;
A dream of what thou wast; a breath, a bubble;
A sign of dignity, a garish flag
To be the aim of every dangerous shot;
A queen in jest, only to fill the scene.

674   O sun, thy uprise shall I see no more:
Fortune and Antony part here; even here
Do we shake hands.—All come to this?—The hearts
That spaniel'd me at heels, to whom I gave
Their wishes, do discandy, melt their sweets
On blossoming Cæsar; and this pine is barkt,
That overtopt them all.

675   MARK ANTONY
Eros, thou yet behold'st me?
                  EROS
                  Ay, noble lord.
             MARK ANTONY
Sometime we see a cloud that's dragonish;
A vapour sometime like a bear or lion,
A tower'd citadel, a pendant rock,

"WRIT IN WATER"

A forked mountain, or blue promontory
With trees upon't, that nod unto the world,
And mock our eyes with air: thou hast seen these
    signs;
They are black vesper's pageants.

EROS
Ay, my lord.

MARK ANTONY
That which is now a horse, even with a thought
The rack dislimns, and makes it indistinct
As water is in water.

EROS
It does, my lord.

MARK ANTONY
My good knave Eros, now thy captain is
Even such a body: here I am Antony;
Yet cannot hold this visible shape, my knave.
I made these wars for Egypt; and the queen,—
Whose heart I thought I had, for she had mine;
Which, whilst it was mine, had annext unto't
A million moe, now lost,—she, Eros, has
Packt cards with Cæsar, and false-play'd my glory
Unto an enemy's triumph.—
Nay, weep not, gentle Eros; there is left us
Ourselves to end ourselves.
Unarm, Eros; the long day's task is done,
And we must sleep.—
                        Off, pluck off:—
The seven-fold shield of Ajax cannot keep
The battery from my heart. O, cleave, my sides!
Heart, once be stronger than thy continent,
Crack thy frail case!—Apace, Eros, apace.—
No more a soldier:—bruised pieces, go;
You have been nobly borne.—From me awhile.
I will o'ertake thee, Cleopatra, and
Weep for my pardon. So it must be, for now

All length is torture:—since the torch is out,
Lie down, and stray no farther, now all labour
Mars what it does; yea, very force entangles
Itself with strength: seal then, and all is done.—
Eros!—I come, my queen.—Eros!—Stay for me:
Where souls do couch on flowers, we'll hand in hand,
And with our sprightly port make the ghosts gaze:
Dido and her Aeneas shall want troops,
And all the haunt be ours.

676   To me, fair friend, you never can be old,
For as you were when first your eye I eyed,
Such seems your beauty still. Three winters' cold
Have from the forests shook three summers' pride;
Three beauteous springs to yellow autumn turn'd
In process of the seasons have I seen,
Three April perfumes in three hot Junes burn'd,
Since first I saw you fresh, which yet are green.
Ah, yet doth beauty, like a dial-hand,
Steal from his figure, and no pace perceived;
So your sweet hue, which methinks still doth stand,
Hath motion, and mine eyes may be deceived:
    For fear of which, hear this, thou age unbred,—
    Ere you were born was beauty's summer dead.

677   Against my love shall be, as I am now,
With Time's injurious hand crusht and o'erworn;
When hours have drain'd his blood, and fill'd his brow
With lines and wrinkles; when his youthful morn
Hath travell'd on to age's steepy night;
And all those beauties whereof now he's king
Are vanishing or vanisht out of sight,
Stealing away the treasure of his spring;
For such a time do I now fortify

Against confounding age's cruel knife,
That he shall never cut from memory
My sweet love's beauty, though my lover's life:
    His beauty shall in these black lines be seen,
    And they shall live, and he in them still green.

678   CORDELIA
O my dear father! Restoration hang
Thy medicine on my lips; and let this kiss
Repair those violent harms that my two sisters
Have in thy reverence made!
                    EARL OF KENT
                        Kind and dear princess!
                    CORDELIA
Had you not been their father, these white flakes
Had challenged pity of them. Was this a face
To be opposed against the warring winds?
To stand against the deep dread-bolted thunder?
In the most terrible and nimble stroke
Of quick, cross lightning? to watch—poor perdu!—
With this thin helm? Mine enemy's dog,
Though he had bit me, should have stood that night
Against my fire; and wast thou fain, poor father,
To hovel thee with swine, and rogues forlorn,
In short and musty straw? Alack, alack!
'Tis wonder that thy life and wits at once
Had not concluded all.—He wakes; speak to him.
                    DOCTOR
Madam, do you: 'tis fittest.
                    CORDELIA
How does my royal lord? how fares your majesty?
                    KING LEAR
You do me wrong to take me out o'the grave:—
Thou art a soul in bliss; but I am bound
Upon a wheel of fire, that mine own tears
Do scald like molten lead.

CORDELIA
Sir, do you know me?

KING LEAR
You are a spirit, I know: when did you die?

CORDELIA
Still, still, far wide!

DOCTOR
He's scarce awake: let him alone awhile.

KING LEAR
Where have I been? Where am I?—Fair daylight?—
I am mightily abused.—I should e'en die with pity,
To see another thus.—I know not what to say.—
I will not swear these are my hands:—let's see;
I feel this pin prick. Would I were assured
Of my condition.

CORDELIA
O, look upon me, sir,
And hold your hands in benediction o'er me:—
No, sir, you must not kneel.

KING LEAR
Pray, do not mock me:
I am a very foolish fond old man,
Fourscore and upward, not an hour more nor less;
And, to deal plainly,
I fear I am not in my perfect mind.
Methinks I should know you, and know this man;
Yet I am doubtful: for I am mainly ignorant
What place this is; and all the skill I have
Remembers not these garments; nor I know not
Where I did lodge last night. Do not laugh at me;
For, as I am a man, I think this lady
To be my child Cordelia.

CORDELIA
And so I am, I am.

KING LEAR
Be your tears wet? yes, faith. I pray, weep not:
If you have poison for me, I will drink it

I know you do not love me; for your sisters
Have, as I do remember, done me wrong:
You have some cause, they have not.

CORDELIA

No cause, no cause.

KING LEAR

Am I in France?

EARL OF KENT

In your own kingdom, sir.

KING LEAR

Do not abuse me.

DOCTOR

Be comforted, good madam: the great rage,
You see, is kill'd in him: and yet it is danger
To make him even o'er the time he has lost.
Desire him to go in; trouble him no more
Till further settling.

CORDELIA

Will't please your highness walk?

KING LEAR

You must bear with me:
Pray you now, forget and forgive: I am old and
foolish.

679　Here is my journey's end, here is my butt,
And very sea-mark of my utmost sail.

680　　　　　BARDOLPH
Would I were with him, wheresome'er he is, either
in heaven or in hell!

HOSTESS

Nay, sure, he's not in hell: he's in Arthur's bosom,
if ever man went to Arthur's bosom. A' made a
finer end, and went away, an it had been any

christom child; a' parted ev'n just between twelve
and one, ev'n at the turning o' th' tide: for after I
saw him fumble with the sheets, and play with
flowers, and smile upon his fingers' ends, I knew
there was but one way; for his nose was as sharp as
a pen, and a' babbled of green fields. 'How now, Sir
John!' quoth I: 'what, man! be o' good cheer.' So
a' cried out 'God, God, God!' three or four times.
Now, I, to comfort him, bid him a' should not think
of God; I hoped there was no need to trouble himself
with any such thoughts yet. So a' bade me lay more
clothes on his feet: I put my hand into the bed and
felt them, and they were as cold as any stone; then
I felt to his knees, and they were as cold as any stone;
and so upward and upward, and all was as cold as
any stone.

681 And my poor fool is hang'd! No, no, no life!
Why should a dog, a horse, a rat, have life,
And thou no breath at all? Thou'lt come no more,
Never, never, never, never, never!—
Pray you, undo this button:—thank you, sir.—
Do you see this? Look on her,—look, her lips,—
Look there, look there!—

582 Ye elves of hills, brooks, standing lakes, and groves;
And ye that on the sands with printless foot
Do chase the ebbing Neptune, and do fly him
When he comes back; you demi-puppets that
By moonshine do the green sour ringlets make,
Whereof the ewe not bites; and you whose pastime

MAGIC ABJURED

Is to make midnight mushrumps, that rejoice
To hear the solemn curfew; by whose aid—
Weak masters though ye be—I have bedimm'd
The noontide sun, call'd forth the mutinous winds,
And 'twixt the green sea and the azured vault
Set roaring war: to the dread-rattling thunder
Have I given fire, and rifted Jove's stout oak
With his own bolt: the strong-based promontory
Have I made shake; and by the spurs pluck'd up
The pine and cedar: graves at my command
Have waked their sleepers, oped, and let 'em forth
By my so potent art. But this rough magic
I here abjure; and, when I have required
Some heavenly music,—which even now I do,—
To work mine end upon their senses that
This airy charm is for, I'll break my staff,
Bury it certain fadoms in the earth,
And deeper than did ever plummet sound
I'll drown my book.

683   Poor soul, the centre of my sinful earth—
My sinful earth these rebel powers array—
Why dost thou pine within and suffer dearth,
Painting thy outward walls so costly gay?
Why so large cost, having so short a lease,
Dost thou upon thy fading mansion spend?
Shall worms, inheritors of this excess,
Eat up thy charge? is this thy body's end?
Then, soul, live thou upon thy servant's loss,
And let that pine to aggravate thy store;
Buy terms divine in selling hours of dross;
Within be fed, without be rich no more:
    So shalt thou feed on Death, that feeds on men,
    And Death once dead there's no more dying then

684 Our revels now are ended. These our actors,
As I foretold you, were all spirits, and
Are melted into air, into thin air:
And, like the baseless fabric of this vision,
The cloud-capp'd towers, the gorgeous palaces,
The solemn temples, the great globe itself,
Yea, all which it inherit, shall dissolve,
And, like this insubstantial pageant faded,
Leave not a rack behind. We are such stuff
As dreams are made on; and our little life
Is rounded with a sleep.

685 A great while ago the world begun,
  With hey, ho, the wind and the rain:—
But that's all one, our play is done,
  And we'll strive to please you every day.

686 Fear no more the heat o'the sun,
  Nor the furious winter's rages;
Thou thy worldly task hast done,
  Home art gone, and ta'en thy wages:
Golden lads and girls all must,
As chimney-sweepers, come to dust.

Fear no more the frown o'the great,
  Thou art past the tyrant's stroke;
Care no more to clothe and eat;
  To thee the reed is as the oak:
The sceptre, learning, physic, must
All follow this, and come to dust.

Fear no more the lightning-flash,
  Nor the all-dreaded thunder-stone;
Fear not slander, censure rash;
  Thou hast finished joy and moan.
All lovers young, all lovers must
Consign to thee, and come to dust.

  No exorciser harm thee!
  Nor no witchcraft charm thee!
  Ghost unlaid forbear thee!
  Nothing ill come near thee!
  Quiet consummation have;
  And renowned be thy grave!

687   Good morrow, masters; put your torches out:
    The wolves have prey'd; and look, the gentle day,
  Before the wheels of Phœbus, round about
    Dapples the drowsy east with spots of grey,
  Thanks to you all, and leave us: fare you well.

ADDENDUM

At the eleventh hour the editor would add one more to the list of lovers:—

What say you to young Master Fenton? he capers, he dances, he has eyes of youth, he writes verses, he speaks holiday, he smells April and May: he will carry't, he will carry't; 'tis in his buttons; he will carry't.

The Merry Wives III. ii.

INDEX OF PLAYS AND POEMS

THE AGES OF MAN

GENERAL INDEX AND NOTES

1. *Pericles* III, i. Lychorida is delivered of the babe Marina in a storm at sea and is believed dead.
2. *The Winter's Tale* II, iii. Paulina shows the new-born Perdita to the jealous Leontes who orders its destruction.
3. *Sonnet* III.
4. *Pericles* III, i.
5. *Titus Andronicus* II, iii.
6. *Sonnet* CXLIII.
7. *King John* III, i.
8. *Sonnet* XVIII.
9. *The Winter's Tale*, I i.
10. *ibid.*
11. *ibid.* A *squash* is the unripe pod of a pea. To *take eggs for money* is a proverbial expression meaning: 'will you be gulled or bullied?'
12. *Julius Cæsar* II, i.
13. *Coriolanus* I, iii. Virgilia, 'my gracious silence,' who looks on war with the eyes of a wife and mother, speaks disparagingly of her young hopeful.
14. *Coriolanus* V, iii. Young Marcius braves his father.
15. *The Merry Wives of Windsor* IV, i. At the end of the Latin lesson the Welsh Parson praises little William's 'good sprag memory.'
16. *The Winter's Tale* II, i.
17. *ibid.* By 'crickets' Mamillius means the chatter of the ladies-in-waiting. Leontes enters to accuse and arrest the queen, and the boy's tale is never told. Grief at his mother's shame kills him.
18. *Cymbeline* IV, ii. Belarius speaks of the King's two sons whom he stole away in infancy.
19. *Cymbeline* V, v.
20. *King John* IV, i. The scene gains by curtailment since the pathos and simplicity of the little prince are later marred by ingenious conceits.
    'A quibble is to Shakespeare what luminous vapours are to the traveller: he follows it at all adventures; it is sure to lead him out of his way, and sure to engulf him in the mire.'—JOHNSON.
21. *Richard III* IV, iii. The Princes in the Tower.
22. *Richard III* IV, ii.
23. *King John* III, iv.
24. *King Lear* III, ii.

25. *Macbeth* IV, ii. The boy's retort 'Thou liest' is more dramatic in the context of the scene, since Lady Macduff has called her husband a traitor only a moment before. The scene is intended to leave us in doubt as to the honour of the Thane of Fife. Up till then Macduff is an uncertain quantity, a dark horse. In IV, iii he shows himself.
26. *King John* II, i. Compare the images in Nos. 2 and 3.
27. *Coriolanus* V, iii.
28. *Romeo and Juliet* I, iii.
29. *Love's Labour's Lost* V, ii.
30. *Twelfth Night* I, v.
31. *Twelfth Night* I, iv.
32. *The Merchant of Venice* III, iv. Portia, not, as one might guess, Rosalind, speaks.
33. *As You Like It* III, v. Phebe loses her heart to the disguised Rosalind.
34. *Cymbeline* III, iv. Imogen is the last of the heroines to put on 'the lovely garnish of a boy' and she is more a woman than her elder sisters.
35. *The Passionate Pilgrim* X. Whether Shakespeare is the author or no cannot be proved.
36. *Twelfth Night* II, iii.
37. *Romeo and Juliet* I, ii.
38. *Antony and Cleopatra* I, v.
39. *Sonnet* II.
40. *Hamlet* I, iii. An earlier example of the paternal manner is found in old Gaunt's dialogue with his son Bolingbroke. *Richard II* I, iii.
41. *All's Well That Ends Well* I, i
42. *A Midsummer Night's Dream* II, ii. Here we pass from childhood to the realm of faëry and the magical.
43. *The Tempest* III, ii.
44. *The Tempest* V, i.
45. *Romeo and Juliet* I, iv. Herrick is the other poet to celebrate the realm of Oberon and Mab with the delicacy and tenderness of Shakespeare and with the same collector's eye for the miniature.
46. *A Midsummer Night's Dream* II, i.
47. *A Midsummer Night's Dream* III, i. Titania entertains Bottom the weaver.
48. *A Midsummer Night's Dream* II, ii. Oberon accuses Titania of making Theseus break faith with Hippolita. She answers thus.
49. *Sonnet* V.
50. *A Midsummer Night's Dream* II, ii.
51. *Othello* III, iv.
52. *The Tempest* II, ii.
53. *ibid*

79. *Much Ado About Nothing* III, i.   The *Venus and Adonis* gives us:

> No fisher but the ungrown fry forbears.

80. *King Henry V* III, vii.
81. *Venus and Adonis.*
82. *Hamlet* IV, vii.
83. *The Taming of the Shrew* III, ii.   If enlightenment is needed, apply to an Irish groom.
84. *A Midsummer Night's Dream* IV, i.   There are the boar-hounds also in the *Venus and Adonis:*

> Another flap-mouth'd mourner, black and grim,
> Against the welkin volleys out his voice;
> Another and another answer him,
> > Clapping their proud tails to the ground below,
> > Shaking their scratch'd ears, bleeding as they go.

85. *The Taming of the Shrew:* Induction.
86. *Macbeth* III, i.
87. *Two Gentlemen of Verona* II, iii.   Crab's incorrigible manners and his master's devotion are further revealed in Launce's soliloquy which opens IV, iv: 'one that I brought up of a puppy; one that I saved from drowning, when three or four of his blind brothers and sisters went to it.'
88. *Venus and Adonis.*
89. *The Merchant of Venice* III, ii.   This pretty toy brings us to the lover:

> Sighing like furnace, with a woeful ballad
> Made to his mistress' eyebrow.

90. *Love's Labour's Lost* IV, iii.   Berowne enlists Navarre and his courtiers who had forsworn the society of woman as affection's men-at-arms.
91. *Venus and Adonis.* A gloss on lines 11 and 12 *supra.*
92. *Timon of Athens* I, i.
93. *A Midsummer Night's Dream* V, i.   Shakespeare's comments on his trade and art are fit but few. Note also the rebuke which Theseus delivers when Hippolyta yawns over the entertainment provided by the artisans:

> 'The best in this kind are but shadows; and the worst are no worse if imagination amend them.'

94. *As You Like It* III, iii.
95. *Sonnet* CVI.
96. 1 *King Henry IV* III,
97. *As You Like It* V, ii.

98. *A Midsummer Night's Dream* I, i. Compare the lightning image in 209.
99. *A Midsummer Night's Dream* V, i.
100. *Two Gentlemen of Verona* I. iii.
101. *As You Like It* II, iv. A *batlet* or batler was used for beating clothes in the wash. 'Peascods were regarded as lucky gifts by rural lovers.'—DOVER WILSON.
102. *The Merchant of Venice* II, ix.
103. *Two Gentlemen of Verona* II, iv.
104. *Romeo and Juliet* II, v.
105. *Romeo and Juliet* I, i. Benvolio and Montague describe the love-sick Romeo. 'Like a change from wood wind, brass and tympani to an *andante* on the strings,' after the rattle of the fight and Benvolio's brisk story of the quarrel.—GRANVILLE BARKER.
106. *Love's Labour's Lost* III, i. Berowne speaks. A *paritor* or apparitor is the officer of the bishop's court who carries out citations which were frequently issued for sexual incontinence.
107. *As You Like It* II, iv.
108. *Love's Labour's Lost* V, ii.
109. *As You Like It* III, ii.
110. *Much Ado About Nothing* III, ii. Other signs of Benedick's condition are that he rubs himself with civet and has had his beard shaved.
111. *Two Gentlemen of Verona* II, i.
112. *Hamlet* II, i.
113. *As You Like It* IV, i.
114. *Two Gentlemen of Verona* III, ii.
115. *Twelfth Night* I, v.
116. *Troilus and Cressida* I, i.
117. *The Winter's Tale* IV, iii.
118. *1 Henry IV* III, i. Edmund Mortimer is wedded to the daughter of Glendower, the superstitious Welshman, whom Hotspur finds worse than a smoky house.
119. *ibid.*
120. *Troilus and Cressida* III, i. After Pandarus's song Helen remarks: 'In love, i' faith, to the very tip of his nose.'
121. *Antony and Cleopatra* II, v.
122. *Twelfth Night* I, i. *Fancy* is the Elizabethan word for romantic love. Love, says Orsino, is the true faculty of imagination. Cp. 89 and 93.
123. *Twelfth Night* II, iv.
124. *The Merchant of Venice* V, i.
125. *A Midsummer Night's Dream* II, ii.
126. *Sonnet* CII.
127. *The Winter's Tale* IV, iii

128. *A Lover's Complaint.* It is a *man* who boasts of these amorous tributes to his charms.
129. *Hamlet* III, i.
130. *Much Ado About Nothing* II, iii.
131. *Twelfth Night* II, iii.
132. *Twelfth Night* I, v. Compare the argument of the first seventeen sonnets:

> Thou shouldst print more, nor let that copy die.

133. *Two Gentlemen of Verona* IV, ii.
134. *Sonnet* LIII.
135. *Sonnet* LXXVI.
136. *The Winter's Tale* IV, iii. There follow a handful of taffeta phrases and three-piled hyperboles which can be matched in many contemporary poets. Orlando's pretty answer (143) is a breath of fresh air.
137. *Romeo and Juliet* I, v.
138. *The Merchant of Venice* III, ii.
139. *Troilus and Cressida* I, i.
140. *Romeo and Juliet* II, vi. Ben Jonson has an attractive version of this:

> Her treading would not bend a blade of grass,
> Or shake the downy blow-ball from his stalk;
> But like the soft west wind she shot along.
> *The Sad Shepherd.*

141. *A Midsummer Night's Dream* I, i.
142. *Pericles* V, i.
143. *As You Like It* III, li.
144. *The Rape of Lucrece.*
145. *Venus and Adonis.*
146. *The Rape of Lucrece.*
147. *Cymbeline* II, ii.
148. *The Rape of Lucrece.*
149. *Coriolanus* V, iii. This fine flourish is presented rather surprisingly to the nonentity Valeria.

We may recall on leaving these rococo fancies that Lysander (Shakespeare perhaps) burlesques them a little:

> O Helen, goddess, nymph, perfect, divine!
> To what, my love, shall I compare thine eyne?
> Crystal is muddy. O how ripe in show
> Thy lips, those kissing cherries, tempting grow!
> That pure congealed white, high Taurus' snow,
> Fann'd with the eastern wind, turns to a crow
> When thou holdst up thy hand: O let me kiss
> This princess of pure white, this seal of bliss!

INDEX AND NOTES

189. *Venus and Adonis*.
190. *Coriolanus* V, iii.
191. *As You Like It* III, iv.
192. *Venus and Adonis*.
193. *Antony and Cleopatra* II, v.
194. *Troilus and Cressida* III, i.
195. *All's Well That Ends Well* IV, ii.
196. *1 Henry IV* II, iii. Lady Percy and Hotspur.
197. *Sonnet* CXVI. France in *King Lear* says:

> Love's not love
> When it is mingled with regards that stand
> Aloof from the entire point.

198. *As You Like It* III, v.
199. *Two Gentlemen of Verona* II, i.
200. *Love's Labour's Lost* V, ii.

> Our wooing doth not end like an old play;
> Jack hath not Jill.

201. *The Merchant of Venice* II, i. This preludes the wooing of
the Moor of Venice in 202.
202. *Othello* I, iii:

> Rude am I in my speech,
> And little bless'd with the soft phrase of peace;
> For since these arms of mine had seven years' pith
> Till now some nine moons wasted, they have us'd
> Their dearest action in the tented field;
> And little of this great world can I speak,
> More than pertains to feats of broil and battle,
> And therefore little shall I grace my cause
> In speaking for myself. Yet, by your gracious patience,
> I will a round unvarnish'd tale deliver
> Of my whole course of love.

This links the Moor as a soldier-lover with King Henry
in 203.

203. *Henry V*, V, ii.
204. *The Merchant of Venice* III, ii.
205. *Romeo and Juliet* III, ii. The simplicity of the close delights
us after the rhetorical opening in the Marlowe style.
206. *The Rape of Lucrece*.
207. *Cymbeline* II, iv.
208. *Troilus and Cressida* III, ii
209. *Romeo and Juliet* II, ii.
210. *The Merchant of Venice* III, ii. This links the last passage
with the next. It strikes a more vibrating note than most
of the play to which it belongs.

INDEX AND NOTES

211. *Troilus and Cressida* III, ii.
212. *Sonnet* CVII. This is a difficult and powerful sonnet. However, as Coleridge tells us, 'Poetry gives most pleasure when only generally and not perfectly understood.'
213. *Romeo and Juliet* V, i.
214. *Hamlet* II, i.
215. *Othello* II, i.
216. *Pericles* V, i. 'Journeys end in lovers' meeting,' but this reunion is of a father and long-lost daughter.
217. *As You Like It* IV, i.
218. *Troilus and Cressida* IV, iv.
219. *Romeo and Juliet* III, v.
220. *Sonnet* LXXXVII.
221. *Antony and Cleopatra* I, iii.
222. *Sonnet* XCVIII.
223. *Sonnet* XCIX.
224. *All's Well That Ends Well* I, i.
225. *Sonnet* LVIII.
226. *Sonnet* XCVII.
227. *Antony and Cleopatra* I, v.
228. *Sonnet* LVII.
229. *Sonnet* LXXI.
230. *Much Ado About Nothing* IV, i.
231. *All's Well That Ends Well* V, iii.
232. *As You Like It* IV, i.
233. *Troilus and Cressida* II, ii.
234. *1 Henry IV* II, iii.
235. *Julius Cæsar* II, i.
236. *Troilus and Cressida* III, iii.
237. *Hamlet* I, iii. Laertes cautions his sister in formal aphorisms. He is his father's son.
238. *Troilus and Cressida* II, ii.
239. *The Taming of the Shrew* V, ii. Kate the curst at Petruchio's command expounds what duty wives owe their lords and husbands. Even Mrs. Ellis of Victorian fame should be satisfied.
240. *The Comedy of Errors* II, ii. A touch of feeling and poetry which is rare if not unique in this skilful imitation of Roman comedy which H. B. Charlton explains as the young Shakespeare's 'recoil from romance.'

Dromio's account of the kitchen wench, all grease—'I warrant, her rags and the tallow in them, will burn a Poland winter,' and so forth—is vigorous, and his geographical anatomising of her reminds one of Donne's *Elegies*. Here and there we find a memorable line:

Ill deeds are doubled with an evil word.

241. *Othello* III, iii.
242. *Venus and Adonis.*
243. *Othello* III, iv.
244. *Othello* III, iii.
245. *The Winter's Tale* I, ii.
246. *ibid.*
247. *Venus and Adonis.*
248. *Othello* III, iii.
249. *Hamlet* III, i.
250. *The Winter's Tale* I, ii.
251. *All's Well That Ends Well* I, iii.   *By kind* means **by nature,** without instruction:

> As cuckoldes come by destinie, so cuckowes sing by kinde.
> —JOHN GRANGE's *Garden*, 1577.

The same idea is expressed by Othello:

> 'Tis destiny unshunnable, like death:
> Even then this forked plague is fated to us
> When we do quicken.

252. *Othello* IV, i.   It is Emilia also who pronounces the most downright and unsparing verdict on the male sex:

> 'Tis not a year or two shows us a man:
> They are all but stomachs, and we all but food:
> They eat us hungerly, and when they are full,
> They belch us.

253. *Much Ado About Nothing* II, iii.
254. 2 *Henry IV* II, i.   Falstaff's inspired refutation of this circumstantial tale consists in remarking to the Lord Chief Justice:

> My lord, this is a poor mad soul; and she says, up and down the town, that her eldest son is like you.

255. *A Lover's Complaint.*
256. *Othello* III, iii.
257. *Cymbeline* III, iv.
258. *Othello* IV, ii.
259. *Measure for Measure* IV, i.
260. *Troilus and Cressida* IV, v.   The man of the world and cynic Ulysses, at once sees through the coquetry of Cressida.
261. *Troilus and Cressida* II, ii.   In this and the three following pieces Helen of Troy is the subject.
262 *Troilus and Cressida* IV, i.

263. *Troilus and Cressida* II, ii.
264. *The Rape of Lucrece.* Lucrece is perusing a crowded and elaborate painting of the siege of Troy. The protracted description of it suggests that Shakespeare had a particular picture or tapestry in mind. The account of Sinon anticipates the creation of Iago:

> . . . like a constant and confirmed devil
> He entertained a show so seeming just,
> And therein so ensconc'd his secret evil,
> That jealousy itself could not mistrust . . .

265. *Troilus and Cressida* V, ii.
266. *Sonnet* CXLVII.
267. *Julius Cæsar* II, iv.
268. *Sonnets to Sundry Notes of Music.* This is probably by another hand, but its inclusion here is venial.
269. *Sonnet* CXXXVIII.
270. *Othello* V, ii. What *is* "the cause"? One actor looked in Desdemona's hand-mirror at his black complexion. The explanation of the speech lies in the sixth line: as Troilus puts it, 'Let it not be believed for womanhood.' Othello is no longer in the mood of revenge and animal passion of 'I'll tear her to pieces.' He is the high priest and she a sacrifice upon the altar of chastity. Some say that "the cause" is the fact that she is impure; others that he speaks of her fatal beauty which betrays man.
271. *Hamlet* I, ii.
272. *Hamlet* III, iv.
273. *Troilus and Cressida* III, ii. The thoughts of Troilus are beyond Romeo's range.
274. *Venus and Adonis.*
275. *All's Well That Ends Well* I, iii.
276. *Sonnet* CXXIX.
277. *The Rape of Lucrece.* Desire is powerfully imagined in the person of Tarquin at the bedside.

> His veins swell in their pride, the onset still expecting;
> Anon his beating heart, alarum striking,
> Gives the hot charge, and bids them do their liking.
> His drumming heart cheers up his burning eye,
> His eye commends the leading to his hand;
> His hand, as proud of such a dignity,
> Smoking with pride, march'd on to make his stand
> On her bare breast, the heart of all her land,
> Whose ranks of blue veins, as his hand did scale,
> Left their round turrets destitute and pale.

278. *A Lover's Complaint.* Note the sudden turn at the end of the poem. Were it to do again, confesses the betrayed maiden, I could not resist him.

279. *Othello* IV, iii.

280. *Antony and Cleopatra* V, ii.

281. *Twelfth Night* II, iv. Time subdues language. The actual meaning is: The women who spin and knit and the care-free girls at their lace-making sing it; it is simple truth and dallies with the innocence of love as in the golden age.

282. *Much Ado About Nothing* V, ii.

283. *As You Like It* IV, i.

284. *Antony and Cleopatra* IV, xv.

285. *Antony and Cleopatra* V, ii.

286. *The Phœnix and the Turtle.* This poem first appeared in 1601 without a title and subscribed William Shakespeare at the end of a book called *Love's Martyr* or *Rosalin's Complaint*, a translation from the Italian by Robert Chester, to which compositions by other hands were added, including Marston, Chapman and Ben Jonson. The Phœnix is the symbol of love and the Turtle of constancy. The poem is at once metaphysical and musical: the Platonic idea of perfect love and purity piped to the spirit in a ditty of no tone.

   The *shrieking harbinger* is the screech-owl: *that defunctive music can* means Who is skilful in singing the funeral service. The *treble-dated crow* may mean here the long-lived raven who was supposed to lay her eggs at the bill; or it may refer to a 'vulgar error' that the crow can change its gender or sex at will. Line 31 means: 'Except in them it would be a wonder.' Should we read *light* in line 34? The poem suggests several parallels in Donne.

287. *Henry V.* Chorus to Act I. This introduces the soldier "seeking the bubble reputation even in the cannon's mouth."

288. *Troilus and Cressida* Prologue.

289. *Coriolanus* IV, v.

290. *2 Henry IV* III, ii. Falstaff recruits the Gloucestershire yokels. The likeliest men, Mouldy and Bullcalf, get off by greasing Bardolph's palm.

291. *Henry V.* Chorus to Act II.

292. *Henry V.* Chorus to Act III.

293. *Henry V* III, i. According to Fluellen, Captain Macmorris is an ass because of his ignorance of 'Roman disciplines,' and Captain Jamy 'a marvellous falorous gentleman' for his knowledge of the wars of antiquity.

294. *1 Henry IV* IV, i. The text (which is emended from the Folio) is controversial and the problem has inspired some excellent pages in *Have You Anything to Declare* by Maurice Baring (210–14). Shakespeare perhaps wrote:

All plum'd like estridges that with the wind
Bated like eagles, having lately bath'd,

meaning by estridge the *goshawk* not the *ostridge*. The Prince of Wales and his companions are compared to goshawks with plumed hoods ready to be flown and beating their wings like eagles lately bathed. The reader who is curious about Elizabethan sporting pursuits and terms and Shakespeare's knowledge of them will enjoy *The Diary of Master William Silence* by D. H. Madden.

295. *ibid.*

296. *1 Henry IV* IV, ii. Falstaff's company consists of 'discarded unjust serving men, younger sons to younger brothers, revolted tapsters, and ostlers trade-fallen; the cankers of a calm world and a long peace.' 'A mad fellow met me on the way and told me I had unloaded all the gibbets and pressed the dead bodies.'

297. *Henry V.* Chorus to Act IV.

298. *Henry V* III, i.

299. *Henry V* IV, vii.

300. *1 Henry IV* I, iii.

301. *Julius Cæsar* I, ii.

302. *1 Henry IV* V, i.

303. *Julius Cæsar* IV, i. Brutus suggests the Hamlet of Act V to us here.

304. *Hamlet* IV, iv.

305. *Troilus and Cressida* I, iii. The Trojan challenge suggests Lancelot and mediæval chivalry. The Greek party seem to symbolise the politics and statesmanship of 1600.

306. *Hamlet* III, iv.

307. *Coriolanus* II, ii.

308. *Coriolanus* I, iii.

309. *King John* II, i.

310. *2 Henry IV* II, iv.

Doll Tearsheet and Falstaff: 'Saturn and Venus in conconjunction.'

The three themes of Love, War and Age unite in this scene of low life:

Fal: Thou dost give me flattering busses.
Doll: By my troth, I kiss thee with a most constant heart.
Fal: I am old, I am old.
Doll: I love thee better than I love e'er a scurvy young boy of them all.

311. *Coriolanus* I, iii.

312. *1 Henry IV* II, iv.

313. *Coriolanus* V, iii.
314. *Henry V* IV, iii.
    'Shakespeare learned his patriotism and foreign policy from Holinshed and the other old chroniclers who followed in the train of that prince of sporting-writers, Froissart. They treated warfare as we treat football—as a spectacular, exciting and fundamentally good-natured pastime, arising from no particular causes except the love of competition and productive of no consequences except the glory of the successful athlete. King Henry's speech before Agincourt is the high-water mark of football oratory."—TUCKER BROOKE: *The Yale Shakespeare*.
315. *Antony and Cleopatra* IV, viii.
316. *Troilus and Cressida* I, ii. As the Trojan warriors pass by, Cressida relentlessly teases her Uncle Pandarus, who plays commentator, and when Troilus passes she asks, 'What sneaking fellow comes yonder?'
317. *The Rape of Lucrece*.
318. *Troilus and Cressida* IV, v.
319. *Love's Labour's Lost* V, ii. The curate, the schoolmaster, the clown, the Spanish magnifico and his page present the Nine Worthies to the King of Navarre, the Princess of France and their sophisticated lords and ladies. Alexander the Great is too much for Sir Nathaniel, the curate.
320. *ibid.* Armado rebukes the jibing courtiers. 'The sweet warman' is Hector.
321. *Henry V* IV, vii.
322. *Hamlet* V, i.
323. *Henry V* III, v. Pistol, the Miles Gloriosus, serves as a foil to Alexander the Great and Hector.
324. *Coriolanus* II, i.
325. *Henry V*. Chorus to Act V. The general is the ill-fated Essex.
326. *Coriolanus* IV, vii.
327. *Julius Cæsar* I, i.
328. *Coriolanus* II, i. This provides an illuminating stylistic comparison with the preceding piece. The grave and cold diction of *Julius Cæsar* undergoes 'a sea-change into something rich and strange' in the varied rhythms, pregnant phrasing of *Coriolanus*. Some nine years development lie between the speeches of these two Roman Tribunes.
329. *Macbeth* V, viii.
330. *Richard II* IV, i.
331. *Antony and Cleopatra* I, iv.
332. *Coriolanus* V, vi. Aufidius has mocked him: "Thou boy of tears."
333. *Othello* III, iii.
334. *Richard II* II, i

335. *King John* V, vii.
336. *Henry V* III, iv. The expedition and mettle of the English forces who have crossed the river Somme extort the commendation of the French. On the eve of Agincourt Grandpree describes their sorry plight thus:

> Yond island carrions, desperate of their bones,
> Ill-favouredly become the morning field:
> Their ragged curtains poorly are let loose,
> And our air shakes them passing scornfully:
> Big Mars seems bankrupt in their beggar'd host,
> And faintly through a rusty beaver peeps:
> The horsemen sit like fixed candlesticks
> With torch-staves in their hands . . .

337. *King John* II, i. *Commodity* means gain or self-interest. The personification (which is matched by Shakespeare's figures of Time and Envy and Luxury and Patience) draws its vitality from the mediæval personifications of the Deadly Sins, the Cardinal Virtues and so on. The same gift is found in the Bible. The poets of the Augustan Age and later eighteenth century lost the power of uniting the idea and the image. Their abstractions are colourless and chill as plaster casts.
338. *King John* V, i.
339. *King John* V, ii.
340. *King John* III, i.
341. *King Lear* II, iv.
342. *King John* IV, iii.
343. *Julius Cæsar* III, i.
344. *Henry V* V, ii. The Duke of Burgundy addresses the Kings of France and England.
345. *Coriolanus* V, iii. Volumnia pleads with her son for Rome.
346. *Henry V* IV, i. Kingship is the subject of the following passages. Pater in his Appreciation of Shakespeare's English Kings writes:

> 'The irony of kingship—average human nature, flung with a wonderfully pathetic effect into the vortex of great events; the utterance of common humanity straight from the heart, but refined like other common things for kingly uses by Shakespeare's unfailing eloquence: such . . . is the conception under which Shakespeare has arranged the lights and shadows of the story of the English kings . . . Shakespeare's kings are not, nor are meant to be, great men.'

347. *Richard II* III, ii.

348 *Richard II* IV, i. The Bishop of Carlisle prophesies that the usurpation of Richard's throne by Bolingbroke will bring civil war and thus he links this play with the Henry V trilogy:

> The blood of English shall manure the ground
> And future ages groan for this foul act;
> Peace shall go sleep with Turks and infidels,
> And in this seat of peace tumultuous wars
> Shall kin with kin and kind with kind confound.

349. *Henry V* IV, i.
350. *2 Henry VI* II, v.
351. *As You Like It* III, ii.
352. *Henry V* IV, i.
   'Shakespeare watched Henry V, not indeed as he watched the greater souls in the visionary procession, but cheerfully, as one watches some handsome spirited horse, and he spoke his tale, as he spoke all tales, with tragic irony.'
   W. B. YEATS: *Ideas of Good and Evil.*
353. *Richard II* III, iii.
354. *Richard II* IV, i. 'He saw . . . in Richard II the defeat that awaits all, whether they be Artist or Saint, who find themselves where men ask of them a rough energy and have nothing to give but a contemplative virtue, whether lyrical phantasy, or sweetness of temper, or dreaming dignity, or love of God, or love of His creatures. He saw that such a man through sheer bewilderment and impatience can become as unjust or as violent as any common man, any Bolingbroke or Prince John, and yet remain "that sweet lovely rose." '
   W. B. YEATS: *ibid.*
355. *The Rape of Lucrece.*
356. *The Passionate Pilgrim.*
357. *Richard II* V, v. In the dungeon of Pomfret Castle immediately before the murder of the King.
358. *2 Henry IV* IV, iv. Bolingbroke's 'dying voice' to his successor Prince Hal who is himself, spiritually speaking, now succeeded by Henry V.
359. *Troilus and Cressida* I, iii.
360. *Henry V* I, ii.
361. *ibid.*
362. *Richard II* V, v.
363. *The Merchant of Venice* V, i.
364. *Henry VIII* III, i.
365. *Richard II* III, iv. The Queen overhears the news of the deposition of Richard in the Duke of York's garden at Langley.

INDEX AND NOTES

366. *Troilus and Cressida* III, iii. The Secret Service is described by the statesman Ulysses to the field-marshal Achilles.
367. 1 *Henry IV* III, ii. *Enfeoft* means surrendered.
368. 2 *Henry IV* V, ii.
369. 2 *Henry VI* IV, ii. Jack Cade's Utopia, one of the earliest scenes Shakespeare wrote, makes a pair to Gonzalo's, his latest work.
370. *The Tempest* II, i. This ideal commonwealth is borrowed from Florio's translation of Montaigne (1603).
371. *Coriolanus* I, i.
372. *Pericles* II, i. The shipwrecked Pericles presents himself to the two fishers (called Pilch and Patchbreech) as:

> A man, whom both the waters and the wind
> In that vast tennis court hath made the ball
> For them to play upon. . . .

373. *Julius Cæsar* I, ii.
374. *ibid.*
375. *Julius Cæsar* III, i. The Dictator speaks.
376. *Antony and Cleopatra* I, iv. *Lackeying* is the famous emendation for *lacking* which has been generally accepted.
377. 2 *Henry IV* I, iii.
378. 3 *Henry VI* III, i.
379. *The Merchant of Venice* II, ix.
380. *Coriolanus* III, ii. *Unbarb'd sconce* means unarmed head.
381. 2 *Henry IV*. Induction. Enter RUMOUR painted full of tongues.
382. *Cymbeline* III, iv.
383. *The Winter's Tale* II, i.
384. *Sonnet* LXVI. The passages which follow are concerned with the ills of society and man's inhumanity to man.
385. *The Merchant of Venice* II, ix.
386. *The Rape of Lucrece*. Compare the Bastard's *tirade* on Commodity.
387. *Troilus and Cressida* II, ii.
388. *Measure for Measure* II, ii.
389. *Timon of Athens* IV, iii. Timon self-ruined and self-banished, digs for roots and finds gold.
390. *ibid.*
391. *King Lear* IV, vi. There is one law for the rich, another for the poor.
392. *King Lear* IV, i. *That slaves your ordinance;* i.e. who makes divine law subservient to his own desires.
393. *King Lear* III, iv. The despot learns to pray for the unemployed and homeless.
394. *ibid.*

395. *Hamlet* II, ii.
396. *King Lear* II, ii.
397. 1 *Henry IV* I, ii.
398. *Timon of Athens* IV, iii.
399. *Richard II* III, ii.
400. *King Lear* II, iii.
401. *King Lear* II, iv.
402. *Timon of Athens* IV, ii.
403. *Pericles* V, i.
404. *Othello* IV, ii. The last three lines are variously emended and interpreted. *Turn thy complexion there* surely means *turn pale at that*, rather than *look upon that*. Othello sees the rose-lipped Desdemona as Griselda: a personification of Patience, and bids her blench; but whether we should read *I here look grim* or *Ay there look grim* is a matter of opinion.
405. *King Lear* III, vi.
406. *Macbeth* I, vii.
407. *Hamlet* V, i.
408. *King John* III, i. Editors frequently follow Hanmer's suggestion and read *stout* for *stoop* in the second line; a word less effective to us than to Elizabethan ears.
409. *King John* III, iv.
410. *The Rape of Lucrece.*
411. *Hamlet* II, ii. *Mobled* means muffled: *cf* a mob-cap.
412. *ibid.*
413. *The Rape of Lucrece.*
414. *King John* IV, ii.
415. 2 *Henry IV* I, i.
416. *ibid.*
417. *Macbeth* V, iii.
418. *As You Like It* V, ii.
419. *King Lear* IV, iii.
420. *The Winter's Tale* IV, iv.
421. *Hamlet* IV, v.
422. *The Tempest* V, i.
423. *King Lear* IV, vi.
424. *As You Like It* IV, iii. When Oliver delivers to Rosalind the napkin dyed in Orlando's blood, she swoons and can support the part of Ganymede no more. She enchantingly excuses herself: 'I pray you, tell your brother how well I counterfeited.'
425. *Henry VIII* II, iv. Queen Katharine's appeal is very like that of Hermione in *The Winter's Tale* III, ii. Hermione concludes:

But yet hear this; mistake me not;—no life,—
I prise it not a straw,—but for mine honour
(Which I would free), if I shall be condemned
Upon surmises—all proofs sleeping else,
But what your jealosies awake—I tell you
'Tis rigour, and not law.

426. *The Merchant of Venice* IV, i.
427. *Measure for Measure* II, ii.
428. *Hamlet* III, iii.
429. *Measure for Measure* II, i.
430. *King Lear* IV, vi.
431. *Measure for Measure* II, ii.
432. *The Tempest* V, i.
433. *Cymbeline* V, v.
434. *The Tempest* V, i.
435. *As You Like It* II, vii.
436. *King Lear* I, iv.
437. *Twelfth Night* III, iv.
438. *King Lear* III, ii.
439. *Timon of Athens* IV, iii. He addresses the common mother of all, Earth.
440. *Sonnets to Sundry Notes of Music.* The poem, it must be confessed, is by Richard Barnfield but is so relevant to this section that it may be allowed to appear, as it does in most complete Works of Shakespeare.
441. *Timon of Athens* II, ii.
442. *Timon of Athens* IV, iii.
443. *As You Like It* II, iii.
444. *A Midsummer Night's Dream* V, i. Theseus shows real sympathy for those who offer well-meant, if tedious, service, and understands the first duty of Kingship.
445. *Timon of Athens* IV, ii.
446. *Coriolanus* IV, iv.
447. *1 Henry IV* II, iv. Prince Hal's four light words warn us how the second play in the trilogy is to end; the rejection which is to leave Falstaff's heart 'fracted and corroborate' is quite deliberate.
448. *Sonnet* XXXIII.
449. *Sonnet* CXLIV.
450. *Macbeth* I, iv.
451. *Timon of Athens* III, i.
452. *Julius Cæsar* IV, ii.
453. *Much Ado About Nothing* II, i.
454. *A Midsummer Night's Dream* III, ii.
455. *As You Like It* I, iii.
456. *The Two Noble Kinsmen* I, v. The movement, expression and

sentiment of this passage seem to me proof enough that Shakespeare is Fletcher's collaborator in this dramatic romance founded on Chaucer's *Knight's Tale*.

457. *Henry V* IV, vi.
458. *Hamlet* III, ii.
459. *ibid.*
460. *Timon of Athens* IV, iii.
461. *Sonnet* CXII.
462. *Timon of Athens* IV, iii.
463. *Cymbeline* III, iii.
464. *King Lear* III, iv. The account which Edgar gives of himself in the disguise of Mad Tom suggests Oswald, of whom Edgar later says when he has killed him:

> a serviceable villain;
> As duteous to the vices of thy mistress
> As badness would desire.

465. *Hamlet* IV, ii.
466. *Love's Labour's Lost* V, ii. Boyet whom Berowne here describes with some bitterness is the professional courtier; Armado, 'a man of fire-new words, fashion's own knight,' from tawny Spain, is the continental courtier; Berowne is the natural courtier of the Elizabethan school:

> His eye begets occasion for his wit:
> For every object that the one doth catch,
> The other turns to a mirth-moving jest;
> Which his fair tongue—conceit's expositor—
> Delivers in such apt and gracious words
> That aged ears play truant at his tales
> And younger hearings are quite ravished;
> So sweet and voluble is his discourse.

All three, it must be allowed, are talkers not doers.

467. *I Henry IV* I, iii.
468. *Twelfth Night* III, ii. The 'Indies,' i.e. America, are to be found in all maps of the period, but the 'new map' was the first drawn on the principles of projection and prepared in 1600 by Wright and Hakluyt. The 'lines' are the radiating rhumb-lines.
469. *The Merchant of Venice* I, iii.
470 *I Henry IV* I, iii.
471. *Romeo and Juliet* III, i.
472. *King Lear* II, ii.
473. *The Tempest* II, i.

INDEX AND NOTES

474. *King Lear* II, ii. Shakespearean "Billingsgate" is always rich and vigorous.
475. *ibid.*
476. *Troilus and Cressida* V, i.
477. *King Lear* II, ii.
478. *Othello* I, i. Iago gives us his character, which can be further understood by noting No. 477 and the account of Sinon in *The Rape of Lucrece*.
479. *Julius Cæsar* II, i.
480. *Henry VIII* III, ii.
481. *Macbeth* IV, iii.
482. *Henry VIII* IV, ii.
483. *Julius Cæsar* I, ii.
484. *The Merchant of Venice* III, i.
485. *The Tempest* I, ii.
486. *Hamlet* III, i.
487. *King Lear* III, vi.
488. *The Rape of Lucrece*.
489. *King Lear* I, ii. "Nature" and "unnatural" are key words, recurring continually in different contexts and indicating the main theme and metaphysic of the play. "Honour" is employed in the same way in *Julius Cæsar*.
490. *Richard III*, I, i.
491. *Richard III*, I, ii.
492. *Romeo and Juliet* V, i.
493. *Hamlet* IV, vii.
494. *Romeo and Juliet* II, iii.
495. *Measure for Measure* I, i.
496. *Sonnet* XCIV.
497. *Julius Cæsar* II, i.
498. *Troilus and Cressida* III, iii.
499. *ibid.*
500. *Macbeth* I, iii.
501. *Troilus and Cressida* III, iii.
502. *Othello* II, iii.
503. *Othello* III, iii.
504. *The Merchant of Venice* V, i.
505. *All's Well that Ends Well* IV, iii.
506. *Macbeth* I, v.
507. *2 Henry IV* IV, iv. The King describes Prince Hal.
508. *King John* IV, ii.
509. *Hamlet* III, iii. Claudius on his knees asks

O, what form of prayer
Can serve my turn? Forgive me my foul murder!—
That cannot be; since I am still possessed
Of those effects for which I did the murder . . .

In Richard II, in Brutus, in Hamlet, in Othello, in Macbeth, Shakespeare presents the divided mind; that civil war and insurrection within the breast of man which has so often proved itself the nerve centre of drama, since the moment when Orestes the matricide first looked on the breast which gave him suck and faltered in his terrible duty.

510. *Measure for Measure* II, ii.
511. *Othello* I, iii. This Book closes with diverse general reflections on man's nature and state.
512. *King Lear* I, ii.- Beatrice says "There was a star danced, and under that was I born"-
513. *The Rape of Lucrece.*
514. *Hamlet* III, ii.
515. *Troilus and Cressida* IV, iv.
516. *Hamlet* IV, vii.
517. *Antony and Cleopatra* III, xiii.
518. *King Lear* V, iii.
519. *King Lear* IV, i.
520. *King Lear* IV, iii.
521. *All's Well That Ends Well* I, i.
522. *Julius Cæsar* I, ii.
523. *Romeo and Juliet* III, iii.
524. *Richard II* I, iii.
525. *Much Ado About Nothing* V, I.
526. *Measure for Measure* III, i. We pass to Death the Skeleton and Time the Shadow, to soul-sickness, sleep and dream. *Serpigo* is a tetter or eruption on the skin.
527. *ibid.*
528. *ibid.*
529. *Julius Cæsar* II, ii.
530. *Hamlet* V, ii.
531. *King Lear* V, ii. Macbeth says Come what come may, Time and the hour runs through the roughest day.
532. *Hamlet* V, ii.
533. *Measure for Measure* IV, ii.
534. *Macbeth* V, iii.
535. *Macbeth* V, v.
536. *King John* III, iv.
537. *Hamlet* II, ii.
538. *Sonnet XXIX.*
539. *Sonnet XXX.*
540. *As You Like It* IV, i.
541. *Hamlet* V, ii. *Gaingiving* means misgiving.
542. *Hamlet* I, ii.
543. *Sonnet XC.*
544. *Julius Cæsar* IV, iii.

INDEX AND NOTES

545. *Romeo and Juliet* I, iv.
546. *Richard III* I, iv.
547. *Othello* III, iii.
548. *King Lear* IV, iv.
549. *Macbeth* II, i.
550. *Macbeth* V, i.
551. *Hamlet* II, ii.
552. *2 Henry IV* III, i.
553. *Timon of Athens* IV, ii.
554. *King Lear* II, iv.
555. *2 Henry IV* IV, iv.   *Rigol* means circlet.
556. *King Lear* IV, vi.
557. *Macbeth* V, iii.
558. *Macbeth* III, iv.
559. *Julius Cæsar* II, i.
560 *Macbeth* III, ii.
561. *Julius Cæsar* I, ii.
562. *Hamlet* III, i.
563. *Macbeth* III, i.
564. *King Lear* I, v.
565. *Sonnet* CX. Is not this the self-condemnation of the Prince of Denmark?
566. *Hamlet* III, i.
567. *Hamlet* V, ii.
568. *King Lear* V, iii.
569. *Macbeth* I, v. The passages that follow show us the dedication of man's soul to evil and the destruction of his kind, to negation and death
570. *Othello* III, iv.
571. *ibid.*
572. *Coriolanus* IV, ii.
573. *Macbeth* I, vii.
574. *King Lear* I, iv.
575. *King Lear* II, iv.
576. *Timon of Athens* IV, i.
577. *Timon of Athens* IV, iii. Timon exhorts the exiled soldier Alcibiades.
578. *Macbeth* III, ii. *Seeling:* this was the technical word for threading up the eyelids of hawks until they became tractable.
579. *Julius Cæsar* II, i.
580. *Macbeth* I, vii.
581. *Macbeth* II, iii.
582. *Macbeth* II, i.
583. *Macbeth* III, ii.
584. *Macbeth* II, i.
585. *ibid.*

586. *Macbeth* III, iv.
587. *ibid*   The first line expresses the traditional theme of revenge
      drama, and the blood feud. It looks back to *Gorboduc*, to
      Seneca, and finally to the *Oresteia* of Æschylus.
588. *Macbeth* V, i.
589. *Macbeth* III, iv.
590. *Titus Andronicus* II, iii.
591. *Julius Cæsar* II, ii. In the passages which follow *supernatural*
      manifestations enhance the *unnatural* actions of man.
592. *Macbeth* II, i.
593. *Macbeth* II, ii.
594. *Hamlet* I, i.
595. *King Lear* I, ii.
596. *Macbeth* IV, i.
597. *Richard II* V, vi.
598. *King John* IV, ii.
599. *Richard II* III, ii.
600. *King John* V, vii.
601. *King John* IV, iii.
602. *Hamlet* V, ii.
603. *Richard II* III, ii.
604. *Richard II* II, i.
605. *Macbeth* I, iv.
606. *Julius Cæsar* V, v. We may add another epitaph:

> A sweeter and a lovelier gentleman,
> Framed in the prodigality of nature,
> Young, valiant, wise and no doubt right royal,
> The spacious world cannot again afford.
>
> *Richard III* I, ii.

607. *Julius Cæsar* III, i.
608. *ibid.*
609. *Julius Cæsar* III, ii.
610. 1 *Henry IV* V, iv.
611. *Antony and Cleopatra* V, ii.
612. *ibid.*
613. *Hamlet* V, i.
614. *Othello* V, ii.
615. *Hamlet* I, iv.
616. *Romeo and Juliet* V, iii.
617. *King Lear* V, iii.
618. *King John* III, iv.
619. *Measure for Measure* IV, iii.
620. *Hamlet* IV, v.
621. *Hamlet* IV, vii.
622. *Hamlet* V, i.

INDEX AND NOTES

623. *Cymbeline* IV, ii.
624. *Romeo and Juliet* IV, v.
625. *Hamlet* V, ii. Note the combination of the Latinised grand style in the second line with the simple native monosyllables —each one a dying breath.
626. *Timon of Athens* V, i. *Embossed* in a word which Shakespeare uses several times with remarkable effect, applying it to enraged animals and inflamed sores.
627. *King John* III, iv.
628. *King Lear* V, iii.
629. *Cymbeline* V, v. Posthumus's gaoler is a philosopher; when he finds his prisoner very ready to die he remarks: "Unless a man would marry a gallows and beget young gibbets I never saw one so prone."
630. *Sonnet* LX.
631. *Sonnet* LXXXIII.
632. *All's Well That Ends Well* V, iii.
633. *2 Henry IV* I, ii.
634. *Hamlet* II, ii. The satirical rogue whom the Prince is reading is Juvenal.
635. *Timon of Athens* II, ii.
636. *The Merchant of Venice* I, i.
637. *2 Henry IV* V, v.
638. *All's Well That Ends Well* I, ii.
639. *King Lear* II, iv.
640. *Romeo and Juliet* I, v. This and the passages that follow draw together old Capulet, Othello, old Nestor, Lear, Justice Shallow; each in turn summons up remembrance of things past and precious friends and grievances foregone.
641. *Othello* V, ii.
642. *Troilus and Cressida* I, iii.
643. *King Lear* V, iii.
644. *2 Henry IV* III, ii.
645. *Much Ado About Nothing* III, v.
646. *2 Henry IV* III, ii.
647. *2 Henry IV* III, i.
648. *Troilus and Cressida* IV, v.
649. *Henry V* III, v.
650. *Hamlet* II, ii.
651. *Sonnet* XII.
652. *Sonnet* LXIV.
653. *Sonnet* XV.
654. *Julius Cæsar* IV, iii.
655. *2 Henry IV* III, i.
656. *As You Like It* II, vii.
657. *ibid*.
658. *Hamlet* III, ii.

659. *Troilus and Cressida* III, iii.
660. *Sonnet* XIX.
661. *The Tempest* I, ii.
662. *As You Like It* III, ii.
663. *The Rape of Lucrece.*
664. *Sonnet* LXV.
665. *Sonnet* LV.
666. *Julius Cæsar* I, iii.
667. *Henry VIII* III, ii.
668. *Richard II* III, iii.
669. *Henry VIII* III, ii.
670. *Antony and Cleopatra* IV, xiii.
671. *Richard II* II, iv.
672. *Richard III* I, iii.   Margaret, widow to Henry VI, addresses
     Elizabeth, Queen to Edward IV. The *bottled spider* is
     Richard, Duke of Gloster.
673. *Richard III* IV, iv. The two Queens with the Duchess of York.
     mother of Edward IV, Clarence and Gloster, join together in
     cursing and lamentation. To the Duchess, Margaret cries:

> From forth the kennel of thy womb hath crept
> A hell-hound that doth hunt us all to death.

The word hell-hound reminds us of Macbeth. Richard who
is "determinéd to be a villain" is an effective but crude
outline as compared with Shakespeare's later study of
temptation, expiation and guilty horror.
674. *Antony and Cleopatra* IV, xii.
675. *Antony and Cleopatra* IV, xiv.
676. *Sonnet* CIV.
677. *Sonnet* LXIII.
678. *King Lear* IV, vii.
679. *Othello* V, ii.
680. *Henry V* II, iii.
681. *King Lear* V, iii. Lear dies in an ecstasy of joy thinking that
     his daughter yet lives.
682. *The Tempest* V, i.
683. *Sonnet* CXLVI. The text of the second line is corrupt and
     variously emended.
684. *The Tempest* IV, i.
685. *Twelfth Night* V, i.
686. *Cymbeline* IV, ii.
687. *Much Ado about Nothing* V, iii.   Compare:

> But, look, the morn in russet mantle clad
> Walks o'er the dew of yon high eastern hill
> > *Hamlet* I. ii

HARPER COLOPHON BOOKS

Lightning Source UK Ltd.
Milton Keynes UK
UKHW011637250419
341603UK00001B/111/P